A MEMOIR

SHATTERED

A VORTEX OF TERROR

a psychological thriller

CONNELL J. J. CHAMBERS

SEOMRAIG PUBLISHING

NEW YORK

SHATTERED
A VORTEX OF TERROR
Library of Congress Cataloging-in-Publication Data

Copyright © 2013 by Connell J. J. Chambers
Original Copyright © 2008 by Connell J. J. Chambers

ISBN 978-0-9859322-1-3 eBook
ISBN-13: 9780985932237
ISBN-10: 0985932236

Cover design & photo by Greta

This story, inspired by actual events, took place over a period of two years. The characters are real. However, I have selected to use pseudonyms for certain individuals, out of respect for their privacy, as well as for the two journals referred to. I have taken the liberty to change the country of origin of the antagonist out of consideration for the family. The events are as true and as accurate as memory allows.

To
Greta

Acknowledgements

There is no order of priority as every cog in a wheel is necessary to arrive at one's destination. An extremely important cog that fortuitously appeared in my life was in the person of Detective Michael Dragonetti. He heard my story and dug beneath the surface, deciphering truth from fiction in the cacophony of voices. At a time when it was too dangerous for me to share with others, I put my trust in his steady hands and strong mind. I do not know where I would be today if it were not for his guidance and words of wisdom. It was my good fortune to be in the hands of a very stealth and astute attorney, Sophia Algoni* who became my voice and savior.

I owe a great debt of thanks and will forever be grateful to Antonia Avery, Joyce Vagasy, Pamela Whidden and Anderson Read* for their unconditional support and for the crucial role each played during my journey, though none were fully aware of the danger I was facing. I want to thank Teresa, my sister, for her sound advice and for her keenness in alerting me to what was to be the final conclusion.

I am indebted to Karen Kohler who took time between her concert schedules, and offered, with her feathered quill to review my manuscript: a generous gift indeed. It is with deep appreciation to Darine Avedisian, in whose hands I entrusted the first reading of the manuscript, for her professional input: to Peter Craig Avedisian, for his unflinching and enthusiastic support from the start. One of the exciting gems I have been blessed with, is the friendship of Barbara Fass Leavy, Professor of English at Queens College, City University of New York, and author of numerous books. Barbara surgically approached my manuscript with her mastery skills and painstakingly edited Shattered.

I state unequivocally that the manuscript could not have been completed without the crucial participation of Greta. After reviewing my journal and the myriad of handwritten pages and notes recording the frightful two-year odyssey, Greta, passionate in her belief that the story must be told, became an integral part of working on the manuscript. Her structural editorial input, laser sharp focus on storytelling and dedication to the facts, were irreplaceable gifts.

* Denotes use of pseudonym

Contents

Forward

E scape is the incremental movement of courage and fear, intuitive thinking and the awareness of the element of surprise. Do not ever change your routine; always be ready for the opportunity of escape. Never change your speed of life, do not panic; never reveal recognition of the predator. When confronted, confront. Never show any change in the natural frequency of your voice. Do not change your home phone number, your locks, and don't change your job. Do not stop the way you live your life. Always arrive at your destination and, if it is difficult, leave earlier so that there is no change in your pattern to those who know you. Every day must be natural. Change transmits fear and predator wins. Do not show fear; show commitment and strength. You have become a warrior in a war that only knows death as the ultimate prize. Do not live for death but respect its reality. Escape is just another way to get to where you were not going. A prisoner becomes a fugitive if he cannot go home. Define why you need to escape. Realize that the strongest place to take a stand to take back your life is where you live within yourself.

If another person decides to draw you into the vortex of his or her reality, you do not have to go. If you participate in the interaction, you are as responsible as the one who sets the trap. How far into the experience does it take to realize that other elements have already taken control of the dynamics? Possession feeds off such a moment; it will consume ownership if not checked, even of your right to sleep.

ONE

Before the End

There they were, clear single-ply tire tracks, just what I had been looking for. Further down, no more tracks. I was puzzled. She may have been here before and discovered to the left of the driveway a garage and the large empty house being renovated. I went into the woods surrounding the house; still no sign of her. Walking back to the car I had an acute sense of being watched. If she were here, she played a good game of hide-and-seek. I drove onto Route 6, traveled south about a mile and parked; still no sign of her, no white car anywhere. I had enough and headed back. Slowing down to make the left turn onto Washington Road, I was startled by a blast of a horn and a flash of high beams. I was so on edge that I freaked out; it was only a pick-up truck. I made the turn and headed straight towards the cabin. I backed into the parking spot facing the right direction in case a quick exit was needed. I glanced around. Chipmunks were busy harvesting seeds; nothing seemed to have unsettled them.

Walking towards the front steps I froze at the sudden sound of leaves being disturbed. It seemed to come from the right rear of the cabin where a loose panel covered the crawl space. The sound stopped when I stopped, then picked up again as I continued to move in its direction. I picked up a shovel from the back of the shed and cautiously approached the panel. Pressing my back against the wall I used the head of the shovel to pull the panel sideways. If she were there waiting, she would assume I would investigate the sound by pulling the panel towards me which would then fully expose me to the barrel of a rifle. The sudden action of yanking the panel must have surprised whatever or whoever was there as a scurrying sound could be heard moving towards the other side of the crawl space. She would now be at the front of the cabin blocking me from getting inside.

I walked back towards the woods and climbed the small rise directly facing the front porch. Leaning against a boulder I had a clear view of the cabin and could observe any movement. I sat for close to an hour, nothing moved. This game of hide-and-seek was stupid and dangerous. Finally, stiff from the cold, I decided to take a chance and headed for the porch. As I approached the glass sliding doors, I anxiously rummaged through my satchel for the keys.

The next thing I remembered was lying face down on the porch, the back of my head hurting. "What happened?" Feeling dizzy, I tried to get up and reach for my satchel lying nearby, and suddenly felt a rush of adrenaline when I noticed a log of firewood close to my feet. "Where had she come from? How could I have missed her?" I unlocked the door and quickly went inside. Sliding the door shut I realized the glass would not be much of a deterrent. One heavy log from the wood stacked would be enough to smash the glass.

It was Brooklyn again, me on the inside she on the outside; but this time, there were no fire escapes and no back door.

Joyce's cabin had a false panel behind the refrigerator, which slid open and revealed a stepladder that led to a loft bed. Moving the refrigerator to the left and sliding open the panel, I stepped in and, pushing the refrigerator back, slid the panel close again and with trembling legs climbed the ladder to safety.

There it was, a small mattress; it was like finding the Golden Fleece. I collapsed on the bed completely wiped out. Here I was trapped by fear of the unknown; fear of being so depleted that making a fatal mistake would bring me face to face with death. I was on automatic; when I closed my eyes, my sense of hearing intensified. Even the smallest natural sound was magnified and played havoc with my imagination. Was she climbing up onto the roof? I hoped she had not discovered the loose panel in the back of the cabin leading down to the garage. If she was hiding under the cabin where the wood was dry; she could easily start a fire forcing me to run out into her line of fire. If I dropped into a deep sleep, would it be the smoke or flames that got to me first? I could not afford to fall asleep.

As I lay there I became aware of the skylight above and the small oblong window to the left of the mattress. This would be my avenue of escape. I looked around the loft but found nothing that could be used to smash open the window. I went back down to get the poker from the wood burning stove, though having to pass by the glass doors would expose me. With the poker in my hand I now felt empowered; I had a weapon and a means of escape. I returned to the loft and lay in bed clutching the poker. Deep sadness and emptiness overcame me as I slipped into sleep. I dreamt of two charioteers arguing as they orbited the earth. One said, *"Let's get him, it's time."* The other one said, *"No, wait, it's not time,"* then in unison, *"let's get them."* They snapped the reigns but the stallions refused to move.

"Oh, my God, they are coming for me, for her, for us. No I will not go. I am alive," I screamed, as I awoke in panic, my heart pounding.

It was now already close to noon. I had forgotten that I was scheduled to open the showroom at 9:00 a.m. We did not have a sale staff on Sundays, and as the telemarketing manager, I would be there alone.

The air was cold, and crisp, close to twenty degrees. I moved cautiously throughout the house in case she had broken in. Passing the sliding door and seeing the log of wood on the porch, I realized she could still be outside. Clutching the poker I went into the shower. The cold water was like shards of ice piercing my body; it felt exhilarating to be alive.

I left the house through the trap door to the garage, and once outside, scaled the stone wall, and cautiously approached the car. I noticed a scuff of white paint on the right side of the slate blue rear bumper. Had it been there before or happened while I was sleeping? I checked the tires making sure they were not slashed. I looked for tire marks. There they were, single ply: were they new or had they been there before? I opened the door to get in and discovered broken glass on my seat.

"It's a trap," I thought, "If I bend over to brush the glass off, my back will be vulnerable. No way, grab the blanket and throw it over the seat and get the hell out of here." I sped away from the cabin and my fears.

Approaching the city, I felt tension begin to build once more. Rachelle had saturated every part of my life.

Was it fate that made me stop at the Futon store that rainy night in December?

TWO

The Journalist

T he steady heavy downpour created an unusual chill on this December evening. Rejected brollies, blue, red, black, ripped and broken, were discarded in wire mesh garbage containers in disgust; traffic was going nowhere; visibility was poor. I finally made the right hand turn onto Seventh Avenue from Flatbush Avenue toward Prospect Park West where I lived. Still early, I decided to stop at *Futon*, a neighborhood store whose owner Bill Murray rented the front section to two women who sold New Age music, books and crystals. Imelda petite and out going, had short, straight black hair and wore large thick glasses. Her partner, Joan, a heavy-set woman with soft brown hair, was the quiet one and usually just observed. Together they ran a Crystal Work Shop in Park Slope teaching meditation and crystal healing. They often expressed a keen interest in having me participate.

The visit was cut short as the store was closing early due to the weather. The rain was causing minor flooding; clogged drains made walking close to curbs hazardous. The hissing sound of tires on wet payments could be heard as traffic wound its way up the avenue. Since we all lived locally I offered them a ride.

"That is thoughtful of you, but we enjoy the rain and would like to walk. Thanks anyway," they responded in unison.

"However," Imelda continued, "I know our friend would appreciate a ride, she lives further down off Atlantic Avenue. Would you mind?" I had not been aware of another person in the store and felt hesitant about giving a ride to a stranger.

"She is a poet, writer and a theatrical director. Maybe you could be of help to each other. Who knows why we meet anyway; both of you may have a lot in common." Turning to the woman she added,

"Connell is an interesting person, writes poetry, loves literature, theosophy, and the sciences."

"Hello my name is Nicole. I will accept the ride," she said softly. I detected an Australian accent.

"Okay, tell me where you live. I don't intend to go too far out of my way so let's go."

She was slim, medium height, wearing blue jeans tucked into dark brown boots, with a rust colored L.L. Bean down jacket, a kerchief on her hair, and dark horn-rimmed glasses. I held my umbrella over her head as I opened the car door for her.

"There is no need to protect me from the elements," she said. "I am in tune with the rain."

"Oh?"

"So, you write poetry. Could I read some of your work?" she asked,

"No. I am selective with whom I share my poetry."

"Are you always so abrupt? I am the assisting editor of *Spirit Path,* a New Age bi-monthly journal. We are looking for new approaches, such as adding a poetry section to increase our circulation. I can't present my work but I could put together a presentation of yours. Have you ever read *Spirit Path*?" she asked.

"I am aware of seeing it in New Age stores."

"Is your work worth reviewing?" she asked.

"I am not looking to be published in a New Age journal."

"Aren't you being an elitist?"

"Maybe, but that is how I feel. The purpose of our contact is to prevent you from getting wet in the rain."

"Do you know that it is possible that this accidental meeting could have a larger meaning?" she said, with a look of anticipation. "Why don't you let me review your work? What harm can come from sharing it with a fellow poet? I will set up a review of your work with my publisher."

"I will let you know if the idea is worth pursuing."

As we turned into Berkley Place, the brownstone buildings, darkened by the heavy rain and off set by the yellow flickering gas lamps, reminded me of fog filled London streets.

"I will give you my phone number and when you feel comfortable, call me."

We exchanged numbers.

"If you are not in a hurry, would you like to join me for a cup of tea in my home?"

"No, thank you."

"My intentions are none other than a cup of tea. If you thought differently, I apologize."

"That is fine; I did not read anything further then the offer of a cup of tea."

"That is a little unusual in this day and age. Are you really a purist who respects another's space?"

"I guess if that is your definition, it fits," I said.

"I like that. It is unusual but similar as to how I view myself. Come on in and I will serve you a cup of tea before you go home in the rain. In my home country, one takes hospitality for granted. It seems New Yorkers have a fear of closeness," she added with a tinge of annoyance.

"Okay one cup of tea, milk, no sugar, served in a china cup and saucer," I replied in jest, as I parked in front of her building and walked around to open her door, holding the umbrella over our heads. She rejected the umbrella, allowing the rain to soak her hair, face and glasses.

"You depend so much on things to protect yourself from the elements," she commented. A little strange, I thought, why would she accept the ride if she was not bothered by the rain? She opened the outer wrought iron gate and the door of her ground floor apartment, apologizing for the security.

The apartment had metal protective bars on the living room windows. The room was of average size, sparsely furnished, a mock fireplace on the left as you walked in. Between the doorway and fireplace was an alcove filled with boxes of all sizes. It was hard to decipher whether she was moving in or out. To the right was a blue upholstered couch with a red cushion, a coffee table, a small armchair and a large floral printed pillow. The rest of the room was empty, except for a few abstract "New Age" posters on the walls.

"Excuse me a moment," she said, as she turned on the portable cassette player, walked to the back of the room, and disappeared.

Chariots of Fire by Vangelis filled the room. The sudden whistling of the kettle broke the moment.

"Water boiled – time for tea," I called out.

"Sorry I took so long,"

She reappeared looking completely different than the woman who got out of my car a few moments earlier. She had changed into a loose fitting eggshell blue cashmere sweater with a jewel neckline and a fitted black skirt; the glasses were gone and her dark hair fell gently on her shoulders. She walked toward the mantle piece, her movements shy and coy, her eyes cast downwards.

"Hello again, would you like your tea now?" she asked in a soft seductive tone. "I only have herb tea."

"Yes, that would be fine. You look so completely different from a moment ago. I would not have recognized you."

"When you get to know me, you will understand," she said with a smile. "I really don't wear glasses and have excellent eyesight. I can see in the dark."

"Then why the masquerade, are you hiding?" I asked lightly.

"No! Well maybe . . . sort of," she said with a playful smirk.

"Hiding from what or from whom?"

"The dark forces lurking in the eyes of voyeurs," she replied as she sipped her tea.

"Actually I am on the international scene and well known in Europe and Australia. When out in public I usually walk in a sort of disguise, you know."

"So what brings you to New York?"

"I have come to teach. I am here on a journalist's visa. I move internationally teaching a theatrical concept based more on the spiritual connectedness between the characters, rather than the emotional-physical expression."

"Some friends of mine in theatre have spoken about new movements, spiritual and so on . . . but I must be on my way now. Good night," I said, as I stood up to leave. "Best of luck in your endeavors."

"Thank you for being so thoughtful. Compared to where I come from, people here don't seem to care for others. It is encouraging to experience your sensitivity as an artist," she said.

"Premature compliments have an adverse effect on me, okay? You don't even know me."

"Oh my, are you protective of yourself! I hope you are not one of those who believe that an accidental meeting is accidental. I am very alert to subtext in conversation," she said, with the air of a schoolmistress.

"Well whatever, I must go, good-bye."

"Wait a moment, when am I going to have a chance to review some of your poetry? I have a feeling it is exactly what we are looking for," she persisted with a sense of urgency and slight panic, as if grasping for a reason to prolong the stay, not wanting me to leave.

"I have to be comfortable with the idea," I said.

"From the way you speak, your sensitivity, your interest in meditation and crystals . . . can't you see this is as if it were . . . predetermined? Don't challenge universal decisions. You belong to the New Age movement," she said.

"Oops! Hold on let's not go universal, this is Brooklyn, it's rainy, and I am not interested in having my work handed over to *Spirit Path* and to you, a fellow writer and poet. Anyway if I decide I will call you, okay? I must go."

"Give me a call within the next few days. The paper goes to print very soon for the March edition. I will let my editor know I have a poet and inform you if he wants to go ahead with the project."

"Listen, I don't think you hear me. I am not interested. I must go, okay?"

"Please, don't throw this opportunity away. Just think, your poetry, two pages, in every New Age Center in the United States, two hundred thousand in circulation. Call me and let me know."

Her suggestion was enticing but I was suspicious of optimistic sounding offers. Who was this woman? I needed to find out a lot more about her. Did I want to be labeled a New Age poet?

Time passed quickly. I had not given further thought to submitting my poems to *Spirit Path* yet I was curious about the publication and picked up an issue. To my surprise there was no Nicole Richards listed as assistant editor but there was a Rachelle Richards listed as a proofreader and coordinator. Were they one and the same, and if so, what else in her story was not true? Was there really a poetry project or was it a guise for something else in her life?

THREE

No Choice

I became aware of the Mayan Prophesies, known as the Harmonic Convergence that would take place on August 16, 1987, through Anderson and Natalia, who managed a New Age store on Waverly Place called *Gem-Stoned*. I purchased *The Mayan Factor* by Doctor Jose Argüelles, an American Author, Artist and professor in the University of California, who initiated the world famous Harmonic Convergence. It was the first globally synchronized meditation and prayers for world peace, a fulfillment, of the Quetzalcoatl prophesy. Quetzalcoatl was an ancient prophet ruler of the Toltec, whose message was of love and wisdom. With new awareness of the deeper meaning of the gatherings, I decided it would be interesting to participate. As it so happened, my good friend Antonia Avery phoned inviting me to join her and some of her friends that weekend at her summer home in Sagaponack, Long Island, to be part of the Festival of the International Sacred Sites; a perfect invitation. On that day in the chilly morning light at 4:00 a.m. Antonia, her friends and I gathered on the beach with approximately fifty other people to celebrate the Convergence.

Antonia came into my life several years earlier. She had a great love of classical music and literature and often invited me to accompany her to concerts at Lincoln Center. Many rich and memorable evenings, discussing literature, social and political issues and current events, were also spent in her home, always ending as usual, by taking Cindy, her white West Highland Terrier, for her evening walk down Park Avenue. We became deep and trusting friends. When Antonia, who traveled extensively, was away, I looked after her home and Cindy. Once, as straphangers on a bus ride together down Lexington Avenue, Antonia, who was an extremely attractive lady, suddenly burst into a beaming smile.

"What brought that burst of joy upon your face?" I asked,

"You," she answered," you helped me trust again; you make me smile. So many small gifts of words come from you; they land within me and I just burst out into a smile."

Her words blew me away.

"No, Antonia, you are the one always so full of energy and laughter." I responded.

"Yes, but only with you because I feel safe around you."

Later, I realized the beautiful gift I had received.

Fall arrived; I settled into my routine, usually going to Popolini's for dinner, where I would sit for hours writing poetry. On the way I often stopped by *Gem-Stoned* to visit Anderson and Natalia. They were an interesting couple: Natalia, a haunting beauty whose family came from India, was involved in esoteric and New Age theories, while Anderson, part American Indian, and an aspiring actor, was a student at NYU. I spent many evenings in their home discussing philosophical concepts and literature late into the night.

Poetry was an integral part of my childhood, at home as well as in school in Ireland. At an early age I was mostly influenced by Byron, Tennyson, Wordsworth, Longfellow, and Coleridge, and discovered William Shakespeare through his sonnets, becoming fascinated with his body of work. During my teens my close friends Christopher Mahon, Mathew Murphy and I would assume and act out the individual characters, switching roles as we walked around campus. Throughout the day we would have great fun continuing to speak the Shakespearean language that flowed easily off our lips.

In later years I developed a great respect and admiration for the fearless voices of Neruda, Heaney, Elliot, Kinnell, Rilke, and Hikmet.

I spent many years in serious endeavor honing my own craft. I attended a course on "The Structure of Poetry" given by Hugh Seidman, a tough professor whose reviews carried weight; I valued his comment that my poem *Time Passing* should be published. Having read *The Death of a Naturalist* by Irish poet Seamus Heaney, winner of the 1995 Nobel Prize in Literature, I attended one of his readings and was impressed by his gift of capturing life, love, war, fear, and contradictions, and delivering them in his rich Anglo-Saxon voice.

I had an affinity with the voice of renowned poet, Galway Kinnell. One day, as fate would have it, I had the good fortune to meet him when he walked into the showroom. We had an amiable chat about poetry and I expressed my deep admiration for his work, especially *The Book of Nightmares*. He suggested that when he stops by the following day, I give him twenty of my poems written at various stages of completion, which he said he would review upon his return to Vermont. A short time later I was excited to receive an autographed copy of *The Book of Nightmares* including a review of the poems written during my recent visit to Ireland, which he said should be left untouched "because of their strong visual quality."

I find it important to talk here about the strong connection I felt with poetry since it was circumstances surrounding the publishing of my poetry that brought about the dire events that started the unraveling of my life.

Winter was now upon us; social gatherings and events picked up as the holiday season approached. Nicole phoned a few times to see if I had made up my mind about the poetry.

I kept putting her off saying I had not as yet given it serious thought. When I mentioned I had not seen Nicole Richards listed in *Spirit Path* but came across Rachelle with the same last name, she informed me Rachelle was her stage name and actually preferred I use it. During another phone conversation she asked if I was familiar with the works of James Joyce, "Of course," I answered, "I recently saw *The Dead* based on his work and directed by John Huston." She was completely aghast that I would go to see a film about death. I did not dwell on the subject.

Christmas was ten days away. Six years had already gone by since my last Christmas with Ingrid. During our marriage we tried to support each other's dreams. The marriage ended abruptly when Ingrid began a relationship with a fellow student she met during her studies in Art Therapy. In the beginning nothing made sense, there were no answers. Once over the initial shock of finding myself alone, I began to revitalize and search for alternate answers, not connected to structural thinking but outside of it. Always curious about why there were different spiritual paths, I decided to wander through the enormous wealth of information available. Slowly I began to realize that my inner thoughts were compatible with my discoveries. This gave me freedom to delve deeper into the complexity and confusion and found that most of the paths led to the same realizations. In these similarities there were differences, and in those differences lay the answer. My life changed and the journey led me to be free of that which, realizing or not, formed my paths, attitudes, selectivity and judgment. I was free; my discoveries permeated my life and my poetic voice. I became an ardent lover of opera and the world of ballet attending as many performances as could fit into my schedule. I went to lectures, travelled and immersed myself in the search of deeper understanding and knowledge. I was curious about everything, a renaissance.

I strolled in the chilly dawn light through the empty pathways of the Botanical Gardens, blanketed in fresh fallen snow, until nine o'clock and leaving the park, walked down to Seventh Avenue. The festive atmosphere in the local streets and shops were palpable. Ornaments glittered in the lights. I went into *Back To The Land,* a health food store, to shop and on my way out glanced at the *New Age Magazine stand: Meditation, Nature, Animal Life, Spirit Path.* Yes, *Spirit Path*! I wondered if the March issue would have a poetry section and whether I should review some of my work and give Ms. Richards a call. I was undecided as to whether this was the right venue for my poetry. I walked out into the snow, now turning black from cars, and people; dogs were limping from salt burns on their paws.

I arrived home as the sunlight was casting its golden touch across my living room, and sitting in the antique wicker rocking chair I had restored, enjoyed the quietness of the moment and the fantastic view my apartment provided me; a plus for New York City. The living room faced west with a clear view of lower Manhattan and the World Trade Center. I moved here from Brooklyn Heights shortly after my marriage of twelve years with Ingrid ended. Ingrid was a talented artist and a few of her paintings hung on the exposed brick walls. On the mantle-piece, photographs I had taken of my friend Sandra, an actress. Photos of other friends and Greta were also on display: an apartment full of memories. Greta was a French Chanteuse and recording artist who performed internationally and at various clubs in New York. She first crossed my path when I managed the showroom two blocks from her home on the east side. I would occasionally see her walk by the Silver Star Restaurant where I sat having lunch and writing poetry at my usual table in front of the large glass windows that wrapped around the corner of

65th Street and Second Avenue. One particular rainy day, gazing out the window watching pedestrians pass by, their presence starved of color, I reflected on what happened to the lightness of step, the strut, the pride of presence, and the haberdashery of old. Deep in thought, my omelet cold, my coffee cup empty, a woman, walking with attitude and beauty, moved into my line of vision as if in slow motion. Later, I knew her as Greta. I first experienced her performance at *Panache*, a supper club on the east side. Her son Peter was the lead guitarist and her daughter Darine her manager. From that day on, I never missed a performance. We became great friends and her presence always enriched me. Though on separate journeys, we shared our joys, sorrows, and successes.

My reflective mood was suddenly interrupted, by the sharp ringing of the phone.

"Seasons Greetings," I said.

"Hello Connell, how are you, my about to be famous poet friend, this is your new promoter, Rachelle. Are you ready to be discovered?" she asked in a light joyous voice. "You know, if you team up with me, I will not only have you printed in *Spirit Path*, but I also have international influences," she added in a more serious tone.

"I will let you know what I decide."

"You have no time to procrastinate, you must decide now." I detected a slight edginess in her voice.

"If you want a decision in your favor, allow me the time and freedom to make it."

"Suppose I know more than you about all this and tell you that it is part of your destiny coming through and you really don't have a choice. Look at the perfect synchronicity. Two writers meeting in the night; one with powerful poetry unpublished; one with access to most of the great publishing houses in New York City. Can't you see, no matter what your decision, it will end up being the one to publish. I know it in the depth of my feelings. It just has to be; this is karma," she exclaimed, in a possessive tone.

"It all sounds fantastic, but I will make my own decision," I said quietly.

"Well don't you think the opportunity is unusual, and since you will be the first to get published, all other works will be compared to yours?"

"Yes, I think the idea is exciting and I respect your emphasis on publishing. I am flattered, but I must come to the decision on my own."

"Do you think it is possible?" she asked curiously.

"Yes I do feel it is possible, but it must be my decision," I replied firmly.

"As long as we are in the same place, the small differences can be worked out. I will discuss our conversation with the *Spirit Path* staff. Don't change your feelings; I don't know how to handle 'change of feelings,'" she said playfully, adding, "Select some poems and let me review. Maybe tomorrow on your way home, you could come by for a reading and some tea," she continued.

"I will call you before I leave my office to confirm."

"I don't like being left to last. Is it possible we can set our meeting up now?" she responded, sounding upset.

"Okay, I won't have time to spend chatting but let's do it. I will come by at eight-thirty."

She was a little abrupt, but was convincing enough for me to take the next step and go through with the reading. Maybe she was right; who knows why one meets? Was it karma or something like that? However, I did not believe too much in karma.

As I slowly walked down the hallway, the last rays of sunlight seemed to give vibrancy to the faded and muted colors of the antique runner leading to my studio. This time I entered the room with a different sense of purpose. I looked around at all the shelves filled with poetry and realized how much I had written.

I pondered what poems to select. Not knowing if Rachelle was qualified to select poetry for publishing, I decided to choose a few poems from the group written in Ireland that elicited praise from Galway Kinnell. *Spirit Path*, I liked those words, *Spirit Path*. Not a bad idea, really, all because of a rainstorm. Maybe that was what was called karma.

The evening traffic was heavy as I wound my way down the West Side Highway, through China Town, along Canal Street, towards Manhattan Bridge. Snow once more began to gently fall as the city lights faded in the night. I was excited at the fact that I finally had made the decision to have some of my work reviewed for publication. She sounded convincing as she presented her ideas in her soft, seductive accent.

"Thank you for keeping your promise. Do you realize how much I appreciate people living up to their feelings?"

"No I don't realize it, but thanks anyhow. My time is limited so let's start."

"Don't rush, I want to be able to absorb your work, it's not often I have both the poet and his work in my home. Allow me the dual pleasure."

"I hope my work is what you are looking for," I responded casually.

"In the way you keep bringing the conversation back to the singular subject of reviewing your work I can see you don't like talking about yourself. Maybe I can be influential in changing that . . . maybe."

She asked if I would like to hear some of her work as an opener.

"Sure why not," I replied. This would give me an insight into the structure of her writing and to what the extent of her knowledge of poetry was.

A delicate scent permeated the air; tea was served with hot milk and *Peek Freans Biscuits* on a gold edged plate. Sandalwood incense burned in a small shell by the fake fireplace as the music of Steve Halpern played. As she read, it was apparent that she had an exceptional voice to deliver the written word. Reciting with a lot of theatrics, she moved through emotions, passions, and anger. She spoke of God as if there was no separation and of the unknown forces that controlled her life. She peppered her work with influences from Buddhism and Middle Eastern beliefs. Her anger at her parents was evident. I assumed the poetry she was reading was her own original work. I was curious as to what she was all about.

"Well, what do you think?" she asked, as I was deep in thought.

"Oh, interesting. Have you reworked any of your poems?"

"Very few, I am surprised you asked. Poets have missions, mine is to reach mankind and remind them of the dangers of misuse of power and the punishment that will be visited upon them if they don't mend their ways. My mission is to get this message across through theatre and the written word," she said with annoyance.

"I asked if you reworked any of your works, not about your obsession with saving humanity. Let's stay on the poetic track."

"Okay, sorry I took off on salvation. It is just that people make me angry," she said apologetically. I let her comment slide by.

"Okay, let's get to my work," I said, as I retrieved four poems from my satchel and proceeded to read them.

I decided to begin with *Time Passing*, about an old man, broken, deaf and lost, and his battle with the farmland before modern machinery took over; *The Heralder*, an old trumpet player, who reminisces about his loved one and the sadness of the loss; *I Hear the Church Bells Ring*, a soul, whose body lies in a graveyard, remembering childhood and the call to prayer; and the last, *When I Was a Child*, speaks about past memories, joys and life's experiences seen through the eyes of a child. Rachelle's reaction to this last poem was immediate and abrupt.

"That's enough; we won't need any works relating to childhood. They have a tendency to awaken in people memories best forgotten. I find the way you work the words disturbing. Your work triggers deep inner responses. I don't feel these poems would work, they are not New Age stuff," she said, with a sweep of her hand, as if to discard all with one movement.

"Let's move on to other stuff of which I know you must have," she added.

"What I have just read to you is 'good stuff,' " I said emphatically. "I selected these poems, specifically relating to freedom of spirit. It is obvious by your response that you have no previous experience as to how to select poetry and are groping in the dark."

"So God speaks!" she said with slight sarcasm.

"I need to reconsider having further poems reviewed but now I must leave," I said annoyed.

"You can't go yet; we have not spent any time together this evening. I was looking forward to meeting you again." She had not heard a word I was saying and spoke like a child who came out to play, and at the moment of play is called back. I was now impatient and anxious to leave.

"Look, I feel it would be unfair to give the impression that there may be any interest beyond coming together for a poetic venture. I have a busy social life . . . so, good night." I gathered my poems, picked up my satchel and got up to leave.

"Good night could be before dawn instead of right now," she replied with a soft seductive look completely ignoring my comment.

"I will call you if I decide to select additional poems."

"I have the power to make the whole world love you or I can destroy you in a matter of seconds, like Medea, so please stop," she responded in a darker voice.

"Good night, again. By the way, that last remark was quite dramatic. You must be an interesting actress."

"Please stay a while longer, just a while longer, please," she begged coyly.

"No, it's time to leave," I replied as I went out the door.

I walked a few blocks to the car pondering her words. "I can destroy you in a matter of seconds." What a strange statement. I mulled it over and then let it go as dramatics.

As I pulled the soft wool blankets over my shoulders, I wondered what she meant.

"I can destroy you in a matter of seconds."

FOUR

Go For It

The following day during lunch, while exchanging idle chat with two of my colleagues, Phil Reinhart and Alex Stepanian, Phil piped up,

"What about this publisher woman, is she worth it?"

I had previously mentioned the chance meeting with Rachelle to Alex and Phil.

"Worth what?"

"Worth it, you know, like getting it on with her, having sex," Alex chimed in with his caustic humor.

"You know how serious I am about my work; it's not a pick up game."

"Oh, no, life is not that simple, someone here wants something. Poets don't meet in this century just to recite poetry. They use poetry as a bridge to have sex," Phil, always the chauvinist, argued.

"Not in this case. She threatened she had the power to destroy me if I did not fulfill her wishes. I am not sure if she was playing with me or if she was serious. This could be a problem."

"Connell, life is short, let it go. You are too serious . . . have fun. Come on, go for her," Alex added, with a twinkle in his eye. The way you describe your conversations, she wants you. You said she was attractive, interesting with a strange sense of humor, and you were curious as to, 'where she was coming from' so find out, push her buttons."

"Her invitation into her home is an invitation for other things," Phil chimed in. "That's not the way I think; in this case it is to get poems published."

I had no desire to elaborate and was exasperated by their comments. The rest of the afternoon was uneventful. At the close of the day, as Phil and Alex were leaving the Volvo Showroom, Alex called out,

"Don't forget . . . go for it. Have fun whatever you do." I was about to leave, when the phone rang.

"Hello Connell, how are you? This is your poetic soul mate. Do you want to share an evening of poetry, music and candle-light with me?" I recognized the deep, soft and seductive voice, yet asked who was speaking.

"This is Rachelle Richards. The weather conditions call for companionship, why don't you visit me? I will make a special Australian dinner. We can celebrate the fact that *Spirit Path* has agreed to publish your work based on my judgment," she continued in a playful, self-assured tone. I was caught off guard since she had previously told me the poems were not right for *Spirit Path*.

"Hold on a moment, you rejected the poems I presented. If I decided to select additional ones, I told you I would call. I have no desire to come over for an evening of celebration for what you claim *Spirit Path* has agreed to do," I said all in one breath.

"Okay," she replied, "I was just creating a beautiful theatrical setting in my mind. I was not being serious, just playing. Don't be so defensive," she replied, lightly.

"Only joking?" I retorted.

"Yes, I have no right to sway you from your creative path. However, I recognized you instantly as my 'ancient soul mate.' You know how God likes to play, so watch out if you don't play my game. You could be forced to," she answered with light laughter.

"And what do you mean by that . . . and what is this thing about soul mates?"

"In the beginning of time, you know, reincarnation, you understand. We have travelled many lives, working together," she emphasized, in the same self-assured tone.

"Let's not get into this stuff, okay? This type of conversation does not interest me."

I knew exactly what was being said but had no intent of allowing myself, or my poetry project to be drawn into her pseudo parapsychological banter. There was a sense of caution moving like an undercurrent within me that I did not fully understand.

"Listen, Rachelle, back to poetry. Okay, I will stop by later this evening to present additional work. No dinner and candles or wine please. Let's keep the process simple."

"If I am to respect what you want, you have to respect what I want."

"Let us not set up challenges. If the decision is in favor of publishing, we will both gain."

"What do you mean, *if* the decision," she said abruptly. "Don't disappoint me. Remember I am a perfectionist and I recognize at an instant a professional creative spirit. You are a very rare and talented person; so don't say *if* in the decision process, say *when*, it sounds better, more convincing to self and others. This is going to happen. I feel it in my body and soul. It's going to be powerful."

"Stop this exasperating discussion. You have not heard enough of my poetry to put your reputation behind it, so let's focus on the reading process," I stated emphatically. "Let's not wander off in dreamland, so goodbye. I will see you later."

"Don't eat; I will put a snack together for you, nothing elaborate. Oh, sorry if I annoy you, not intentional, I hope you know that. Bye, see you soon," she said softly.

Why would I put effort into this project? It was not like me to change my tempo at another's suggestion, especially related to my poetry. She was an attractive woman, intellectually refreshing with an alert literary mind, and seemed to be well grounded. However, I was not physically drawn to her.

As usual, traffic was heavy, snow had turned to sleet: a city of lights and people, success and failure, wealth and poverty.

"Where do I fit in this mosaic?" I wondered, as I watched the lights of Brooklyn Bridge and lower Manhattan move closer.

FIVE

The Red Pillow

I arrived in Brooklyn about 8:30 p.m. and decided to stop home, change into warmer clothes, and continue the rest of the way on foot. The long walk to her home was brisk and enjoyable, and, feeling in good spirit, I was full of anticipation and commitment to the effort. Why not just relax?

A red candle burned in her window; its soft light diffused the ugliness of the windows steel bars.

"Welcome my poet, thank you for challenging the elements. Come in to the warmth of my home."

Christmas lights gave her living room a welcoming glow; Luciano Pavarotti's voice could be heard singing *Silent Night*.

"Your home tonight has a warm atmosphere," I remarked.

"It is my home and you are welcome to visit whenever you wish. I made a few small changes just for you. I have not put up Christmas decorations for years, so what you see is a celebration of you in my life," she said with a soft smile.

"Thank you, Rachelle, what am I to say? You flatter me." I remembered I had made up my mind to relax, but I was curious, why would I be a celebration?

"You are special, you stay in your place, and have not intruded in mine, even though I have invited you to. I don't mean half the drama I express to you. It's just me, playing my own theatrical games, okay?"

My eyes caught the steady pattern of steam blowing from the kettle's spout. I watched the movement for a moment enjoying the dance. Rachelle, silhouetted against the light outside, moved towards the window. For a moment I observed her theatrics as she enjoyed her own sense of mystery and the atmosphere created by the steam.

"Are you ready for the reading now?" I asked

"No, not yet, let us share a meal. I don't eat very much, just steamed zucchini, carrots and cauliflower."

"No meat for dinner?" I asked jokingly.

"No meat, I am surprised you would ask. I even have problems eating vegetables and fruits. I feel I could survive without eating if I could discover a way," she replied.

"To each his own, Rachelle. Let's get back to poetry."

"After we eat, okay Connell? Take it easy you are so intense."

I was feeling uncomfortable and decided to change the conversation.

"I guess you have completed your Christmas shopping and are ready to enjoy your parties?" I asked, trying to make small talk.

"No, I don't like Christmas. I have made no plans and don't attend parties," she responded defensively.

I had touched a sensitive chord. Now I was curious as to this abrupt reaction.

"Well, I am sorry I asked. Did Santa Claus bite you when you were looking up the chimney as a child?" I asked, trying to make light of it.

"My childhood is best forgotten. Let's get back to your poetry and leave Christmas and my childhood out, please," she begged, with a pained expression.

My curiosity getting the better of me I pressed on.

"What was so bad about Christmas that you seem to have blocked out its true meaning of celebration and joy?"

"Nothing, I just don't like December, and Christmas happens to be in December. I hate being alone this time of the year." Her gaze shifted as if recalling a sad event.

"Sometimes in sharing memories and pain we feel better. Would you like to talk about it?" I asked, attempting to reach out.

"No, it's not important," she said with a wave of her hand. "Why would anyone want to listen," she half mumbled to herself, looking forlorn, eyes cast down.

"I am willing to listen; I am not offering an answer, only a platform for you to share."

She seemed very touched. However, the memories being so deep and sad, she did not think anyone was ready to help her unload her life long burden. She thanked me for my sensitivity. Then from what she called, "painful memories," her mood shifted saying, "Poetry, that's the order of the day, okay, let's read."

I felt my poems *Life After Death* and *Spirits Who Take Us to a Higher Plain,* were more inline with what she was looking for.

"Your work borders on brilliance. I am deeply moved by your understanding of 'Universal Law.' Very good," she said, with a big grin on her face. "But now, I need to see more of your body of work before making my final presentation." She came and sat on the floor by my left foot. I accepted her accolades with a grain of salt and remained seated on the couch, my right arm resting on the cushion.

"Let me have the red pillow behind you," she said as she reached across, stretching her body close to my face, not giving me a chance to hand it to her.

"You don't have to stretch, I can hand it to you."

"Are you afraid of my closeness?" she asked coyly.

"No, closeness doesn't bother me; assumptions bother me."

She sat on the cushion as we discussed the poems I had read. The candles were burning low and the music was soft. She acted shy and seemingly somewhat reserved. I wondered if her tough act was just that, only an act.

"So what happened when you were a child?" I asked again.

"Do you really want to know?"

"Sure!"

Nobody spoke for what felt like an eternity. Then finally breaking the silence, in a quiet dramatic voice, she said,

"I lost my brother when I was six years old in Australia. He was killed while we were crossing the street. I will never forget it as long as I live. It was horrible; his hand was ripped out of mine in one second. I don't want to talk about it any more."

"It's important to speak of your emotional and physical pain. Otherwise it will consume you."

"Where does your awareness of psychological matters come from?" she inquired.

"Life and listening. Why don't you get off the floor and sit on the couch so we can talk face to face?"

"Okay, but I would like to sit next to you. I feel so strange right now," she said, looking pale.

"Are you okay?" I asked, concerned.

"Yes, I will be in a moment. Anytime I talk about him I feel ill, but it will pass. Please hold me, please," she said, sounding sad and vulnerable. "Please, hold me Connell, for a moment," she repeated as she put her head on my shoulder.

I wondered about her life as we sat in silence. Who was this woman? I found her closeness okay, and liked her and yet I kept experiencing a strange feeling in my solar plexus warning me to be careful. I proceeded to gently move away.

"Why did you move away? I feel the sudden change; are you afraid of my closeness?"

"No, not really."

"I think you are one of these men who project a sense of mystery that draws people to him, but denies them intimacy," she said.

"That's an odd remark."

"You have great shoulders for a weary head to rest on." The tone of her voice had changed.

"It's getting late but before I go let me state that if you decide you want to share your sorrow, I am a good listener."

"*All* my sorrows?" she asked raising her eyebrows.

"Is there more?"

"Yes, a life full," she said, looking straight into my eyes, anticipating a response.

"A life full . . .?"

"Yes," she said quietly, "for over thirty-five years, through many countries, possibly many lives."

"Let's not leave reality in the pursuit of pain."

"You really don't believe in karma?" she expressed with a genuine look of surprise.

"No, not really. I like the idea, but I really don't believe past lives effect our actions and choices of today."

"We shall see," she said in a half whisper. "What if I prove to you karma exists, and that I have knowledge as to why we have met, and the importance of the work we have to do? If I can prove to you that I am capable of experiencing communication with you without any contact, and give you specific proof, will you begin to believe?"

"I am always open to new experiences, but right now, I must leave."

"You are always 'leaving.' You don't seem to function in other people's time frame."

"Not always, Rachelle, my real purpose for being here is to review poetry; however, we went off on a tangent."

"What are you doing for Christmas?" she asked, out of context.

"Christmas, ah yes. I forgot. I have a series of engagements with friends."

"Do you need company for any of your engagements?" she asked softly.

"No, I don't."

"Just asking. You see what I mean about not including others? It's like you have your life functioning just for you. How interesting to observe," she said with a little sarcasm.

"That's me as you see me, I guess. Remember this whole connection relates to poetry so let's both focus on it. Please don't make any final decisions without my consent."

Each time I tried to relax in Rachelle's company, the need to be cautious was a constant. I had become curious as to what she was all about, this trauma in her life, karma, soul mates, purpose and commitment. I still wondered if this was the right contact for me.

"Can I join you Christmas day if you have no plans?" she asked again out of nowhere.

"No, that won't be possible. I already have plans."

"Who will you visit?"

"Members of my family. Let's change the subject. Where I go, and what I do, is my business. I don't intrude and I am sensitive to intrusion."

"So, how about doing some socializing around Christmas? If we are going to go forward with this project, I don't see any reason why we can't be friends also. I would like to have you as my friend," she said warmly.

"Friendships evolve over time. Right now, coming here is not to socialize. If this eventually leads to a friendship, fine," I emphasized. "For now relax and let go of your mild obsession." I knew I was being played with.

"You are so different," she continued, "Is the rest of your family like you? I hope to meet them someday." She wasn't giving up.

"Why do you assume that you will get to know them?"

"It has already happened in 'thought.' We cannot stop its manifestation," she insisted. I inquired about her family.

"Those who consider themselves family live in Australia. I miss my home, my mother, brother, sister, and my two children, especially around Christmas, but they don't correspond with me anymore," she said, "It's all connected to the pain I carry through life. That is why I feel you could be the friend I never had. I need to experience the 'connection' we have and fulfill the 'commitment' to the connection. When two strong people come together like us, it strengthens the universal bonding of mankind, like a marriage of souls," she insisted, now looking directly into my eyes.

"Hold on, you are getting carried away, connections, commitments, friendships, marriage of souls. What are you talking about?" I said.

"You are frightened of those words, aren't you?"

"No, but they are out of context; let's get back to the printed word, poetry."

"What about friendship?" she asked.

"If it is to be, it will be."

"So there is a possibility. That's a start, we could be great friends," she said jokingly, "Let's toast to a new friend."

Something gnawing at my gut again kept saying, "Keep your distance."

"Let's get back to poetry. Remember, it does not necessarily mean that I will go with *Spirit Path*, okay?"

She became furious at what I had just said, her face reflecting disbelief.

"Don't dare change your feelings. Feelings cannot be changed once they are expressed."

She lifted her cup of tea, which by now had become cold, tilted the cup to her lips and looking straight at me over the rim, said, "If you change your mind, I will kill you."

Her eyes, glittering in the candlelight, were those of a wolf before it devours its prey. Something hit me that felt like hot liquid in my solar plexus. It was time to leave. I quickly got up and walked to the door. Phew! What a confused bundle of energy. If only she could unload her emotional baggage.

Weird . . . weird . . . weird, I thought, as I walked out into the chill of the night.

SIX

Intrusion

The next day I was still somewhat disturbed and confused by Rachelle's comments, when Phil stopped by my office and asked,

"Did you and that woman ever get together?"

"If I interpret the question meaning sexually, no. Something is not right. I can't pinpoint it, but I sense a danger. It seems Rachelle was traumatized as a child and it plays a major role in her life. She claims everyone has isolated her. I don't know if I should help, or not get involved."

Phil and I often discussed relationships and courtship. We respected each other's opinions though he could not quite understand the respect I held for women. The sudden entrance of Alex abruptly stopped our exchange.

"Still wearing those California crazy colors? Alex, you don't wear bright plaid jackets in winter," I said, goading him.

"Why not, the sun is shining in California, so I wear my summer colors," he countered gleefully.

I loved these two characters; they were very good for me. Phil was an impeccable dresser, handsome, attentive, curious, a perfectionist and yet insecure, always falling in love, but incapable of handling relationships. He was divorced and now in love with an airline stewardess, yet still looking for fresh conquests. Alex was slightly bald, rugged and dressed in a more comfortable style. He was smart, caring, alert, and worldly and felt he had all the answers.

"Mister Wisdom has lost his words," Phil said, looking at Alex with a smirk.

"Guys, go back to work. Sometimes things can't be explained," I responded.

Did I really want to help? In no way did I want to get closer to her. I pondered these questions.

A few days passed with no contact. This quiet period gave me time to think and refocus on the purpose of our meetings, which somehow, had wandered away from the main subject, poetry.

I had spent considerable amount of time reviewing my work with her. Though praising my poetry, her continual procrastination confused me. What was her ulterior motive? During the past weeks of work, I realized that there were too many inconsistencies in what was supposed to be a professional project. She now wanted to meet in various cafés, restaurants, and social settings to continue our discussions and plans. Only later I came to realize that she assumed that our meetings were dates. And, there was that strange inner voice that consistently kept saying, "Not now, this is not your platform." The decision not to publish still felt correct. I had not as yet decided when to tell Rachelle; I trusted that she, being professional, would understand.

I sat in my studio and thought about my poetic life - books, dictionaries, pads, pens and binders stashed upon binders, full of my writings. When did all of this start? I cannot recall ever deciding to write poetry; it seemed to have "just happened" and became an enjoyable daily experience. The earliest poem that I was able to find in my notes dated back to when I was fourteen.

I did not write for any acknowledgement through my work, yet received respect and recognition for it.

My bookcases reflected my journey over the past six years. Some books aroused memory, some, still not read. Each page of knowledge unfolded another view of the same theme. My discovery on each step came with the deep realization that nothing was new, just different. I drifted into the history of my books, touching the sources of each new step that influenced my life: volumes of works of Teilhard de Chardin, the writings of Thomas Merton, Tibetan Studies, and the *Tibetan Book of the Dead*, given to me by Dorothy Soyer.

Dorothy was a writer, poet, actress, a student of Zen, Jain Teachings, with interests in anthropology and Tibetan history. We were in an intimate relationship for about two years during which time we moved in the creative world of writers and poets. Our friends were part of the literary movement of New York City. Our styles were very different yet complemented each other. As Dorothy began her studies of Shamanism, the ancient form of healing, taught by Professor Michael Harmen at the New School, she seemed to move away from our center of communication to her need to be alone. Her research was not solely limited to this ancient healing; it was used to expound on her anthropological studies.

Henry my landlord Eli's Abyssinian cat, wandered into my room. I watched him as he moved around this familiar haven, his place of escape from Eli's children. I looked out at the grey winter sky, which appeared closer to the trees that stood naked to the winter winds. The happy sounds of children could be heard as they quickly moved and played. The quietness and privacy of my home made it a beautiful meditative sanctuary. My study was where I immersed myself in my books, extracting gems of knowledge that wove into the tapestry of my daily life. My home was the refuge I fiercely protected. When Rachelle suggested a few times we have a meeting in my home, I experienced an adrenaline rush, a near panic. My feelings were that if she did visit, it would be very hard to get her to leave. Why did I experience a sense of danger; it troubled me.

I watched Henry move in the jungle of books on the floor, stopping every now and then to rub his scent, claiming territory. Yes, claiming territory was what my home was about.

Henry jumped up on my lap, purring, into a snugly position as I nodded into sleep.

I jumped at the sound of a buzzer and for a few seconds was unable to orientate myself. I could not make out if it had been the phone, alarm clock, the smoke detector, or the door buzzer. Yes, it was the door buzzer. I guessed it was probably a mistake as usually nobody came to my door unless I knew before hand. Ignoring it, I went into the kitchen and prepared a cup of tea. The buzzer rang again. I went down stairs, looked through the front door glass panel, and saw no sign of anybody. I opened the door and went down the stone steps. Nobody, a mistake, I thought. I walked back up the stoop. Just as I was entering the doorway, I heard the sound of footsteps behind me and quickly turned; my body experienced a sudden chill.

"Hello Connell, so this is where you live, quite an expensive location. May I come in?"

"Rachelle, what are you doing here and how dare you sneak up on me. No, you may not come in."

"*No?*" she said, surprised.

"That's right, *no*," I replied in the same tone.

"Does this mean I am not welcome in your home, Mister Chambers?" she questioned in a tone somewhere between annoyance and control. "Exclusion and indifference, Connell, are as dangerous as dynamite and detonators. Do you understand what happens to me if I am excluded after all I have shared?" she demanded in a tense darker tone.

"Rachelle, you only shared a moment of your childhood. Unexpected visitors do not sit very well with me. I did not invite you and do not appreciate the intrusion," I said firmly, "so, I wish you good day."

"Do you really understand who you are dealing with? This kind of exclusion is dangerous for people as evolved as you and I are," she reemphasized in a demanding tone.

"Please go about your afternoon," I said, trying not to get into any confrontation. I did not intend to give any credence to an "accidentally passing by" excuse.

"No tea together in the afternoon light? What a pity," she responded in a changed tone.

"No tea, Rachelle, especially in my home," I said, lighter yet still firm.

"I will continue my walk, but be careful. Little Rachelle can get very angry if she is not invited in. She has been outside too long. She is tired of her lonely place. Please be gentle with her when she gets aggressive," she went on, in a softer conciliatory tone.

"I will keep Little Rachelle's moods in mind. Bye." I went inside, closed the door, and walked upstairs, irritated and angered by her intrusion.

When one walks three blocks east and twelve blocks north, locates a house number, rings the door bell, hides and makes themselves invisible, then sneaks up coyly and says, "So this is where you live. May I come in," I close down completely because of the premeditated action and blatant lie. By now I recognized that Rachelle loved to involve herself in mystery and drama. She loved to play with "soul-mate" and "accidental meetings."

The doorbell rang within two minutes. I ignored it. All became quiet as night approached.

SEVEN

Ulterior Motive

Fifth Avenue bristled with last minute shoppers. Dark limousines lined up in front of Bergdorf Goodman, Saks Fifth Avenue, Lord and Taylor. At Rockefeller Center, Christmas hype had reached a crescendo. The sound of jingle bells ringing was everywhere. Tourists crushed against each other trying to get a glimpse of the ice skaters: others, snapped photographs of the life-size white angels and the giant Christmas tree.

I remember how we all gathered in the kitchen on Christmas Eve, in Ireland, to help our mother prepare the meal that she would serve the next day upon our return from church. Each of us was assigned a job, which we accepted without the usual grumble since it was for our Christmas celebration. Besides the turkey with its giblets, which I hated, the meal included the usual plum pudding with warm *Bird's Custard* poured on top, which I would devour, and of which my brother Daniel was proudly in charge. Our final task of the night before going to bed was shining our shoes until we could see our reflections in them. Mother starched and ironed our white shirts and readied my sisters' dresses. It was very important to her that we all looked proper and presentable. The priest of our church in Castlecomer held the Chambers family as a model to emulate. This of course, did not sit well with us, or the children of other families who we knew would retaliate against us. During our

40

half-mile walk to the church, my brothers and I constantly tried to make each other look disheveled pulling out the shirt of one or undoing the shoelaces of another. Mother, holding her brood of six together, constantly fired visual threats with her eyes while at the same time staying aloof as she proudly walked her children to the "House of God."

I walked by Scribner's Book Store on Fifth Ave between 49th and 48th Street and decided to go in. I wandered towards the poetry section and browsed for a while. This section was on the balcony: poetry, poetry and more poetry from Thomas Merton, and T. S. Elliot to Dante's Inferno. Inferno! Why did that word suddenly remind me of Rachelle Richards? Maybe I viewed her life's pain a "purgatory on earth." I wondered if what she had shared with me really took place and if so, how one in pain learns to survive.

I found Galway Kinnell's *The Book of Nightmares* in which his poem, *Under the Maud Moon*, deals with his nightmares and thought why not give this to Rachelle, as his work in some way may awaken her ability to deal with her own emotional nightmare. Why not try to be of help. I bought the book and headed back to the office. By the time I arrived Christmas fever had taken over; the office party was in full swing. At 5:00 pm we all began to head out.

I decided to drive uptown to say hello to my good friend Sarah, whom I had not seen for a while and whose company I enjoyed. She was helping her friend at his flower shop during the holiday season. Sarah was from Montana, and was studying dance with Merce Cunningham in New York City. Her favorite saying was, "Everything is perfect in the Kingdom of God." On arrival at the shop Sarah was alone, ankle deep in discarded flower stems and leaves; chaos abounded. I realized she was on overload and needed help. She explained the owner of the shop was dying of AIDS. By midnight, I was tired and left for home.

My apartment was quiet. Christmas Eve, Silent night, Holy night, just the way I wanted it, peaceful and alone. The red Christmas candle burnt in the open fireplace playing shadow games across my room. I curled into bed, enjoying the sensation of the slow dropping away of all the noise of the day. Sinking deeper into the softness of the pillows, I was suddenly blasted into wakefulness by the harsh loud ring of the telephone. "Damn it," I exclaimed as I woke, "who the hell would call me so late!"

"Hello, who is this?" I said with annoyance.

"Hello Connell, Happy Christmas. This is your soul mate calling you from 'Christmas past.' I waited all day to call you. I have been calling since midnight; you never answered. Were you home?" she inquired.

"No, I wasn't!" I said abruptly. "Do you realize what time it is?"

"Where were you?" she asked, in an off-handed way.

"That's not your business. It's very late. I am going to hang up. Call me in the morning if you have something to say."

"I have a lot to say, I have missed you and realize that I have grown fond of you, and I want to see you again. I could not sleep waiting for you to come home," she said softly.

"What do you mean by 'come home'?"

"Are you afraid that someone likes you? If this is true it saddens me," she said.

"Listen, I am tired, in no mood to discuss anything, so good night!"

"Can I call in the morning?"

"Okay, not too early."

"Where are you having dinner on Christmas Day?" she continued in a monotone voice.

"At my sister's house in Farmingdale," I said, "Why do you need to know?"

"Can I join you, since I have no plans?" she asked timidly.

"No, that will not be possible. Goodnight."

"Where is your humanity?" I heard her say, as I put the phone down.

Humanity? I offered to listen, that was it. Did I really need this?

Christmas morning, crisp and beautiful, the sun was shining brightly and I felt great. Greta was in Australia on a five-week singing engagement. I called my close friend Amy Hawthorne, to confirm I would be coming up as planned. She was overjoyed. I drove up the Henry Hudson River Drive to Piermont, where she had a beautiful house built on the banks of the Hudson River. When I arrived, I found Amy tending her garden. We walked to the conservatory overlooking the Hudson where we sat enjoying each other's company. Coffee was fresh and strong. The cookies, baked by her Italian mother, were served on an unusual platter, the glass faceplate of a deep-sea diver's facemask. Ken, her husband from whom she was separated, was an interior designer, and their home had many unusual artifacts. Amy was a gentle person and quiet companion. We sat peacefully, not needing much conversation, as we watched two swans floating gracefully on the chilly waves of the Hudson. The afternoon arrived too quickly; she had to leave to dine with her family, and I to dine with my sister and her family. We hugged and said goodbye.

I arrived back in my apartment and prepared to drive out to my sister to enjoy the ritual of turkey, ham and stuffing, topped by Christmas pudding with hot custard and trifle. Nobody made trifle like my sister.

Again, as if by some grotesque design, the phone blasted from the wall.

"Hello, Happy Christmas," I said.

"Hello, Connell. It's Rachelle. How are you?"

"Fine, and peaceful," I responded. "How are you?"

"Horrible, just horrible, but it's okay, I don't want to spoil your Christmas," she said sounding agitated.

"What's the matter?" I asked, forgetting our earlier conversation.

"I told you this is a very bad time for me. I have nowhere to go, no relatives here. It's just everyone gets together in America. I miss my family, so it's horrible. Are you still going to you sister's?" she asked, off handed.

"Yes, this afternoon."

"Can I join you? I will be very quiet."

"No, it is a family gathering."

"I need to be with people. If I am alone I will go crazy. Can't you call and just tell her you have a friend who is alone, and who just needs the atmosphere of a family gathering. There is no purpose in my request except to be with people. It does not really matter with whom as long as it is a family atmosphere. I will be proper." I felt she was handing me some sort of sob story and resented her constant harping about Christmas Day and yet she sounded so depressed. I was uncomfortable and told her I needed to discuss this with my sister, and could not promise her anything.

"I will accept whatever she says," Rachelle said.

I told her I found it confusing that in all the time she had been in New York she had not made any friends. She answered that her life was dedicated to a pure spiritual path, that it was very hard for her to be understood in today's society, and that she would rather be alone than tainted by the ugliness that exists.

"Life is being able to be who you are, and still experience different types of people. Why do you feel that you have attained some level of purity that cannot be tainted by human-ity?" I asked curiously.

"You are different, sensitive, and strong headed, but you don't seem to be tainted by a capitalistic way of life. That is why I would like to be among people who understand Christ's Mass, and in the company of a family who is in touch with the 'pure spirit of Christmas.' I don't need to be introduced into your fam-ily circle, or to appear as your girl friend or partner. If you feel that this would make your sister uncomfortable, I will under-stand. My honest reason is that I don't want to be alone, and my choice is to be in your presence."

I knew she was buttering me up but I needed time to pull back and think. I was of two frames of mind; she was saying all the right words but the longer she spoke, the more convo-luted her reasons sounded. I was disturbed, felt entrapped and needed to call my sister for her input. I told Rachelle I would call later.

Outside the afternoon sun spread its low angle rays against the skyline of lower Manhattan. Seagulls floated in the cool clear air. Silence blended. I phoned my sister.

"Happy Christmas. Are we still on for dinner?"

"Yes, we will be dining about six. I am happy you are com-ing," she said.

"I need to ask your opinion on a situation and whatever way you respond is okay with me. There is a person who is reviewing my poetry for possible publication in a New Age journal. She is from Australia and asked if she could join me for Christmas dinner with my family since she does not want to be alone. We are just friends. And, she promises to be proper," I added jokingly.

"My home is open to my family and friends. I have no prob-lem if you bring someone. If it's okay with you, it's okay with me."

"Thank you, I wish I could open my home as freely as you do. I will let her know. See you later."

On the surface everything seemed fine. Yet, there was something gnawing inside me that said, "Don't do it."

I usually listen to myself, but since this was Christmas, I put aside caution. Little did I know in doing so, this action would come back to haunt me. I phoned and told her to be ready by five.

"What a beautiful Christmas gift. I have been alone every Christmas since I came to America. I am very grateful to you, my new friend, and to your sister. Is she special like you, Connell? Do you realize what this means to me, do you?"

"Let's not get carried away, I did not invite you nor did my sister. You invited yourself. We just agreed to your request to be with a family for Christmas dinner."

"I am sorry I got carried away; it's just a beautiful thing you did, making it happen. You are right. I did rather invite myself. I will behave in whatever way you wish as long as I can be with your family, in their home, seeing you among your own," she expressed, in what seemed to me false admiration. Something was still telling me, there was an ulterior motive at work underneath her act of "innocence."

"By the way I have moved into Park Slope, I now live at 151 Garfield Place. I will be waiting on the door steps at five."

I was surprised by her move. When I arrived she was already waiting dressed in a navy blue costume, a white blouse, and wearing one string of pearls; her coat draped over her arm. I held the car door open and she sat down in a very affected manner.

"You look quite smart today, Happy Christmas," I said as I slipped behind the steering wheel. She leaned across and gave me a kiss on my right cheek.

"Thank you for this present," she said.

EIGHT

Tensions Crack

We rode for a while mostly in silence.

"When did you move?"

"Last night," she answered.

"That was quick. How did you find an apartment so fast, especially in Park Slope? How large is it?"

"Four rooms on the fourth floor."

"That must be quite expensive. You had told me since you were here on a Journalist Visa, you were only allowed to make seventy-five dollars a week. You must be paying about eight hundred to a thousand dollars. How can you afford that rent?"

"I don't pay any rent. I know the owner of the building. He is a special friend," she replied.

"Oh, now you have a special friend. If he is so special, isn't it odd he supplies you with an apartment, but does not throw in a Christmas dinner?"

"You are speaking with anger in your voice, Connell, are you jealous?" she asked with a grin?

"No! I find it confusing. There are facts about your life that don't seem to fit. How do you know this person?"

"We met in London and he brought me to America; he shall remain nameless. He continually pressures me to have an affair with him and become his mistress, but I refuse. However, he is convenient now in my life. Some things are changing for me and

47

I have my sights on a new venture that seems promising, so this is only temporary," she said.

"Have you met someone else?"

"I think I have, but time will tell. For the moment he too shall remain nameless."

We continued driving in silence on the Long Island Expressway until Exit 44. As we entered onto the Wantagh Expressway, I wondered who this person in my car really was.

"So you have one male friend who supplies you with accommodations, another with the possibility of a relationship and me, who fills in the emptiness of your Christmas. You know you have successfully made a fool of me," I said annoyed.

"You are sensitive," she said.

"I don't understand why you have to set-up this whole sad story, which is now full of holes. I hate to be used and manipulated."

"Sorry, but I honestly did not use you. Your openness and what I interpreted as your commitment to help spawned my actions. So why are you annoyed?"

"Let's drop it for now." I felt, that if I responded, the mood would carry over into the evening.

We exited the Expressway onto Route 24 West towards Farmingdale.

All the houses were alive with the most spectacular display of Christmas lights. Reindeers in the sky, Santa Claus on the roof tops, red, blue, pink, green, yellow, orange, white lights. Everything twinkled and glittered. Christmas songs and carols saturated the air. What a spectacular expression in this friendly and close knit community where my sister lived for twenty odd years. When we turned onto Walnut Avenue, snow banked the sidewalks; the decorations were more subdued, more personable. As we pulled up in front of Teresa's home, the sound of

Adeste Fideles could be heard. My two nieces, Geraldine and Teresa Junior, were at the door waiting to greet us.

"Hello, Uncle Connell!" Geraldine said in her usual jovial, happy voice, her face alight with the true joy of seeing me. I opened my arms wide to greet my six-foot tall niece. How fast she had grown, I thought, I used to carry her on my shoulders or sit her on my knee in the playground in Prospect Park. I introduced Rachelle, who reached out her hand, but held her body back.

"My name is Rachelle, I am happy to be here," she said.

I was amused to see the difference of these two women, Geraldine, so wide open and innocent, Rachelle, controlled, well traveled, scarred by life's problems, trying to do her best, it seemed. Maybe I was being too strict and demanding. We all moved into the cozy cheerfully decorated living room. Christmas cards were scattered throughout. The dinner table was covered with a white linen tablecloth. Two candles adorning either end, with sprigs of holly and red berries placed around their base, made the table festive. Teresa entered the room dressed in a shell blue dress, her soft red hair contrasting with her light complexion.

"Welcome to my home. Happy Christmas," she said, reaching past me to shake hands with Rachelle. Teresa always greeted everyone with warmth, which immediately made them feel comfortable.

"Thank you for inviting me to your home for Christmas. It is a very kind act. Connell was right when he said you were special."

Teresa gave a quick smile and returned to the kitchen to put the final touches to her Christmas dinner. A flurry of questions followed from my nieces as they buzzed around helping get dinner on the table. Rachelle stood apart from us with a look of self-righteousness. My reaction was to attend to her, but instead remembering her theatrics, I told her to relax and make herself comfortable.

"I am your guest," she said in a loud whisper, "please treat me with respect: do not leave me alone. You are excluding me and denying me the specialness a guest should receive," she demanded, a little louder.

"I came here to be with my family and nobody here stands on protocol. No one is a guest here. You are the one who is acting aloof. Remember you invited yourself and we complied. So don't twist the facts and stop being childish or we will leave right now," I said in a low determined tone. At that moment Tom entered and walking towards Rachelle said in his musical Irish accent,

"Hello there, so you are Connell's new friend? Take a seat; don't stand there, rest your feet young lady. What do you like to drink?"

"Didn't Connell tell you I don't drink?"

Tom, his face weathered and always jovial, was a kind man who loved his wife, children and home. He may have been the purest Irish Man I knew in mind, body, and soul. Proud of who he was and pure in his expression of it.

"Hello Tom, how are you?" I broke in.

"Fine," he replied as he passed me, drink in hand, heading toward his ritualistic responsibilities of carving the turkey, which had just been brought out. Tom was the cook. He loved steak, ham, and fowl, basic and good meals, his potatoes always served on time.

I looked towards Rachelle, who by now had gotten the message. She was sitting on a straight back chair against the wall, her head and shoulders erect. Her small blue leather handbag and her blue suede gloves, neatly folded on her lap, as were her hands, palms down, one over the other, with fingers curled inwards. Both her feet were positioned so properly perfect, equal distance from the front legs of the chair. She sat there motionless; only her eyes moved as she watched the silver trays and bowls arriving at the table. I was reminded of Madame Tousaud's Wax Museum in London.

"Rachelle, don't be so formal, relax! Come walk with me, let us go outside for a few moments, and I will show you the grounds. Would you like that?" I asked, looking into her eyes.

"Yes, please, let's walk for a moment. I do need to relax," she said with her eyes downcast, as she slowly stood up. We walked out into the evening chill. "Maybe," I thought, "if I put my annoyance at being manipulated aside, she might act differently."

"I like your family, your sister is very beautiful; there is a sense of spiritual joy in her home."

"You have only spent about fifteen minutes in their presence, how can you assume that?"

"Connell, you forget that I spend most of my life in the spiritual realm. I know things about people in a matter of seconds. You would be surprised as to how much I know about you," she answered, waiting for a response.

"What difference does it make who I am or what I am about? It actually is none of your business," I said firmly, forgetting my resolve.

"Yes it is my business. I want to know every thing there is to know about you. You seem to exist at a different vibration level than most. You are self-assured and secretive and seem to have a mystery as to what it is you are about, and I would enjoy discovering the mystery. So I have made it my business to know," she said, gaining more confidence as she spoke.

My "mystery" or "secretiveness" was not familiar to me. I never gave much thought about how people saw or perceived me. I was comfortable with myself.

"So now you want to become a sleuth?" I said as we walked back into the house.

Turkey was served, accompanied by mashed potatoes, turnips, green peas, carrots, stuffing, gravy, and wine. Since it was an informal dinner, everyone sat where they wished. Geraldine's fiancé Keith and his family by now had joined us. I offered Rachelle a chair to my right in order that she would be more comfortable.

"Would you like red or white wine?" I offered.

"I don't drink alcohol," she snapped.

"Oops! Sorry I asked. How about water then?"

"That's better; it surprises me that you did not realize how pure of spirit I am." Her voice rose loud enough for the statement to be heard. "You act as if we just met," she added, in a twist of mood, more jokingly. I ignored the statement, and poured the water, spilling a few droplets in the process, possibly displaced annoyance. Vegetables were passed. Rachelle took one potato, one carrot, one spoonful of turnip, and a spoonful of green peas. She placed them in a circle on her plate.

"Turkey time," I said lightly. "Do you have a preference for light or dark meat?" I asked.

"Meat? How dare you belittle me? You are acting as if this is the first time we have dined together. Are you ashamed of me, what is up with you?" she said, directly at me, but again loud enough for others to hear.

"Rachelle is possibly nervous; she has not dined with a family in a home at Christmas for the past four years, so excuse her mood," I said quietly. There was a strange silence. All you could hear were knifes or forks making contact with plates. Stuffing was served and the special turkey sauce was passed around.

"So you have been alone for four years in America?" Teresa said, opening conversation.

"Yes, all alone until I met Connell. He has been so kind, especially today," she answered softly.

"Connell told me on the phone that you were a new acquaintance, involved in publishing. From his conversation I was under the impression that you did not really know each other," Teresa remarked in her usual directness.

"That's true," I said, in a confirming tone.

"It's more than that," Rachelle said, "we have become very close, I have grown very fond of him, yet he acts in an aloof manner, sort of self-protective," she said with a subtle smile.

"It's as one wishes to see it," I said as a matter of fact. "Each of us knows our own truth, so what's the point?" I added trying to diffuse the moment.

"You see, Teresa, Connell is embarrassed. He does not want to admit we know each other for many lifetimes, definitely four hundred years ago. I know this for a fact, God made me aware of him. He is my soul mate," she said, with an air of authority, her shoulders straight, face, in a stone like expression, no movement except for her eyes that scanned the table waiting for reaction. Silence seeped across the table. Tom's eyebrows moved upwards slightly, but he never missed a movement as he sliced the turkey. Teresa's face showed no response, Geraldine's eyes shot to mine; I cast my eyes downwards.

"It's true," Rachelle stated, breaking the silence. "Don't you know anything about reincarnation? Don't tell me you are all pure Catholics in thought and expression. Even God spoke about reincarnation," she said, trying to break the tension. "Well Connell, what do you have to say, are you suddenly just a pure Catholic?" she said, annoyed, as she dug her position deeper.

"Anyone want another drink?" Tom said, "What about you, Connell?"

"Okay, Tom, wine." As I lifted my glass and reached toward Tom and the bottle, Rachelle's face showed frustration and anger, yet she held her composure.

"How dare you put me on the spot? You will pay for this," she said in a whisper looking at me, then not at anyone in particular, continued, "Connell, as you know, is a very deep man, you should be proud of him."

"Who cares as long as he is happy, what's the difference, as long as he is a good Irish Catholic; how's the wine Connell?" Tom said, moving away from the subject, as was his nature.

"I recently saw the movie, *The Dead* written by James Joyce; excellent production and direction," I said to change conversation.

"Oh! When did you see it?" Rachelle asked, her face expressing mild surprise.

"Over a week ago. Remember, I mentioned it to you?"

"With whom did you go?"

"Myself!"

"I am surprised that you went to a movie without asking or telling me you were going," she proclaimed, just loud enough for the statement to register. "How could you find time for a movie if you are so busy?" I did not bother to answer. We continued with small talk as we finished dinner. Rachelle, ice cold in expression, never raised her eyes. Geraldine and Keith shared their plans for their wedding. Rachelle expressed her appreciation of marriage and the importance of one's dedication to a commitment.

"I have not been to a family wedding in years; I bet your wedding will be beautiful. Maybe Connell will take me as his guest," she said, waiting for a response; Geraldine's eyes shot to mine. My family did not manipulate people, so Rachelle's personality and manipulations were very obvious. We usually did not get into confrontations with each other or with guests.

"How is mother fairing in London?" I asked Teresa.

"Fine, fine, a little lonely, feels a bit isolated, would love to receive more calls and letters," she replied without being judgmental.

"You don't contact your mother, how shameful; you seem casual about relationships and commitment," Rachelle said, with an air of condemnation.

Trying to keep my cool, I told Rachelle that my relationship with my family, especially, that of my mother, was completely off limits and not up for discussion. If she believed that pretending we were in a relationship gave her the right to pass judgment, she was absolutely mistaken. I sensed she was pushing to create a rift. I reminded her that she invited herself, and to act in like manner.

"You are very cruel and single minded; we have to talk again later," speaking now in a loving tone trying to establish the semblance of having a history of confrontation.

I was seething with anger and now knew I had been set up. Her behavior and rudeness to my family as well as to me was embarrassing but I did not want to cause more friction and spoil the Christmas celebration. That strange feeling in my solar plexus returned. I did not remember if the trifle was up to Teresa's high standard.

The evening came to a quiet close. Guests, left, Teresa junior kissed me good night, Geraldine, walked out with Keith; Tom went to bed. Rachelle stood up and while keeping her body stiff reached her hand out to thank Teresa,

"You have shared with me your joy, and I hope as Connell and I get to spend more time together, we will see much more of each other. It has been a beautiful evening," she said with a warm smile. Teresa looked towards me, our eyes made contact, and we knew Rachelle's performance was without substance.

We drove north to the Long Island Expressway in silence and headed back to Brooklyn. I needed to confront her behavior and was angry at having been seduced by her sob story of needing to be with a family on Christmas day. I finally found my voice.

"What was your purpose in trying to establish we had an ongoing relationship? You know this is not true, so why make a fool of yourself in front of my family. They are not naïve, everyone was aware of where you were coming from. Do you know how stupid it all must have looked to them?"

"So what is wrong in creating an atmosphere of tension, it produces a reaction, and I made you angry. This shows me that there are feelings involved here. You may think they are of anger, I know better, I study subtext, and you actually like me. You are denying these feelings by controlling me to respond your way. The context of what I set up is of no importance, the reaction was what I was looking for, and I got it. You underestimate me," she said with a smirk on her face. "If you did not have some interest in me you would not have responded to my needs and brought me with you," she went on, in a more serious tone.

"Rachelle, I think you bring too much theatrics into your life by mixing reality and make believe. You don't seem to know the differences between feelings and compassion. So stop dreaming, it is not healthy."

"You are actually afraid of me," she said in a tone of surprise. I did not respond, as the comment was unfounded. The rest of the journey continued on in silence. We turned onto Garfield Place and on arrival at her building I remained seated and said goodnight.

"Don't you want to come up, I am not a monster. Don't be so heavy; you know I enjoy drama; it's what my life is all about," she said in a light tone.

"No," I said.

"Okay, thank you for all your kindness. Maybe I am confused as to how to tell you I like you and want to spend productive time with you. You know, your presence intimidates me. I respond by putting you on the defensive, in order that I know where I am at," she said sort of to herself, yet looking at me. "Are you engaged on New Year's Eve?" she added casually.

"Goodnight."

"It would be nice to be with you and celebrate," she said coyly as she got out of the car.

"Goodnight, Rachelle, I am already committed. Goodnight," I said as the door closed. I could not believe her audacity after what she pulled earlier. I drove through deserted streets still fuming with anger at being set-up. Fresh snow covered the park. There were no Christmas sounds; restaurants and stores, were closed. Cartons and wrappings monopolized the garbage cans. Santa Claus had delivered. Brooklyn had gone to sleep.

I was genuinely concerned with Rachelle's many mood swings and her concept of how we related to each other. She seemed to have a separate agenda. Even though we had another meeting scheduled, the project was going in the wrong direction and I was brooding over how to bring it to closure. Since this was her "trauma period" as she called it, I decided to discuss it with her after the New Year. No need to add to her overloaded memories, if that was what they were. I knew she was very manipulative, yet somewhere in there was a scared person, screaming out for attention. In no way did I want to get involved. Now I needed to focus on the New Year and my poetry. My responsibility to the voice of poetry was important.

NINE

Exclusion

New Year's Eve, the liquor stores were doing a brisk business; people were hustling heading "somewhere." I was heading nowhere. Even though I had received invitations to a few parties, I decided to spend New Year's Eve at home reading, and writing.

My phone began ringing in early evening with friends calling wishing me Happy New Year. Things finally quieted down until one more call came in at eleven thirty.

"Hello Connell, this is Rachelle. I am surprised that you are home. You told me that you had plans. Are you okay? I was worried about you. You have not called or come by. I am really worried about you," she said in one breath.

"Stop worrying about me. Actually I think you are worried about yourself. If you want to be a friend, then stop your obsessive behavior."

"Who stepped on your toes today?" she said playfully.

"Nobody, my day has been peaceful," I answered less harshly.

"Why do you always have to run to a defensive position, why?" she asked.

"The way you want to insinuate yourself in my personal life annoys me," I said quietly and hoped, effectively.

"Why are you still at home so late on New Year's Eve?" she asked, ignoring what I had just said. "Since we are only a few blocks from each other, why can't we celebrate together? I would love to be with you tonight. Why should I deny liking you, when I know why we have met? Don't disappoint me, please."

"Did you hear what I just said, Rachelle, you're doing it again? I purposely chose to be home tonight. I came through on Christmas day and included you in my family plans. You abused the hospitality that was extended to you; I learned my lesson and will not make that mistake twice. So please, back away, and stop this calculated intrusion."

"I don't mean to intrude, but I know you don't mean it. How can you like me and not like me, enjoy our exchange, and not want more? I think you like me more than you want to admit and you are dealing with misplaced emotions," she said, in a quiet tone.

"I am very clear about my emotions and what I want. When it comes to you and me . . . there is no 'you and me,' there is no relationship. Since you are incapable of understanding that, I think it best we bring this contact to a close."

"What about our project, will it continue if I back off?" she asked.

"My feelings about it have changed," I said, feeling a little awkward.

"Your feelings have changed?" she said. "Feelings once expressed and felt, grow, and cannot be changed. I am surprised that you think they can," she said, sounding annoyed, "That is Universal Law."

"It is my decision, my poetry, not Universal Law."

"I am too vulnerable and sensitive for this type of treatment. I will not bother you again. If you don't want to see me, and that is the message, then I am sorry I ever offered to help you. You have made a terrible mistake. Only God can change the plan of the Universe," she uttered in a low dark tone. "You have no idea of what you will have to deal with by this rejection," she continued in the same dark voice.

"Stop playing your theatrical games, I will not present a false picture of hope. If my abruptness hurts, I am sorry. What brought us together was a poetry project and nothing more."

"Then I go into this year alone, just like before. I thought that you liked me," she said feigning rejection.

"Rachelle, I enjoy being alone and it is now five minutes to midnight, so goodnight."

I put down the phone without waiting for a response. Within one minute, the phone rang. I turned down the tone, lifted the receiver, cut off the call, and left the phone off the hook. I realized the more I gave in, the more she wanted. She was indeed a very needy person.

Next morning, planning to join some friends and fellow artists at a New Year's Day party in Manhattan in early afternoon, I put the phone back on the receiver. As soon as I did so the phone blasted out its shrill ring, as if waiting to disturb my tranquility. I answered. It was Rachelle.

"I have been trying you all morning. Your line has been continuously busy; who have you been speaking with?" she asked. "I was worried; I thought maybe something was wrong."

"Rachelle, I told you before, stop this obsessive behavior," I replied abruptly.

"Can we spend a few hours together today and celebrate the New Year in the sunlight?" she asked softly.

"No, I don't have time, I am late for my engagement," I said quietly.

"Not even a New Year hug? I am alone, and like Christmas, this is a painful time for me."

After the fiasco at Christmas, I had no desire to be responsive to her needs. However, this being the holiday season, was I now being callous and lacking in compassion?

"Just a hug, Connell, I promise," she pleaded. I knew I was being manipulated, but since it was on my way to the city, I agreed, "Okay, just a hug, then. I will ring your bell, come down; hug time."

"I will be ready when you ring," she said joyfully, as she hung up the phone.

I pulled up outside her home. She arrived at the door in beautiful attire with her brown hair loosely flowing upon her shoulders. I walked to greet her, "You look elegant, Happy New Year," I said, stepping back.

There was always that voice within that said, "Be careful, you don't understand, be careful."

"What about my hug? I want my New Year hug," she said in a girlish way. "What happened to my New Year hug?" she said again, a bit more demanding, but with a soft smile.

"It's here," I said as I opened my arms to give her the hug. She rigidly moved towards me, arms by her side, eyes cast down, and in a submissive gesture raised her eyelids as I hugged her. I held her for a moment and wished her a Happy New Year. As I released the hug, her body remained rigid. I looked at her, and in that instant, in what seemed out of place, her eyes shifted to a look of aggression.

"Are you okay?" I asked.

"Yes, why do you ask?"

"Your expression changed," I said, "and your response to my hug was not what I would call receptive. Anyhow, I must leave or I will be late," I said, moving away.

"Connell, I am sorry if I upset you," she said.

"I am not upset, confused, yes. Usually, when one gives a hug, one gets one in return, that's all," I said. "I've got to run now, bye."

"Don't go, please, stay a moment," she said, her eyes wide open, "stay just another few moments, please, I want just one more moment," she continued in an almost begging tone. "You don't know what your hug means to me. I can't hug back because you seem insensitive to me. I feel you hug more as an obligation of sorts, like, 'let's hug, get it over with, I've got to go,'" she said softly but firmly. I was annoyed yet I knew she was right. My purpose for stopping by was to give her a hug and go to where I wanted to be, with my own friends. As I was thinking this thought, she said,

"Why don't you take me with you and surprise your special friends. It would be an expression of friendship and a sort of commitment to what we are about."

"Rachelle, any answer to you now would be the wrong answer," I said firmly.

"I have a place that needs respect also, so I am asking you to take me with you, that is my wish. I want to be with you today and tonight. I like you a lot and want to spend quality time with you, don't you understand?" she asked in a demanding tone. "Why are you so stubborn, Connell, am I ugly, or are you ashamed of being seen with me? You know by not taking me, you are rejecting me. This I cannot understand, since I know you like me, and are confused about what to do with me. Well Connell, whatever your decision is today, I will accept, but remember I will not disappear. I like you," she said, adding, "Before you run off I would like another hug."

I hugged her again. It was more convenient to open my arms than to confront. She wrapped her arms around me allowing her body to come completely against mine.

"Is this much better?" she asked in her earlier frail voice.

"At least it shows you are alive," I joked.

"It's all yours if you wish it," she said in a whisper.

I released my arms, kissed her on the left cheek and walked to my car.

"Happy New Year. I will miss you, Connell," she called out, now speaking in a normal voice.

I arrived a little late and found the party in full swing. I mingled with my friends making small talk and exchanging greetings. Drinks and food were served, and midnight came too quickly. We all hugged and moved out into the night chill and the New Year. I arrived home at 2:00 a.m. crawled into bed, closed my eyes, and feeling content, within seconds fell asleep. Suddenly the phone rang.

"Hello," I answered in a cheerful voice thinking it was Greta calling from Australia where she was still on tour.

"Connell, I was so worried about you. I have been calling you since 10:00 p.m. are you okay? I have been so worried I have not been able to sleep," Rachelle said.

"Rachelle, what are you doing calling me at 2:00 a.m.? You're just curious about where I go and what I do. Do me a favor and stop this crap. Goodnight!" I said, putting the phone down. Within seconds, it rang again. I picked it up, "I am warning you, don't call me again," I said annoyed.

"Are you okay, Connell?" This time it was Greta calling, "What is the problem, you sound annoyed?"

"Nothing," I said, "Sorry, I just got a call from someone who annoyed me, but everything's fine."

We chatted for a short while then said goodnight.

I drifted into sleep.

TEN

A Horrifying Tale

January, a time to reflect, a month of chilly winds, of raindrops frozen in mid air on their journey down. Trees resembling those in Japanese drawings against changing skies: long, cold shadows. People seem lonelier in winter; smiles more genuine. I enjoyed kinship with those who walked bundled up in the cold winds. There is alertness in movement, quick entrances and exits from stores, cars, and theatres. Around Lincoln Center, from a distance, I could observe people silhouetted in the late evening sunshine, their breaths pulsating the air in quick conversational exchanges, the quick hugs and flip of long scarves and shawls.

New Year was a time to stroll, a time for resolutions. Mine was to have a manuscript of my poems published hopefully by an established house. After spending a few days working in the tranquility of my home, it was time to head out and re-stock my refrigerator. *Back to the Land*, the best natural food store in Park Slope with organic oranges, apples, yogurt and milk, was an oasis for distilled water buffs. Re-supplied with all my special choices, I waited in line reading one of the health magazines I picked up.

"Hello Connell, I have been observing you for a while in the store and couldn't help but admire you." A soft seductive voice seeped through the store and street noise.

"Oh, fancy meeting you here, Rachelle!" I said surprised, experiencing a strange sensation in my stomach. I dismissed the feeling, chalking it up at being taken off guard.

"How was New Year's Day?" she asked.

"Fine, quite enjoyable, actually."

"I miss your poetry; we must conclude our selection this week as the March issue will be finalized in January. I must run; I am late for an appointment. Let's have dinner soon," she added in a business like tone, disappearing as quietly as she appeared.

"We must conclude our selection this week . . . let's have dinner soon," she had said. Not a bad idea, I thought, if we could bring closure to the project. I had to make sure she did not interpret this as a date. However, whenever I agreed to any of her suggestions, it fueled her fantasy of being in a relationship; that was the gamble. Did I really want to have dinner with Rachelle? Absolutely not, I intended to use it for closure. I knew it would not be easy because she always arrived with an agenda. If only she was able to keep the obsessive part of her personality in check, working with her on the poetry would have been agreeable.

Social events in New York City were still on the quiet side. I called Rachelle and informed her of the place and time. The response was immediate. I believed and hoped she understood this was a working dinner only.

The Raintree Café on Prospect Park West and Ninth Street, which had been an ice cream parlor in the nineteen fifties, was an excellent choice. The ambiance would be perfect. It was in my neighborhood where I would feel more comfortable and have better control of the evening. January six was damp and rainy. Rachelle appeared in her doorway dressed in a dark blue tailored, wool overcoat. She walked towards the car, slowly, with an air of confidence. I decided not to open the door for her or make any gesture that could be misinterpreted.

On arrival at the Raintree, we sat by the window, with the lights of the Park to our left. Conversation was sparse, as if we both had a need for silence. I felt comfortable and at ease and hoped this would allow for normality in communication.

"You are very peaceful today," she said, "I like you this way best." We placed our order.

"Why do you continue to eat fish in my company?" she asked quietly.

"I am eating fish because I wish to eat fish," I said.

"You are very complex and full of contradictions. Maybe, if we spend more time together, since we are neighbors and friends, I could learn from you, especially on how to be strong."

"How long have you been in America?" I asked, ignoring her comment.

"I am here on a journalist visa, which expires in four years, so there is no fear that this will be a short friendship," she said, not answering my question.

Her response, hit me like a red flag.

"So you feel we will be friends for a long while?" I asked as casually as possible.

"Yes, a long time. Do you realize that by knowing you, I have begun to know myself again? I am very grateful to you for not being nice to me just to please me. This pleases me very much."

"I never know how to take your comments. At times you tend to be very complementary, then in a flick of a switch you change. Are you trying to keep me off guard?"

"That is not my intention; it's just that my defenses continue to pop up. I find myself wanting to be vulnerable in your presence, and in doing so your power threatens me. So to prevent any hurt to myself, I create a character of sorts, which I can call upon at will. Then I sit back and watch the part of your personality, normally hidden, surface. When this happens I don't feel vulnerable anymore," she said in a monotone voice.

"Why are you giving credence to being subject to another's power? I asked.

"I am not, I am just protecting myself."

Rachelle stated that she attended some meetings locally and that there was a possibility that our paths may have crossed before we met at the Futon store. After small chatter, we focused on what needed to be done regarding the project.

"We are on the cusp of the final stages of publishing and will need one more set of poems to solidify the project. Another evening needs to be scheduled for a reading at my home. I like what I have seen so far and with this final reading, we will be able to go forward."

"I understand but I have not made a final decision."

"I am aware of that; anyhow I have to interview you for my company. If that is acceptable, we can do it now."

My intention had been to put closure to the project that evening, but being curious about the interview, I agreed. At this point Rachelle brought out her note pad and proceeded. Most of her questions related to where I went and what type of meditative groups I belonged to. Being wary, I gave general answers, never naming any specific group or place. I felt the need to keep my movements, friends, and acquaintances private.

"There is a lot of avoidance in your answers," she said curiously.

"I expected the interview to be about poetry, not about where I go and what I do. Let me get the check. Rather than drive I will walk you home," I said.

We left the restaurant and walked along the Park to Garfield Place. The rain had stopped. Rachelle said she loved the romance of strolling. At moments in our silence she would look at me, stare, and then look away. She repeated this action a few times. A few yards away from her doorway she asked,

"Have you lost interest in our special connection?"

"What special connection?"

"The interest you showed before Christmas to help me banish all my childhood traumas," she said curiously.

"I said I would listen so that you could unburden yourself, but I am not an analyst."

"I don't need you as an analyst. I have already spent a small fortune on them since coming to America. I felt, as you had pointed out, that it was healthy to share with friends."

I was very familiar with America's pastime with therapists and analysts, so Rachelle's comments seemed natural. We arrived at the dark stone steps of her building.

"Goodnight, and thank you for joining me for dinner," I said.

"It's still early. Why rush away? I would like to share that part of my life we touched on before. Give me an hour and I will make you a pot of tea, served with excellent healthy cookies."

"Okay, an hour." This was as good a time as ever. I was curious about the reality of her stories and not sure what to believe.

Entering her apartment, I was surprised to see it well furnished, and not sparse like the one on Atlantic Avenue. Everything was in place, music was playing softly; we took off our shoes leaving them by the door.

Rachelle went to the kitchen, filled the kettle, and lit the stove.

Sitting on a well-worn leather swivel chair I observed her movements; she was smooth, coordinated and well rehearsed.

She returned to the living room carrying a black lacquered tray upon which was placed a small antique teapot, two white floral print porcelain cups and saucers, and on a matching plate, finger snap cookies that I recognized from the local health food store. She gently placed the tray on the oblong smoked glass coffee table between an antique silver candle stand and a delicately balanced incense burner whose smoke spiral crept upwards playing in the flicker of the candlelight. She poured the tea, stopping approximately a quarter of an inch from the rim. Handing me the cup, she asked, why I had select the leather chair. When I answered it looked comfortable, she said she felt the reason I selected to position myself there in her company was that it was a safe place, and that I would always be in control. She was challenging a response.

"One choice we have in life is to observe, I always wish to exercise that choice. If from that place I create discomfort, so what, I am comfortable sitting here."
She was trying to pull me into a confrontation.

"You are so far away from me. Come here, sit close to me," she said, as she patted the cushion on her couch.

"You selected to sit over there, not me," I said.

"You are right, once again, I did choose to sit here," she said. She stood up, walked to the far side of the room, and picked up a large cushion.

"This is what I use with my clients when I am counseling." Putting the cushion on the floor to the left of the chair at a forty-five degree angle, she squatted down into a semi-lotus position. "So, now, let's have tea and biscuits," she said playfully, "Are you strong enough to listen to my childhood trauma and not run away?"

"Sure."

"And your tolerance?'

"Absolutely!"

"I warn you if you help me release my monsters, I will be indebted to you for the rest of my life," she said looking straight into my eyes.

"You don't have to be indebted to me for anything. Just share what is comfortable."

"My birth was a mistake," she said in an off-handed manner, yet watching my eyes for a reaction to the quick switch.

A mistake, I thought, what an odd word.

"There are no mistakes," I said emphatically.

"I miss him desperately. If I had not been born, he would not have died," she said, her eyes cast down.

"We were playing Hop-Scotch together, he was laughing, his eyes were laughing, and the air was warm and breezy. We played together all day . . . we didn't say much; we just played and played.

'I'm getting hungry, Nicole, can we go home now, can we?' he asked.

'Let us play a little longer.'

'But I am hungry,' he asked again.

'Let's play a little longer,' I repeated.

'No, I am hungry, I want to go home,' he said.

'A little longer, just for me,' I insisted.

'I will die of hunger,' he said playfully.

We started crossing the quiet street towards home and almost reached the other side, when I grabbed his little hand in mine and in a running, skipping movement began pulling him back across the open street, 'No, Nicole, no,' he was crying, 'I want to go home, I'm hungry.'

The scream, I will never forget the scream. It burns my mind, my soul . . . the scream, the screeching of tires, the metallic shudder of the truck, the thud, as the truck ripped him from me. I can't go on, Connell. It was horrible. His hand was still in mine. His body was gone. The scream, horrible, it was horrible." She became quiet as the tears streamed down her face, her body shaking. I reached and put my left hand on her shoulder,

"That was a long time ago. You were only a child," I said.

"It was my fault."

I kept my hand on her shoulder as she quieted down.

"They all blamed me, my brothers and sisters. There he was playing, he was only six years old, only six." She began to sob out of control.

"How old were you?" I asked.

"Seven," she said in a broken voice, "We were so close. Even though we were young we knew special things."

I remained quiet as she attempted to compose herself.

"Can I move closer to you, please, I feel so cold and alone?" she said, as her sobs quietened.

"Yes, pull the cushion over," I said.

She rested her back against the chair to my left with her right elbow on my knee.

"I always get cold when I speak or think of him; it's as if part of me is dead. You must think I am crazy," she said.

"No, I don't." I felt compassion for her and for what she must have gone through.

"Thank you; I appreciate what you are trying to do. You have become very special to me," she said softly, resting her head on my lap for a few seconds, "I wish it would stop. My head pounds as if my blood is boiling. It drives me crazy. I wish it would all be over."

"It *is* all over, Rachelle," I said searching for the right words, "You allowed the memory to be released and flow out like a river."

"Would you like some more tea?" she asked,

Still spinning at what she had just shared, it took me a moment to answer,

"Yes, please."

I got up to stretch my legs, walk about and try to absorb what I had heard. The wind had picked up outside, its sound playing with the hissing and banging noise of the old radiators in the apartment. When I walked back to my chair, Rachelle was sitting in it, sipping her fresh cup of tea.

"This is a nice chair, come sit here," she said as she gestured to the cushion on the floor. I chose instead to sit in the middle of the couch. She reached over, lit a new stick of incense and sat back.

"Now that I have composed myself, I can proceed. Were you insecure as a child?" she asked.

"What! No, I am as I always have been. As you perceive me, this is how I am. Go on with your story," I said as I picked up my cup and saucer and reached for the Ginger Snap cookies.

"I could not sleep, speak, eat, or drink; every time I would try, I would become violently sick. I could not digest anything; my body became skin and bone . . . nightmares became unbearable. My mother, who was always warm and nurturing, went crazy. She would grab me and beat me until I could not cry anymore, my body full of welts, my face and head cut and bruised. Father said nothing: absolute silence. He never spoke to me or touched me again; he became withdrawn. To them I was dead. Rumors began circulating around school and among my friends that I had gone mad. I became known as 'Crazy Nic.' I believed I had caused my brother's death. The pain was so bad I felt I was bleeding to death. If I died I would be free, never to hear the horrible scream, never to see my mother, or father. Yes, to die. I would be able to see my brother again."

As Rachelle spoke, she seemed to have gone into a trance. I wondered how much of her story was true. It was hard to separate the dramatist from fact.

"Did your father ever speak to you again?" I asked, as I watched my forefinger press onto the crumbs on the plate.

"No, things got worse for him. My mother made a decision to change her whole life. She no longer focused on her family and children. Father slipped deeper and deeper into depression. His black silence dragged me with him. He stopped sleeping, went out into the night, and would return only after we went to school. One morning I was very sick, and could not go to school. Father was sitting on the front porch arguing with mother; mother was shouting.

'Get out of my home, you drunkard, get out. Don't set foot in this house again. I need nobody, get out. I hate a man who crawls and begs to a woman. Go drink yourself to death.' She walked back into the house, slamming the screen door behind her. I was standing a few feet inside the door when she saw me and screamed,

'Now you are killing your father; you won't kill me, I will destroy you first. You are banished to the dark world of demons, cursed, you will never be able to love another, you murderer! Get out!'

She grabbed me by my soft pink blouse, with her left hand, as she viciously beat me across the face with the front and back of her right hand, her rings cutting my face. I curled into a ball on the floor. I suddenly realized the beating had stopped as quickly as it started. Mother was still screaming. I heard the louver doors squeak open and slam shut . . . silence . . . absolute silence. Father, upon hearing the screaming, had come in, grabbed mother and dragged her out into the garden; she became silent. He walked to the gate opened it slowly, looked back at the house. I ran down to him, my vision blurred with tears, clothes disheveled, and feet bare spinning so fast in the heartbeat of despair.

'Stop, daddy, stop, don't go, please daddy. I will die if you go. Daddy, daddy, don't go.'

I cried out as the gate shut with a finite click. He was outside and I was locked in forever.

'Goodbye, Crazy Nic, may God protect you. Goodbye, evil one,' he said, his face puffed from alcohol, his eyes deep, sunken, desperately lost.

'You killed us all,' he said, as the tears glistened on his weather worn face. His hand touched mine through the opening in the garden gate.

'I will miss you, little one, I must go,' he said, as his head turned away. I fell onto the grass and pushed my face into the earth. I remember pulling the grass and its roots, trying to stuff my mouth with clay and roots to suffocate my scream and my life. Father never came home again. He was found dead near the edge of the woods, with his coat rolled up like a pillow under his head, a dirty old blanket over his body, empty alcohol bottles on the ground. Mother, who by now had successfully achieved her own business in real estate, turned to me at the funeral, her eyes glazed,

'When will you stop, who will be next? You killed your father as you killed your brother,' she said. I squirmed under her power and damnation. I looked at father's face, peaceful, no more screaming; I felt the pain of loss in the depth of my being. I walked out towards the roadway into the warm Australia breeze, they were all there. I felt like Christ being crucified.

'Evil, evil, witch, you bitch, God will send you to hell . . . evil, evil, murderer, child killer, die, die, better off dead, evil, death possessed . . . evil, devil' the words whipped through my mind, body, and soul. 'God, kill me also. I cannot live like this, I will go mad.'

I got to the roadside, sat down in exhaustion. Mother caught up with me.

'You are banished to the world of dark horrors, no longer my child, never born from me. Go evil one. Take your journey to your death.' She walked away from me, as I became nothing. I have no recall of how I arrived at my home. The doors were bolted; I was locked out.

The morning dampness had settled into my frail body. As I awoke on the porch, I heard life in the house. My brother came out and gave me some warm milk. I could not swallow. He gave me some bread and fruit in a table napkin. His face was bruised; somebody had beaten him, since the funeral.

Mother, flying through the door, lifted me and in one movement, before I could get to my feet, threw me onto the front garden.

'Get out, you no longer live here,' she screamed.

'Mother!' I screamed back, as the back of her hand ripped across my mouth.

The road was empty and wide. There were evil monsters over the hill. They were very hungry. They only fed off children. Since cars were introduced they had become very angry. My parents were the ones who kept them away from our home. I began walking in my bare feet, in a light cotton dress, and with the napkin of bread. Up the lonely road, the monsters were waiting. As I approached the hilltop, I opened the napkin, broke the bread into small pieces.

'Here monsters, good morning, I brought you breakfast.' I began to drop the small pieces on the side of the road, hoping they would understand. Where were the monsters? I could not see them. I walked and walked, my feet blistered, my eyes were glazed in tears and dust when I saw a farm truck loaded with sacks of grain parked on the side of the road; nobody was around. I climbed up on the back of the truck and hoped that if I hid behind the sacks I would pass the monsters' territory. I began to cry silently as the world I was born into closed gently around me. I believed I was dying. My eyes closed into what felt like a warm stinging sweetness."

Rachelle, who had been curled up in the leather chair, her body trembling, reached over for the hand woven Indian blanket on the ottoman and wrapping herself in it, came over to sit next to me.

"I feel strange . . . please hold me . . . I am so cold," she said, as she now curled into my side.

"Rachelle, this trauma possibly wounded you for life," I said looking at the cold pathetic, trembling person who so often presented herself tall and full of confidence.

"You are talking about events that took place over thirty years ago but are still vivid in your mind. Is it possible by keeping that pain alive you re-enforce your own existence by re-identifying yourself through theatre?"

I had asked her to release her trauma but now wondered if I had made a mistake. This was more than I had ever imagined, and was it all true? I put my arm over her shoulder trying to comfort her.

"You are so distant in your holding, are you afraid of me? Why is it that everyone is afraid to get close to me, am I ugly?" she asked, looking up at me, her eyes damp with tears.

"No, you are not ugly, maybe hard to fathom. As I listened to your story I went from feeling sympathy and compassion into total confusion."

The wind was blowing against the window as silence crept into the room. The incense had burnt down . . . cookies, gone . . . tea, cold. Could I really help? Was I inviting danger? How would I know if this was the right thing to do? I was exhausted, sleepy and needed to go home. Rachelle now seemed to be resting comfortably. I gently took my arm away.

"No, no, please don't go yet. Please, just hold me a little longer; please Connell, just a few more moments."

"Okay, just a few more moments," I said.

I put my arm around her again. She turned her body towards me, her shoulders and upper body across mine.

"Hold me gently and let's be silent. Your presence is so strong, I can feel myself reenergizing second by second," she whispered.

The night winds whistled against the old windows continuing to synchronize with the old radiator; the apartment was very warm. I thought about how life "plays games." I began to nod, the hour was late; I had to leave.

Rachelle had dropped into a deep sleep on my lap. I wanted to ease away without disturbing her. I moved my hand to support her weight as I carefully lowered her head onto the couch and covered her with her blanket. Her breathing stayed deep, she made a few groaning sounds. I waited a few moments to make sure she was asleep then checked the incense, candles, and put out the light. How strange the evening turned out to be.

I put on my dark taupe overcoat, scarf and shoes, which I had nearly forgotten by the wall, and without making a sound walked to the door. I unlocked both locks quietly and with a hand on the doorknob, slowly opened the door when a hand touched my shoulder from behind, startling me.

"You can't leave now. I won't let you sneak out on me after opening me up. You can't leave me in this vulnerable place. Don't go Connell, I need you," she begged in a seductive voice. I looked out enviably into the stark hallway and the stairs in their silence, my hand, still on the doorknob, her hand, still on my shoulder. I turned to face her, her blouse hung open, skimming her bare breasts, her feet were bare, her other hand motioning me back in; her eyes were soft in the semi-darkness.

"Stay with me, Connell, you have helped me. Don't go now. I just need to be held, I feel so vulnerable. You have opened me up."

Staying was out of the question. It had been a long and exhausting night.

"Good night, Rachelle, you will be okay; you have made it so far. At least tonight you will have a peaceful sleep," I said, as I opened the door wider to leave.

"Please, the light, it's bright. Close the door for a moment. At least hold me before you go."

"It's late Rachelle, I must leave and you need to go to sleep."

"If you reject me, you have no idea how dangerous I could be."

"We had a good evening, productive and constructive. Let's not cross over," I said as I walked out the door.

"You will be sorry, I am very special but maybe you cannot see that."

I gave the words no heed and walked down the four flights of stairs.

The cold wind felt refreshing on my face; I pulled my collar up. As I walked away from the building, I heard a scream then another scream that seemed to come from her window; it gave me chills. I looked up; she was standing silhouetted against the light waving gently. Exhausted and sleepy, I walked up towards Prospect Park West. It was 4:25 a.m.

I lay in bed and watched the slow gentle seeping of dawn. I thought of Rachelle and the complexity and confusion of her life and how sad, painful and desperate her loneliness must be. Maybe I was thinking too much. I prayed for answers. I visualized her at peace, all of her trauma falling away. I fell asleep.

The ringing of the phone awakened me. I tried to ignore it but it rang about twenty times and then stopped. I drifted back to sleep. The phone rang again.

"Hello! Who is this?" I said abruptly.

"Hello, Connell, I miss you, please come back. I am scared, I can't sleep, please come back," she said softly.

"Rachelle, I need my sleep. I have to get up shortly to go to work. We have already said goodnight, so please once again, good night."

"I am sorry if I upset you, but if you leave me open and vulnerable like this, I can not be responsible for my actions; I feel unprotected," she said, sounding angry.

"I told you I would try to help if I could and be open to listen, so please trust me. But let me make one point clear, I am not interested in a relationship. Now, please, I must sleep, so good night." I put the phone down not waiting for a response and slipped back to sleep.

Rachelle called me the next evening at home.

"Thank you for listening to me last night. I hope you were not too disturbed by what I shared with you. I wish I knew how

I could free myself of this trauma, Connell. It would mean so much if you could give me some insight into it and advise me with your words of wisdom."

I was not quite sure as to how to approach this. Her story was so bizarre and the parental abuse so horrific, that if true, it was difficult to digest. I had only offered to be a good listener. I had to be cautious.

"According to your story you seem to indicate that by ignoring the pleas and cries of your brother to go home and instead insisting he stay, you carry the guilt of his death. You must approach this drama by reviewing the facts. Yes, you did pull him across the street but it was the truck that struck him. It was a horrific accident, but it was exactly that . . . an accident. Yet the part that you did play was one of wills. Subsequently it was easier for your parents to blame you than to blame themselves for their total negligence in not having adult supervision for their two very young children. By keeping this guilt alive, it becomes your monster. The monster eventually becomes your pet and you begin to despise and want to destroy anyone who makes it disappear.

You talk about your communion with God, yet you depend on man to give you identity.

You seem to obsess over anyone who helps identify your existence and if they satisfy your need, they will be denied their right to leave unless it is you who banishes them. It seems to me, from what you have shared, nothing of your childhood trauma has been resolved."

I invoked the name of God, as I knew that was always her point of reference. While saying all this she did not interrupt or say a word. I was surprised that after a brief moment, she said good night and hung up the phone.

ELEVEN

Death by Proxy

Rachelle phoned inviting me to join her at a Poetry Convention in Washington, D.C. where she was scheduled to speak, and would be honored if I would accompany her. I told her that because of my busy schedule it was not possible.

"Are you afraid of me? You are, aren't you? Don't be afraid, it would be purely platonic."

"Rachelle, besides not having time, I don't think a Poetry Convention is where I want to be."

"There is a good possibility that some important people, especially publishers to whom I have spoken about you and your poetry, will attend. Why would you miss this opportunity? Look at it as if the universe has set up a connection and you are rejecting it. That's not safe you know."

"I don't get what you mean by 'not safe'?"

"It's not safe for you to reject me ever, Connell."

"To understand what one wants to do or not, has nothing to do with safety. Even if I wanted to go, it would not be possible. Do you understand? Are you on some quest?"

"No, but the more you leave my gift plate empty, the emptier you make me feel."

"Anyhow, I don't think going to a poetry convention is productive. Poetry becomes diluted in a crowd. I prefer a more solitary life. It allows me to be more connected with my creative voice."

"Boy, do you isolate yourself. Before I leave for Washington as planned, we have to finalize this poetry selection. Let's schedule a time and place to work. Let's not go to the Café. It is more focused if we work in your home or mine. We have processed most of the work in my home, yet it would be a nice change to switch to your place."

"My place has never been a place for meetings. It has always been a place where I work creatively alone."

"Okay, so let's set it up in my place. You must find my apartment boring."

"Not really. I just go there for you to review and select the poems. In any case you don't seem satisfied with any one of them."

When I arrived at her home, I was pleasantly surprised to see that she had dropped the veil of semi frumpiness, and looked attractive in a simple cotton dress. I wondered if she hid behind a façade. It was a strange moment.

"How sweet of you to be on time. I guess this is boring for you; no final poems selected. Maybe your work is not suited for Spirit Path. You seem to speak in the subtext of language in your poetry. Maybe that's the gift of the poet, the mystery. What do you have to say about that?"

"Nothing really, it is your observation."

"Does it bother you?"

"No, not in the least. Sometimes words have power, sometimes not. Do you or do you not want the poems? If not let's stop right now. Make up your mind."

"Are you aware of your words and action towards women? You believe you are a gentleman, while you set up situations so that women are flattered, like the umbrella, when we met on that beautiful rainy night. You are sensual and very masculine and yet you look at me and do not see my sexuality. Do you find me unattractive, boring or even intrusive, maybe indecisive?"

"Rachelle, first if you consider a natural act such as offering to hold an umbrella over a woman to prevent her getting wet on a rainy day as toying with them, then it seems to me you know very little about social graces. Thank you for your discourse about how you perceive me. Let's not dwell on your insecurities."

"Alright, let's get going."

We chatted for a while and then got to work. It seemed as if nothing I shared from my poems were accepted as possibilities. By now, after having worked about an hour, I had become wary about this project. Since neither of us had eaten, I suggested that we go out locally and have something to eat.

"Oh, we are going to have dinner together, that's nice."

"No we are just going out for a bite."

"I wish to stay in," she said in a soft voice.

"Okay, that's fine with me," I said with indifference.

"I am surprised that you give up that easy. I have some vegetables on the stove. Let me heat them."

While they were warming, she set up a small round table in the living room against the wall directly opposite the front door of the apartment.

"Why place the table there?" I asked curiously.

"I like to be in control and have access to everything. I position things in my home so that when you enter, you see the table with a bottle of wine and two shiny glasses, sort of cozy, do you agree?"

"It makes no difference to me."

As I spoke, she proceeded to light two red candles.

"Why the candles?"

"Why not, don't you think it looks romantic against the rough brick wall?"

"More cozy than romantic I think."

"You're very cautious in the way you select your words."

"Not really."

"You are such a game player, no wonder you are such a great poet."

"Rachelle, if you think that I am such a great poet why is it taking so long to select some of my 'great' poems?"

"In time Connell, it will all fall into place, and when that happens and I succeed in the completion of my plan for you, you will be remembered; absolutely, here and around the world. People's lives, in many countries, have changed because of what I am capable of doing. It's sad because some could not adjust and their lives fell apart."

"If what you are saying is true and the outcome so earth shattering, why has the literary world not heard of you, other than the self-promoting accolades?"

"You will see I have exciting plans as to where I intend to take you."

"I guess I have to do some background research on this lady with whom I am going to have a plate of vegetables and a glass of red wine."

"It's not wine; there is no alcohol in this home. You don't seem to know a lot about me."

"That's true, but there is no need to be defensive. It is a wine bottle and whatever is in it looks like wine."

"Do you think that when an actor is on stage, in character, and has to drink wine that it is really wine?"

"Of course not! It really does not make a difference to me. You have a lot of trigger moments. So, it's a non-alcoholic wine, like a veggie-burger?"

"Sort of."

We chatted, had a few real laughs and shared personal experiences. Rachelle spoke of her journeys to Tibet, Israel and Lebanon, where she worked with orphans in Beirut. She claimed to be the founding director of the Australia Actors Theatre Studio, and performed in Sidney and Paris. She studied speech and drama at Trinity College at Cambridge, and performed with the London Shakespearean Theatre. In New York, she studied with Stella Adler. She claimed to have studied different religious and spiritual pathways using them to link modern theatre techniques with Buddhist principles and practices, so as to create a harmonious center from which to interact in the world. At these moments, she seemed pleasant, and attentive, though at times, she would suddenly sit straight-backed, with a blank stare, as if in a photo shoot. This was the first time I became aware of something about her eyes. When in conversation, she barely blinked her eyelids. After our "vegetable snack," which consisted of a few slices of one small steamed zucchini, and a sip of "non alcoholic" wine, we went back to work in the living room. Rachelle sat on the couch and proceeded to light some more candles. I sat in the armchair at the end of the table facing the window, watching the smoke from the burning incense snake upwards through the soft light, as I wondered what this was all about. Was it poetry, or her way of luring people into her trap?

"Come join me," she said raising her eyebrows.

"I am comfortable where I am."

Rachelle came over to where I was sitting and made a subtle but aggressive move as if she was going to sit on my lap. As she attempted to slide her arm around my shoulder, I saw she was naked under that "simple cotton dress."

"Why don't you want to make love to me right here on the chair, Connell?"

"Rachelle, cool it, the answer is no. Stay focused."

"You make me angry and aroused you bastard," she said as she began to cry. She reached over in an attempt to caress me. "Rachelle, stop this, calm yourself and sit down."

She began undulating sexually, then suddenly exploded with a horrendous scream as if experiencing an orgasmic release; her dress had now fallen from her shoulders down to her elbows.

"You must be gay, why don't you fuck me? Are you afraid of caressing a woman, afraid of sexual intercourse?" she screamed in anger.

"Absolutely not! Rachelle cool down, take a deep breath," I said trying not to loose control of the moment.

She continued her aggressive attempt for a while and suddenly fell silent.

"Are you okay now?" I said, ignoring her dramatics.

"No, I am not okay. Whether you know it or not, we have just had sexual intercourse three times. We made love; you have assaulted my psyche. My spiritual womb bleeds with your penetration while you sit there."

"So, you actually believe that in the past few minutes while I was sitting here we had sexual intercourse. I seriously think you have lost it."

"I know that it actually happened on a psychic level and if that makes me satisfied, so be it. It is becoming part of what we are about."

"So, why don't you broadcast to the world that I made psychic love to your soul," I said, trying to be light for the moment, hoping it would defuse the tension.

"I will broadcast it to the world. I will never let you go until you penetrate me on all levels," she screamed.

Her outburst stunned me.

"Rachelle, what is this all about? It sounds like a Shakespearean tragedy."

"Do you like Macbeth?"

"It's fine."

"I asked if you liked Macbeth, not what you thought about it."

"Why is it of importance?"

"I sometimes apply part of the story to my life, as if I was alive in the drama. I can understand the tragedy. You don't seem affected by things that happen. You isolate yourself from the social movement of mankind. Maybe as a poet that is how you escape reality."

"So why do you want to continue with this charade?"

"I'm a poet too; therefore you know what I mean."

"Not really, let's close this one-sided analysis now as I have to leave soon."

We made an attempt to work for another hour with no progress. This was repetitious and I wanted to leave.

"What are you doing? Why have you stopped working? Read me some more."

"I believe you don't know what you're looking for, or you're not looking for anything except to prolong this game. Fun is fun, but that's it. I have to go."

"Why not stay for awhile? I'm sorry you feel this way. I do ramble, don't I? It's the therapist in me. Thanks for making me aware. Sometimes when we are together, I get lost in fantasies. I get romantic thoughts, like the way you, as a poet, can come to my place in many personalities yet you remain still."

"It's time to leave."

As I was preparing to leave I glanced at the poster above the small table of Hamlet dying.

"That's an unusual poster to have near a dining table. It's bizarre," I said.

"Death by proxy is always close by . . . poison, poison," she repeated.

I got up, picked up my poetry and left. It was something out of a Fellini movie; frames of reality flashed in black and white; air impregnated with a conglomeration of anger, desire, raw passion, and bizarre claims of psychic intercourse; judgment calls on my refusal to physically participate in her sexual demands; the promise that she would not let go until I penetrated her on all levels; the bleeding of her spiritual womb by my psychic penetration; her empowerment to make the world remember me as a "great poet." This barrage on so many levels was nerve shattering and terrifying. What was I doing here? Who was this woman? Though she was attractive and intelligent, her social behavior, as earlier demonstrated, had a great deal to be desired. What had I gotten into? There was an urgency to extricate myself as quickly as possible. Why had I let this continue? Did the sub-conscious thought to have my poetry published, stop me from cutting her off completely? I should have ended the contact long ago. I had to rethink this situation. The dichotomy was frightening as she spun her complex web. Webs are spun in silence. If you are not looking for a web, you fail to see the spider in plain sight.

TWELVE
Pent Up Passion

In spite of my misgivings, when Rachelle called I agreed to the meeting. I told her this would be the last one and a final decision had to be made, either way, to bring it to a conclusion. When I arrived at her home I found her to be upset and moody. She sat as usual on the floor next to me as we read through the last group of poems. After an hour we took a break and while discussing a specific theme of poetry, she expressed her disagreement by suddenly slapping her hand hard upon my knee and quickly stroking my thigh, grabbed my groin. As I pulled her hand away, she burst into tears.

"Cool down and stop crying, we have to talk right now."

I told her to get up off the floor and sit on the couch, and re-emphasized the sole reason we got together.

"You have your opinions about things," she answered, as her sobbing subsided. "You don't seem to realize that things in life are set in motion before we experience them on a physical plane."

We returned to the project but focus was lost. Rachelle was still upset, and blamed herself, for disturbing the constructive atmosphere that "we were building."

"I realize that you don't know what you are looking for, and I have lost interest," I stated.

"I feel really bad. I am sorry," she said as she moved closer. "I just get crazy when I listen to your voice. Could you please listen to mine for one moment?" she pleaded. "I have a lot of pent up passion for you. You seem so far away from me, please, don't resist me; hold me, caress me. It doesn't have to be physical. We don't have to remove our clothes."

She curled up on the couch, and seemed to drop into some sort of a trance, as she repeated, "penetrate my soul." I was careful not to make any physical contact, as that would immediately be taken as encouragement. No matter how many times I discouraged her, it meant nothing. This made working together almost impossible. I had to get out of there. I walked down the creaky linoleum-covered stairway thinking I may have been insensitive. But, I was on constant alert not to give reason for any of my actions to be misinterpreted.

Rachelle phoned a few nights later. She was very apologetic for her behavior and said she had deep respect for my efforts to keep things in perspective and about healthy closeness. She begged to let us finish what we started at our last meeting and promised to keep her feelings in check.

I accepted her words at face value, and agreed to return.

Her living room, where we worked, was very cold. This did not bother me, as I actually enjoyed the chill when working in my own home; however, Rachelle complained. She made a pot of tea, and suggested I bring the remaining poems into the kitchen, as it was much warmer.

The living room, bedroom, and kitchen were all laid out in a straight line, like a railroad apartment. We passed through the bedroom to get to the kitchen, and stopped to pet a cat that was curled up on the bed.

"Now you have met my new lodger," she said.

The heat in the bedroom was unbearable. She told me she had never been able to turn it down, that the control was possibly frozen with rust.

"Maybe you could take a look."

I tried to turn the valve, but it was impossible to budge. I leaned forward to make another attempt, it would not move. I stepped back and bumped into Rachelle who was standing close behind me: her hands reached over my shoulder and across my belly. As I turned around to face her, all she had on was an old faded lace slip.

"Rachelle, you have got to stop this."

She stood in silence trying to look seductive and sultry while at the same time looking as if she would cry at any moment.

"Please hold me, I feel so stupid. I had promised myself not to take advantage of you, but I failed again," she begged, as she wrapped her arms around herself.

"Now I must love me, because nobody loves me. My mother and father never loved me. Will someone penetrate my soul?" she begged as she broke down crying uncontrollably. I wondered whether this was real or another one of her acts; she was good at theatrics. I made it clear I was not going to have sex with her.

"Oh yes you are, whether you experience it or not. It is happening to both of us on so many levels. Nobody has made me feel so alive and pulsing with passion," she concluded. I walked back into the living room to quickly collect my thoughts. She followed, crying, saying rejecting her made her feel dirty. Maybe I was missing the story. I suggested we sit and discuss parameters. We discussed attitudes towards sex and friendship. She said my input was too convoluted. I realized nothing would ever change and I had to put an end to it. Enough is enough, I thought. It was time, once again, to go down the stairs into the night.

THIRTEEN

Festering Madness

It was now obvious Rachelle's real interest was based solely on her desire for a sexual relationship. When she called to arrange another meeting at her home, I refused. I told her that instead, I would meet her at Cousin John's Café in the neighborhood. I intended to inform her of my decision to pull out, and thought it better to select a public venue to do so.

After a cordial greeting, Rachelle opened the conversation.

"We will need a bio of four or five lines for the publication. Did you bring any final poems for review?"

"No, I am pulling out of the project."

"Without my permission? What do you mean? That is impossible."

"I have decided not to go ahead, that's all. It was your initial suggestion that we make an attempt, then you took it on your own to go ahead without my consent."

"No, you can't disappoint me and make a fool out of me at this stage."

"Don't get so bent out of shape; people change their minds everyday. Nothing was finalized."

"This was my idea from the beginning and you will not sabotage it, not now, never. You have no idea what my investments are in this; they go beyond publishing and have nothing to do with poetry. It has to do with soul mates. I guess you know nothing about that. You have no idea what you have ignited within me so please reconsider before it is too late."

I told her there would be no Spirit Path connection. Rachelle was furious and would not accept my decision. I had not taken into consideration that her job may possibly be in jeopardy.

"You cannot do this," she begged, "I shared intimate moments of my life with you; they cannot just be left out there. You must stay with me. It is our connection. It was predetermined on the rainy night we met. Don't you get it? It never really was about poetry."

When I stated that choices were based on free will, she reiterated that it was a command coming from the universe through her to bring me back onto the path of righteousness which was God's will. Going against His plan would bring me misery and destruction. "You have to stay close to me for protection. To part ways would be to invite festering madness." In order to dilute the tension within the dynamics of exchange, I needed a release valve. I told Rachelle that we were still neighbors. She responded, saying, it was not about what people do but of honoring the connection. We left the café in silence and parted ways. As she walked away I glanced back at her, she seemed completely deflated. During the sporadic communication that followed, Rachelle kept emphasizing the need to keep the friendship alive. She eventually stopped calling; I began to believe her obsession with me was over.

My work schedule kept me busy, and early springtime brought a new vigor to my life. I once again enjoyed my pre-dawn walks in Prospect Park and the fascination of the glistening morning dew on the grass caught by the rising sun. I would sit on the spreading roots of an old oak tree, which I named my "Bodhi Tree" and meditate. Many hours were spent writing poetry and reading. I soaked up photographically the beauty of the blossoming of spring in the Botanical Gardens. Evenings were spent in social engagements.

March arrived and I had one of the occasional dinners with Ingrid, enjoyed spending time with Amy, and attended one of Sandra's readings. Sandra needed new headshots so we decided to experiment taking pictures outdoors during a hurricane; the results were exciting.

The highlight in April was attending once again Greta's club performances at Erv Raible's Eighty-Eight's. One evening I invited Sandra. As usual I attended every performance along with other devotees including her very close friends, Leon Matrakis who always arrived with an entourage, and Bill Stansmore. Peter attended when in New York and Darine kept busy making sure everything ran smoothly. I often invited friends to join me to celebrate Greta. After inviting Amy to one of the shows, she was so enthralled about the performance that she immediately planned a dinner party at her home in Piermont in honor of Greta. Darine, Peter and Bill, whom she had met the night of the performance, were also invited.

Amy had taken great care to prepare a delightful meal. We retired to the living room after dinner. The white birch logs were burning in the fireplace and the ribbons of lights from the Tappan Zee Bridge reflected in the Hudson River. The ambiance was perfect and at Amy's request, I read a few of my latest poems. I was thoroughly at peace.

I spent the night at Amy's home and returned to the city the following morning. One late afternoon at home, Rachelle called; I was surprised to hear her voice. I asked how she was and if everything was okay.

"No, it's not," she answered, "I am in a terrible state. I can't handle this anymore."

"What are you talking about?"

"Everything, I can't talk. Nobody wants to listen to me."

"I am listening to you now. Why don't you tell me what's wrong?" As I was waiting for a response I heard what sounded like a match being struck. "What was that?" I inquired.

"Nothing!" Suddenly I heard a male voice asking her to put the cigarette out at once.

"No I won't," I heard her answer,

"Put it out, and give it to me, you can't smoke in here," he insisted.

I knew Rachelle did not smoke; something was wrong. I asked her where she was and she said she had to pick up some medication.

"For what?" I inquired.

"I am very depressed. Everything is spinning out of control."

I asked her to give me the phone number so that I could call back in case we got cut off.

"That would be nice," she said.

At this point a man took the phone away from her and asked me who I was, and what I knew about her.

"We were working on a project together."

"Mister, whoever you are, this is an outpatient clinic . . . you know what that means?"

"No!"

"It's for the..................."

There was the sound of a struggle and the phone went dead. I called back the number and was informed that it was an out-patient clinic for the mentally disturbed. I inquired where they were located. "Clinton Avenue off Flatbush," was the surprising answer. I asked to speak with Rachelle and was told there was nobody there by that name. I insisted and stated that I was just on the phone speaking with her, "Sir, I just told you this is a clinic for mental patients." The phone clicked off.

FOURTEEN

Disturbing Illusions

In early June I began receiving a series of strange letters and cards from Rachelle as well as long-winded messages left on my answering machine.

The first letter of the series dated June 10, began with "Saturn has moved to Sagittarius giving respite to the dense energy which has been surrounding Capricorn and Aquarius." She then apologized for her behavior and begged to keep in contact, saying how much she "missed terribly our intimate connection" the "sharing of our poetic souls," and "the exquisiteness of breathing together."

Alarms immediately began to ring. I knew she was trying to draw me back into her web. I believed I had acted out of compassion in letting her unburden herself by listening to her story. Was my idea of being compassionate unrealistic? My actions were interpreted as best suited her. Whatever my response, it would make no difference. She had her own mind set. I had to move quickly and find some answers.

Then, one evening on my machine, she left a message.

"At this very minute June 14 at 1:30 a.m., the moon is in conjunction with Venus, so I wanted to call you to share the wisdom that is influencing this week from *Tao, Book of Days* which says, there must be a principle that is recognized relating to the foundation of life that brings people together. It would be nice if you would call me, I would love to talk with you."

While listening to the message my downstairs door buzzer rang; I ignored it.

Two nights later, on the 16th, I clicked on the answering machine.

"Well hello, you do seem to be out late these days. I called you Monday and – um – you were apparently out –so – I just had one or two things to say – don't you think it's getting a little bit silly to not call me – I mean it really is sort of quite proud and angry of you to do that and perhaps *snobbish* – and – imposing your thoughts?"

The buzzer rang.

"Anyway just to finish," here it sounded as if she lit a match, "if you called me it would not necessary encourage or discourage me - it's – I am encouraged by *something higher* than a cliché like that; I am guided by *God in His perfect wisdom.* So it has nothing to do with what you or I toss or not toss into the situation; therefore it would be nice to hear from you – and – um – maybe you could - ugh, kind of rise above – this silly idea. I hope you are well anyway – and – um - that everything is going well with you."

The buzzer again!

Another message immediately followed. This time she spoke as if performing on stage complete with theatrical affectations.

"Your hostility and unforgiving attitude are completely unbearable. I can only wish that you could be responsible. I can't take it anymore."

Buzzer!

Rachelle spent a few hours buzzing, then, possibly calling from a nearby phone booth, left another message.

"Don't you think you should come down and talk to me? It is silly to go to all that trouble to just not talk. Let us meet somewhere private and talk." Now crying, "Please come down and let me in. Connell, are you there?"

I knew letting her in would further complicate matters and it would be impossible to get her to leave. I was confused and frustrated; the barrage kept up until she tired.

Sunday the nineteenth being a beautiful day, I strolled down to the Seventh Avenue Fair in Park Slope. Bright color balloons floated, some attached to railings, danced in the breeze. Musicians, lost in their rhythm, played in the summer sun. Laughter was spontaneous, as the neighborhood became a carnival; a conservatory of music blended with the neighborhood of song. Some played as if their souls had waited to express. Others, their hands sweating in the nervous anticipation of participation, danced and laughed. I loved the way they looked, the sound of their instruments and their songs. Jazz competed with the beat of African, Jamaican and Haitian rhythm and the splitting open of fresh coconuts by a glistening, sweaty Rastafarian. Music sheets flapped in the wind, a voice releasing notes weaved in the language of music. Notes flew away, as the music touched all. The sun was warm and the smell of a summer fair was in the air. A touch upon my shoulder startled me.

"Rachelle, it's a surprise seeing you here; were you following me?" I asked with a grin, yet it was close to the street where she lived.

"I did not realize you would attend a street fair. I considered you more of an elitist. Maybe you should have called me."

I told her I did not need to call anyone if I wished to stroll at the fair. She said she was impressed and that like her, a poet out here among artists, living our art. "You never responded to my letter of apology on June 10. I am sorry about the things I said and am happy to find you here relaxed and an active participant in our community. There is hope for you yet. I miss our intimate connection. Are you going to spare me some time? Maybe we can integrate into the community together? If you have not eaten could we have a snack together?"

"No, I am enjoying the afternoon in my neighborhood, that's all," I answered.

"What about my letter, are you going to keep it?"

"I have no reason to. You expressed yourself and that's that."

"There will be more letters, more words, more conversation. You have released a river of thoughts, emotions and playful tricks. I could be a real good friend, Connell."

"I have to return home. Enjoy the rest of the evening."

"Together?"

"No, I have a dinner engagement."

I walked back up the avenue feeling nervous. My thoughts went back to the street fair, the smell of burgers and of fresh coconut milk mixed with the beat of music.

In the evening I took Greta to attend a performance of Judith Sainte Croix, a good friend of mine, at Merkin Concert Hall. Judith was a gifted composer greatly influenced by the history and the music of the Hopi Indians. I spent much time early in her career to support, give advice and lend an ear to her work.

A couple of days later, while in the East-West Bookstore, I picked up a catalogue listing summer workshops, programs and events at the Omega Institute and discovered they were offering a five day retreat starting on August 29 in Rhinebeck, New York on "Tibetan Path of Love and Compassion" given by Lama Gelek Rinpoche from the 13th House of the Dalai Lama. Believing this might open a different and deeper understanding of compassion. I decided to sign up for the course.

I received yet another two-page letter dated, June 29.

"I was attempting to escape the truth of my feelings for you and the aching vulnerability I feel with you. I want to stay here and be with you. I am aware that I expose myself to possible rejection. I do this because of my trust in the special connection that lies between us.

I promise I will never hurt you again, ever. And neither will I leave. I only ask that you give me the reassurance I need to feel safe and I will give it back to you a hundred fold. I hope I will see you before I go to the Ashram on July 7th. Please call me."

This letter was so off track from reality that it was upsetting and unnerving. None of these words sounded safe to me, " . . . aching vulnerability, . . . connection that lies between us . . . and neither will I leave." and so on. Was she delusional or a clever manipulator hoping that being flattered, I would oblige her with a response? I was not that naïve.

Then on July 4th, while listening to a long convoluted message left by Rachelle on my machine at 1:25 a.m., the ringing of the front door buzzer began. Her last comment left on the tape was that she hoped I would contact her so that we would see each other before she left for her trip on Thursday.

A couple of days later another letter arrived dated July 3.

"I am sitting in the living room of a large rambling old house in the suburbs, writing you. I wanted to say these things to you in person while looking into your eyes, feeling your gentle soul stirring in its beauty and grace again. I want to reach out and touch you, to feel your body next to mine, to whisper love softly in your ear. I have wanted to express my love for you, but all of these things have been impossible because of the barrier that exists between us. I feel sadness at the harm I have done to our beautiful contact – the souls of poets dancing on magic moonbeams. So many times we have cuddled up together, so many times we have sighed our souls to one another."

She wrote at being frightened that upon her return from Washington, I rejected seeing her, Then, of dark voices filling

Connell J. J. Chambers

her mind with doubt. By spending time alone she now was able to contact the powerful and compelling forces that were at work in the inner life and made a commitment of giving herself to our union. She included an 8x10 headshot of herself in the letter, and asked me to send her a picture of myself.

The letter was disturbing to read. It was frightening how fast her fantasies solidified into reality.

At the initial reading of her letter I sensed having heard the words before, but did not make the connection. Yet upon the second reading I realize it was almost verbatim to the phone message she left on my machine on the 4th of July at 1:25 a.m.: so much for spontaneity. Now I could see how she developed her thesis from deep feelings of love – forgiveness – sex and desire with unions and connections. Her letter was exasperating. Her words were cloaking a game of cat and mouse. I understood the subtext of her letter, and her saying she was "going away" was ruse to elicit a response. Why did she send me her headshot and want a picture of me in return? No way!

After numerous calls from Rachelle, I finally agreed to meet her the afternoon of August 4th at a local café on Flatbush Avenue in the hopes of destroying all her "romantic" illusions. Having already gone through this many times with her to no avail, I still found myself at a loss as to how to handle the situation. I did not want to give her any encouragement, yet by agreeing to meet with her, was I giving her false hope? What was real and what was not? Was she playing me for a fool? This was a place in which I had never been. Without experience in knowing how to navigate these dangerous psychological games, I was at a disadvantage.

On meeting at the café, I opened the conversation by first mentioning seeing her name listed in a journal as leading a course in a workshop on "Harmonizing" and was impressed with the write-up. Without loosing a beat, she said she had written it herself. For the rest of the meeting I tried in every conceivable way to make her accept the obvious. She was convinced we were soul mates and that it was all in God's plan. None of what I said seemed to matter. Before leaving, in order to discourage her phone calls, I told her I would be out of New York for a while and unreachable.

A few days later, another letter from her arrived. She said she hoped our meeting was a new beginning and would pray for my journey, adding, *"Please thank your mother for her prayers."*

What was that about? My mother's name had never been mentioned. Another illusion!

On Tuesday, August 23rd, Rachelle called at my office saying there was a lot of stuff going on that she didn't understand. She was hurt and wanted me to stop running away from her and having relationships with other human beings. She let me know what my continuous evasiveness could create in her.

I told her she was repetitious and that her actions alone were responsible for how she felt; her convoluted conversation had nothing to do with me.

"It does not have anything to do with you. It is in and of me," she answered. "It does not have to do with human things and I acknowledge that. Don't you understand?"

"Rachelle, I am busy."

"It is all so confusing. You go out of your way to not make me feel secure while I stay open and more vulnerable to you. I was giving, yet I was being mistreated. I have tried to make amends and acknowledge what I did was wrong, yet now I have been just left here, just kind of, there's a lot of stuff going on."

"I have got to go. I really can't get into this kind of conversation. I have work to do, goodbye."

I hung up the phone.

FIFTEEN
Omega

The twenty-ninth of August was almost here and I was eager to begin the course with Gelek Rinpoche. I spoke with Judith a few days earlier who informed me she would be in Woodstock and invited me to stop by after the retreat. I arranged to meet Natalia and Anderson at our local bookstore to search for books on Tibetan Buddhism. Locating the books on a bottom shelf, the three of us hunkered down to browse. Anderson picked up *In Exile from the Land of Snows* by John F. Avedon.

"Take this with you," he said, handing me the book. A voice directly behind me called out, "It is all a lie." I froze. It was Rachelle's voice.

"That's her," I whispered to Anderson as I rose to my feet. "Hello Rachelle. What are you doing here?"

"Aren't you going to introduce me?" she asked.

"Connell wants to become a Tibetan Monk," Anderson chimed in immediately. I panicked. All she needed was a hook to zero in and find out what my interests were or where I went.

"Goodbye Connell, I will catch up with you before you leave," she said as she spun around and left.

I turned to Anderson, "You may have blown my cover."

We walked outside, hugged, and I got into my car and drove off. What did she mean by, "I will catch up with you before you leave?"

I headed towards Flatbush Avenue in my Passion Red 740 TGA Volvo, anxious to be leaving Park Slope and its dangers. Glancing in my rear view mirror I caught a glimpse of Rachelle running block by block trying to catch up with the car. She finally reached the back door when I got stuck at a traffic light and yanking the door open, attempted to get in. But before she could do so the light changed again and with the door still open, I accelerated away, then, slamming my foot on the brake for a split second to cause the door to slam shut, accelerated once more. In my rear view mirror I saw Rachelle continue her pursuit of the car. My heart was pounding. What if she managed to jump in front of the car knowing I would have to stop and then jump in? What would the scene be as I tried to pull her out of the car? Would she scream, "attack," "rape," anything? Was she armed? I was panicking. I could still see her. There were traffic lights at every two blocks. I had one eye on her and one eye on the traffic lights. She ran past my car as it approached Flatbush Avenue. As the light flashed to red, she ran towards the car. Before she made contact I accelerated through the red light making a right turn towards Grand Army Plaza, then another right on Prospect Park West, past my home, a right turn on Ninth Avenue then a left towards the Brooklyn Queens Expressway. My heart pounding, my hands and feet trembling, I was finally clear of her. In my panic it had never occurred to me to automatically lock my doors.

I was on my way to where? An ad, in a summer magazine, "compassion," an adventure, an escape into the world of Buddha, a student for five days. It was late evening when I arrived. There were red barns, white cabins, people old and young milling about. As we all booked in and signed up for our course, we were given color tags to identify our group: fifty budding Buddhists heading to a wooden pavilion in the woods, a place that would become home for the next five days. How simple we all must have thought this exercise would be. Would my world change; would I recognize the important differences; would it be so different that I would reject it? So many questions; how long is it going to take to become quiet?

As night settled in, the conversational murmur among strangers ceased. Silence was to me like a fresh breeze. The sounds of the night in the woods lulled me. Would I be able to sleep, to rise at 4:00 a.m. when the retreat was scheduled to start? It had been a long time since I slept a full night without intrusion. I realized I was in a room that had no phone, no electricity, nor bathroom, "To sleep, perhaps . . .?"

Sleep took over like a fever. I woke up chilled and to my surprise it was ten o'clock in the morning. Omega Institute was alive with new arrivals. The energy was a mixture of a communal, a Woodstock moment and the unknown certainty of an Ashram. I went to the central café; the menu was inundated with vegetarian and vegan choices and magazines relating to New Age ideas and courses. And there it was again, Spirit Path Magazine, which I now nicknamed 'The Flash Point' magazine.

August twenty-ninth arrived with a fist banging on my door. I jumped up. "Oh my God, it's her." It took me seconds to realize where I was; it was 4:00 a.m. the beginning of the retreat. Dampness hung heavily in the pre-dawn air as I stepped out into a journey of *Love and Compassion.*

We moved like shadows in the damp and silent dawn toward the dark wood pavilion protected and shrouded by a heavy morning fog. We filed into this vast emptiness consisting of large window spaces without glass and without doors. The stark angles of its structure were shrouded by the fog, which permeated the inside and the outside. A place of non-definition, a place of silence, this is where I needed to be. I had brought my meditation cushion and mat with me and placed them at a forty-five degree angle to the right of the circle where Gelek Rinpoche would sit.

The only sounds were those of preparation as we sat in our individually selected places in awkward anticipation of the arrival of Gelek Rinpoche. An hour past and there was no sign of him.

"Ha, ha, ha," a boisterous laughter shattered our quietness. There he was wrapped in saffron, sitting on extremely large pillows, his round face beaming with joy. He appeared as if from nowhere.

"You are all westerners, right?" he said as he smiled. "Do you know how I know? It is because nobody is smiling, nobody is talking. You are all very, very serious, right? This is very important today. It is about love and compassion. What if you all died right now? You would have to be reincarnated back into this life to try again to laugh, to smile, and to be funny. Have you ever found a sullen Buddha? But you can find a laughing Buddha. That is why laughing is so important. Laughing Buddha had to perfect joy in order to be able to laugh at seriousness." Gelek stood up, walked out, without saying another word.

A young monk came in and requested we stay where we were until breakfast time. One member of the group asked at what time?

"What is time?" the monk asked, "You have chosen to be here away from time. You will know breakfast time," he said as he left.

We sat in our awkwardness in the cold dampness. After an hour and a half the monk returned.

"If you still want breakfast you should hurry; we stop serving in fifteen minutes."

After breakfast, we were informed, by Gelek that in order to fully absorb and understand the depth of love and compassion, we would have to shed all known sense of comfort.

"It is only in emptiness that we can become receptive." For the next five days and nights we would learn to live in an awakened state of our spirit not our body. So forget sleep, solid food, liquids or any communal dialogue. We would experience all experiences and need to share, as individuals, the experience of the self to the self. There were always about three or four young student monks accompanying him, part of his entourage, there to assist us through the process if need be. Personal health conditions would be respected but previously be shared with the group.

Tibetan Buddhists believe that sentient beings exist in all forms of life calling for reverence for life known and unknown. With this new thinking our ability to feel, perceive, and to experience subjectivity were heightened. In our pre-dawn silent, slow meditative walks, I felt the moon could hear me. How many nights had I wandered in doubt and fear saddened by the complexity of the never-ending assaults that had now become a way of life. I nodded to the moon in reverence, as it had become my night companion.

At any moment of day or night Gelek would spontaneously start conversations with the group, and he himself, serve small individual Tibetan delights for the palate. I had never realized how something so small could be fulfilling. Then all would become quiet again.

Every morning Gelek began the chant and within a few moments our voices harmonized with his, then without realizing, the discourses would begin.

"Death, be prepared. There is no reason to regret if you are prepared. Ask yourself 'Am I prepared?'

Remember be prepared. Helping another is good, though sometimes it looks as if your help was a disastrous mistake.

How do we avoid getting into circumstances we find ourselves in? What were the conditions in your life that led to the circumstances? What were your needs? What were the causes and what were the effects? View, before you judge another."

I felt he was speaking to me directly.

The days and nights began to blend into one.

He went on to say that *Purification* should be a daily action like breathing, and had to become natural. It would bring power to the base of one's life. It allows you to get in touch with the fact that you are impacting other beings. You become grounded and connected, allowing you to integrate in actions and effects. It allows you to take refuge and live the deeper meaning of compassion. I listened intently to all he was saying.

"Enlightened ones," he said, "are our external future expressions of selves. Not really knowing whether the being that is challenging all aspects of your sanity and safety, even your life, is an enlightenment being of purpose or a failed spirit desperate to attach itself to you to be pulled into the light using you as the vehicle. You must always, through this ordeal, believe and direct your actions to learn to affirm dedication and intention," he said.

"Regret must be understood in its effectiveness, must be experienced and equally purified. To meditate the experience is equal to being right next to the result.

Your posture no matter how fatigued you will become, becomes important in relation to stages of development of self, in danger and fear. Remember you are not the shadow spirit. Posture empowers the energy system. Standing upright in front of fire weakens the assailant even if you die."

The five days went by quickly. Somehow I had sensed Gelek understood the inner turmoil I was going through without anything being said. We spent much time walking together and I experienced an intimate closeness. On that last day we were

each asked to share why we had chosen this Tibetan course on
Love and Compassion. I shared my journey with him and the
rest of the group. Gelek listened, and then spoke,

"You must shatter her."

"But . . . " I started in without getting any further,

"You must shatter her," he repeated emphatically.

As I walked towards the large bonfire I remembered Gelek's
words about karma, that it was fast growing as a result of each
one's needs, and if not attended to could grow much more dis-
proportionate to the initial action; if not looked at to see the
fault in it, it would become destructive. Mindful awareness is
the power of action. And again, "If you speak of the person
preaching, preaching is tied to illusion."

Time to leave; however, I was not ready to do so just yet! I
needed some time to myself before going to Woodstock. I took
a rowboat out onto the small lake rowing to the middle of it and
pulled in the oars. The lake was covered with water lilies and so
peaceful, I meditated for a few hours. That night I slept in the
car before driving off the next day to see Judith. We were happy
to see each other and I shared my experience at Omega. Late
in the evening, while talking about crystals, I showed her the
clear one-inch quartz crystal I kept with me during the retreat.
Judith held it in her hands and said she felt a very strong vibration frequency from the stone. I placed it on the shelf next to
where we were sitting. The crystal emitted a soft glow, which
brought a smile to our faces. At the end of the evening, Judith
made up a bed for me on the enclosed porch that extended out
over water. I fell asleep to the rippling sound of the flowing
mountain stream.

SIXTEEN

Threats

Returning one day earlier I went directly to the office. Before leaving for Omega I set up an interview for Anderson with my general manager, Frank Costa. Anderson needed extra income for his forthcoming wedding to Natalia. I was eager to welcome him on his first day with the firm, and to share my experience with Gelek Rinpoche.

Rachelle called at 11:30 a.m. to invite me to dinner that night at her home. How did she know I had returned a day earlier? In order not to feed her illusions and give her false hope, I declined the invitation. Her reaction was swift, saying that if I continued to refuse I would have no idea as to Uranus' activity within her astrological makeup. She threatened that refusing the invitation to discuss matters would be dangerous and disastrous and that I would be made to suffer the consequences.

"Your reaction is based on an actual fear that you really do want to have dinner with me, but, are frightened to become intimate. If I found out that I was wrong about who you are really, I would kill you."

There was so much danger and entrapment in her words. I could see, as usual, this was going nowhere and I desperately needed to put an end to her obsession. I suggested a meeting with her analyst, which Rachelle agreed to; however, she insisted on meeting with me emphasizing that it had to be today. This gave me chills. I told her it could not be today but to go ahead and make an appointment. When I asked for the name of her analyst, she told me, it was none of my business.

"If you make an appointment and I'm late, how will I get a hold of you?" she gave me the number.

"Whom shall I ask for?"

"Olivia Rambert." I thanked her and hung up the phone. I intended to call her analyst later in the week. By now, I had gotten into the habit of scribbling down her phone conversations. Around 4:30 Rachelle called again. She was furious.

"I am freaking out. Since you cannot reach out with love, I will become dangerous. I will do something damaging to your life that you will regret. It could have been beautiful and real. The only alternative is making us into enemies."

She compared herself to the poet in the play *The Night of the Iguana* who had committed suicide and was found in a lake. "I am an Iguana at the end of the rope. Tomorrow I will be evicted from my house."

"Why are you being evicted?"

Here she had paused long enough for me to finally get a word in. She had previously told me she had been living rent free in the building owned by a man she met in London, who was responsible for bringing her to the United States. She claimed that when she told him she was having an affair with me, he asked her to leave and a court case was now pending on that.

"Why would you tell him something that wasn't true?"

She just kept on going, totally ignoring what I had just asked.

"What do you think I have been doing for the last eight months? I cannot live with this feeling; it's not right. I keep knocking at the door; all I get is 'Go away, I will call my father.' "

What was she talking about? At whose door was she knocking? None of what she was saying made sense.

"I don't need to use past circumstances, to be intimate, caring and loving; I feel that I want to go out and hurt something. I feel I am being lynched. I don't make judgment about you." Then within the same breath in a completely different tone she continued. "I wrote a poem that I want to share with you."

I told her I was not interested and had to get off the phone. She promised to put it in the mail and hung up.

At 6:30 p.m. she called again, her voice seething.

"I cannot be put on the back burner. I am angry, in pain and put under great tension. I am at the end of my rope. You have to take some time for me."

I told her to work it out with her analyst. She emphasized that analysts did not give credence to a holistic human being and that, since she experienced everything wholly, fully and spiritually, was wrongly treated. In the same breath she claimed she had been a confused alcoholic and men used her. "Now, it is about what I want," she added, boiling with indignation. She kept repeating the same things over and over. I tried several times to interrupt, telling her I could not deal with this, that I was at work and had meetings scheduled.

"Then, come after the meetings. I need to be a priority."

Her thought pattern suddenly shifted and she continued speaking as if in a trance. "It only comes back if it is *ignored*. Drastic things begin to happen – it's a sickness; it comes through me, in my sleep and in my wake state. You are a dictator. Your house is so sacred. I do not know this selfish, ruthless, caricature of a human being. This is ridiculous. You must set a time."

At 6:45 again,

"If I found out that I was wrong about who you are really in depth, I would kill you. I found out you are me! We have to be whole together in spirit and love otherwise we turn into horrible enemies. You have never invited me into your home, not even when you found me on your doorstep. I have just been sitting for ten months experiencing – nothing else for ten months – just experiencing."

I was angry and was finally able to get in a word and told her I had to hang up.

Arriving home at night I found three messages left on my answering machine, all from Rachelle. On the first one, crying and sounding distraught, gasping through sobs, she was begging me to pick up the phone.

On the second one, she sounded less upset. Finally, now in a demanding tone and a sense of annoyance,

"Connell, are you there? Can you please pick up? I am not having a beautiful afternoon, evening or night." (This referring to my taped greeting) "It is just too trite to speak like that. I would really appreciate a phone call. Please pick up the phone."

While playing all these messages the front door buzzer kept ringing.

The phone calls never let up whether at home or at work. Rachelle hounded me and knew my every move. She refused to accept that I had no interest in a relationship; the threats were deeply disturbing. I had no idea how to extricate myself from this situation. I was frustrated and exasperated. I had no peace and no escape. The promised poem, she claimed to have written, arrived.

> In many years I have not seen his face,
> Felt his heart; touched his smile.
> Yet in this time around we meet
> On yet another lonely mountain,
> Catching each other in the breeze,
> Never sure if this is just illusion,
> Just a shadow of our fate . . . .

Two more stanzas followed. Since her words were always cloaked in contradictions, so also was the poem. I felt the poetic voice, not hers. Her main purpose in sending the poem possibly was based on the lines, *yet in this time around we meet on yet another lonely mountain.* My antennas shot up. Was this reference to soul mates?

Around mid September, I received a package accompanied by an exquisite card from my good friend Pamela Whidden in California. At one point, chatting on the phone with her, I shared my frustration and confusion as to how to deal with Rachelle's obsession. Pam understood and recognized on many levels the threats and danger. In the package was what she called a "Rescue Remedy" for healing, with notes and instructions. Included were healing stones, herbs, crystals, a Tarot card, a Tiger Eye, and for a wide variety of stressful situations, a blue envelope. "The basic principle" she said, "behind 'Rescue' and 'All Bache Flower Remedies' is that it heals the emotional level so that the body can heal itself. Also you can't overdose because if your body doesn't need it, it doesn't use it." Also enclosed was Anderson's Medicine Bag for Success and Prosperity. "The Blue envelope is to be disposed of however you see fit. It is called a 'Bye, Bye Spell' and sends the person we wish out of our lives onto bigger and better things. You can burn it, bury it, flush it, or throw it in the lake, river, or ocean, whatever is right for you. Kiss it, say, 'Bye, Bye, Rachelle', fill it with unconditional love and get rid of it. Connell, the stones, and herbs I channeled, asking to help you with your healing and to protect you when you forget. I thought the stones would cleanse the elements, but apparently, you are meant to put out fire with your water." Following Pam's suggestion and my office being near the Hudson River, I walked to the banks of the river and tossed my blue envelope in. sending it off with "unconditional love." As I watched it float outward, a boat sped by creating turbulence and to my astonishment caused the blue envelope to return to where I was standing. It spooked me. It eventually floated back out only to be caught again in an additional wave, carrying it once more towards the embankment; I turned my back and walked away.

SEVENTEEN
Disturbances

No sooner had I arrived home, my answering machine began a series of clicks. In an instant I knew it was Rachelle. She managed to hack into the answering machine to retrieve my messages, then, by punching in a code, could monitor the sounds in my home to know if I had arrived. This would continue for hours. Seven messages were already registered. As I listened to each one, the front door buzzer would start ringing in what seemed to be a synchronized pattern between messages.

"Are you there, Connell? Are you asleep? I really need to talk. Wake up please and pick up the phone?"

"If you are there, pick up the phone please? Hello Connell! Connell! Answer me please, are you there?" Then in a more subdued voice, "If you are there, can you pick up the phone? Please, Connell. It is very, very, very, important that you pick up the phone."

The last message, delivered in a slower more deliberate cadence, was followed by New Age music.

I considered disconnecting the phone or simply taking it off the hook, but concluded that it would play into her hands. It would indicate that she had the power to disrupt my life or intimidate me. I wanted to sustain a semblance of normalcy, a strategy I hoped would work.

The messages continued throughout the night: It was impossible to fall asleep.

Finally, exasperated, I picked up the phone. It was now 3:53 a.m.

"Who is this?"

"It's Rachelle, who else."

"Do you realize what time it is?"

"Time is what *I* as a person need. You're leaving it so loose."

"At this moment I don't consider it important."

"I consider this very important. It's just highly frustrating, waiting for something. Everything else is ten thousand times more important. It sends a clear message; I have a holistic attitude. I constantly feel I am imposing on you. I need to express, to discuss things. The work I do on this planet is much too much."

Lying in bed on my side, I scribbled on a pad, as usual, as fast as I could, her disconnected words and sentences. Doing this, allowed me to redirect her abusing words to paper rather than absorbing the assaults.

I let her ramble on and hung up.

The weather on Sunday afternoon was warm. I walked to St. Francis Xavier Church and sat in the quietness for a few minutes to meditate. I felt isolated and somewhat blocked from the meaning of the Mass that was in process. As I was about to leave, the priest raised the Host, spoke ancient words of the Eucharist then raised the Chalice. I knelt and experienced a voice deep within and asked the voice to comfort me and bring me peace. I had no awareness of my deep sobbing until I realized that tears were streaming down my face and seeping through my fingers. I felt the sensation of a hand resting on my shoulder and the tension I was carrying seemed to dissipate; the feeling of love rising up within overwhelmed me as all the negative thoughts and anger fell away. I rose from the pew, genuflected and walked out into the afternoon sunlight as I pondered the experience.

Rachelle's messages kept coming and now reflected her change of mood, as she began to read from different books on astrology, I Ching, psychic studies and other numerous references. She would call me in the night and read; however, when asked if she was reading from something, she would answer, "You underestimate me." If I did not answer the phone, it did not matter; she would proceed talking into the machine. She had completely evolved from her role of victim to one of victimizer.

On one of her many recorded messages, she said,

"In order for one to achieve the great renunciation of self, he who can totally surrender is ordained by heaven. When men have a common focus, unity will be attained; with unity, recovery is possible. So there it is, the wisdom influencing the week. It would be nice to speak with you, in a place when you are not rushed or pushed for time. I am going to be home tonight, probably late; I would love to hear from you . . . if you can bring yourself around to pushing those buttons. Bye, bye!" Buzzer!

Another message left on the 26th.

"This is about me and who I am. I need structure; I cannot have everything so loose. It's been weeks since we spoke. I gave you space and time. It's very difficult for me to do all this wanting. I have something that I need to talk about that is important. Could we make time to sit down?"

Then completely unrelated, "Why are you so fascinated with the play *Dance of Death*?"

By Wednesday, the 28th Rachelle's phone calls and her ringing of the front door buzzer of my building had now become exasperating; it no longer was sporadic. Her intrusive behavior had intensified. On this particular evening before dusk, she took it to another level. Arriving home I found a series of calls left on my machine with no content except to please call.

While having dinner the door buzzer rang. Being aware of her pattern, I waited until the count of ten, if it was her she would ring again. However tonight her pattern changed; she kept her finger on the buzzer for three to five minutes at a time. This was new. Maybe she would get tired. Did she know I was home? I had not caught sight of her in the neighborhood upon arrival. Twenty minutes went by without any let up. I believed I could outlast her, but what if she began ringing the buzzer of other apartments? She had never shown respect for anyone's privacy, especially that of my landlord, who, rightfully so, had absolutely no tolerance of any form of invasion into his home. I began to worry as to what action he would take.

I went down the stairs to the hallway and could see her through the glass of the front door sitting on the low stoop to the right of the entrance, looking relaxed, her right arm raised with her finger pressing the buzzer.

I returned to my apartment quite concerned as to what would happen if the other tenant or a member of Eli's family entered or left through the front door, giving Rachelle clear access to enter the building. Once inside, she was capable of creating a story that would be believable and thus freely walk up the stairs to my apartment. The thought scared me. This would be disastrous, I would be trapped and there would be no telling of what she would do. I was left with no alternative but to call the police. She had to be quickly removed from the steps. I watched from my studio window for their arrival. The continuous ringing of the buzzer only added to the tension.

Finally two police cars pulled up; four officers approached the stoop. Now that I had called the police to remove Rachelle from the front steps, no matter what the final results, the dynamics had changed. The buzzing had stopped; the police cars were still there. Why was it taking so long? I was full of apprehension as I rocked nervously in my wicker chair.

Suddenly the phone rang, "Are you Connell Chambers?" They asked if I had phoned the police and if so for what reason. I explained the situation and the disturbance it was creating for me, and the rest of the habitants of the building. They asked if I knew who she was and why I wanted her removed. I gave them her name and again mentioned the harassment. After a moment of silence, the officer requesting I let them in or that I come down.

I told them I would come down but that she must not be allowed to enter the building.

As I opened the front door, I had no idea what the consequences would be. A police officer stood to my right in front of Rachelle who was still sitting on the side stoop.

"Is this Mr. Chambers?" he asked her.

"Yes, this is my friend Connell. We were having tea together and I came outside to have a cigarette – he does not allow smoking."

After verifying that I was indeed Connell Chambers, he asked if it was true I neither smoked nor allowed it in my home. "Absolutely!" I answered.

"Why are you not allowing her to go back into the apartment; she says you always have tea before sunset by the window."

"She has never been in my apartment and everything she is saying is not true." I went on to explain about the continuous harassment night after night, her obsessions and her baseless claims of a relationship. Rachelle explained it all away saying that it had taken place a long time ago and that now we were together.

As this dialogue simmered to a halt, I realized the police had repositioned themselves. One was standing on the top step slightly off to the side in front of her, another two steps further down standing in the middle, and the third close to the last three steps.

Rachelle still relaxed, sat there for a while. Nobody spoke. She would glance up at me with a soft smile on her lips, yet her eyes were ice cold.

"Can I go back in now?" she asked, "I guess we have to brew a new pot of tea?"

"Ma'am, the only place you are going is to the police station if you don't voluntarily come down from the front stoop of this person's home."

"What have I done wrong? He is the one who is a liar."

"You are trespassing on private property, harassing a tenant, and disobeying a police officer. So please, come on down off the steps."

"What if I don't?"

"You will be arrested, charged and locked up in jail, along with criminals – prostitutes – you don't want that do you?"

"Criminals and prostitutes are God's missionaries on earth. They have more spiritual power than anyone else. I am not afraid. I am here doing God's work."

With that said, she got up, looked at me and said, "I will be back in a while darling. Keep the tea warm."

She walked casually down onto the pavement and I walked down with the last officer who told me since she voluntarily moved down to the pavement, they could do nothing, as that was public property. The officers got into their cars, leaving Rachelle standing by the tree. They told me to call them if she stepped again on the private property, adding, they would keep a check on her while driving around during their normal night patrol and then drove away.

I was furious as I realized the front door was wide open. I quickly ran up the steps into the hallway, and as I flipped the lock in place, I saw Rachelle walking up the steps, head lowered with eyes staring up at me, like a zombie. I went up to my apartment; the buzzer rang once.

Three hours passed since the police had gone. Before going to bed I looked out towards the tree where they left her and saw she had gone back down and was standing there leaning against it, making gestures with her hands clasped together as if in a ritual, raising them upward toward my window. It was eerie.

I woke up around 6:00 a.m. and looked out hoping she had left. She was standing in the same spot as still as a statue. I felt confusion, anger and pity all at the same time. I knew I was facing an even more serious problem. I now had to focus on leaving for work and would have to cross her path. As soon as I reached the pavement, she approached with her arms stretched out and speaking in a childlike voice said,

"Hold me please, I am cold and frightened."

I had to be cautious, but needed to break the impasse. I placed my hands firmly over hers; her arms were rigid. Looking straight into her eyes, I told her to go home, get some sleep or she would get sick. She kept repeating in the same childish voice to please hold her. I let go of her hands, again stressed that she go home, and quickly walked around the corner to Sixth Street to where I had parked my car the night before. Wanting to avoid her, I backed down the street and continued my journey to work.

I wondered if she really had spent the entire night under the tree or gone home and returned at sunrise. She was an actress and liked drama. How much of this was real and how much was acting? I could not take the chance.

On Saturday, October 1, at 12:30 a.m. Rachelle rang once more.

"I can't function on this level until things complete themselves. The third of October is the anniversary of my father's death and his birthday. I am like my father; he also was not recognized."

"What does recognition have to do with things?"

Connell J. J. Chambers

She felt she was being relegated to only one aspect in my life. "You keep making choices to avoid being with me, someone who knows you, and loves you. Why would you go to strangers? You make that choice over us and feel that by throwing me some crumbs I may go away, you're wrong. Why can't you share with me what you experience with others?"

She continued with her usual false illusions as to who she was in my life and the pain it was causing her. Poetry, she felt, would allow us the direct line to our soul to give to another what another human being needs, which she was not getting from me; "God is between us, and I need . . . " I did not let her finish. I told her I did not need a pseudo preacher to add to my social life, and that what I needed was to get off the phone and get some sleep. Ignoring what I said, she continued on about God, the planets, and the earth being on the verge of destruction. At this point I was positive she was reading out of some New Age book.

"We, the world, are close to total annihilation. Anything that promotes separation contributes to the destruction of the world. It is destructive if it is not allowed to be intimate. You create denial for intimacy to exist on other levels. To ignore that is like a crime of the heart and soul. Do I scare you, since you can only take me in small doses? Life can be scary."

"What I know for a fact is that I find nothing scary about you; you are a fraud. You pathetically try to interweave your illusions into the written words of others. That, I find pathetic. Of great importance to me is to get off this phone and stop listening to verbal vomiting. I am tired of it; I have had enough. I need to get my sleep."

She did not miss a beat and immediately shifted her monologue.

"I keep getting messages that you don't want to see me. It is very important to be able to discuss without judgment as to what this has all been about."

"Since you say you realize that I don't want to see you. Why don't you accept this as fact?"

"I need to communicate on an intimate level, not on a therapeutic level. So when I feel I am being kept out of the way it reminds me of how the Japanese tortured pregnant women by tying their legs. It may be a spiritual need for you to really consider the reality of what is going on. Even if it is because I need it, in itself, that is a giving gesture, and it is healing for the giver. I want you to know that I do appreciate how much you are able to extend yourself to me at this moment. It expresses your size and nobility and I think the more of you for it."

"Rachelle, you are full of contradictions and I have had enough of you."

I hung up the phone. It was 2:06 a.m.

EIGHTEEN

Acid and Sweat

Looking for "Awakening the Mind of Enlightenment" at a local bookstore, I was hunkered down searching the bottom shelf, when suddenly I realized Rachelle was standing less than six inches behind me.

"It's over, you bastard," she said, pulling something out of her pocket as she lunged forward towards me,

"Acid, my darling, are you ready for a drink?"

I spun around coming up towards her hand and face as she threw the liquid from a metal container into my face. Stepping back, she released a blood-curling scream.

Everything happened so fast; my face was soaked with liquid. Oh, my God it's acid. I swung in an upward chop motion hitting her wrist causing the object to fall as she ran from the store. As I picked it up I saw it was a small container with a label reading "Holy Water That Kills Evil Ones." I ran outside but there was no sign of her. I rushed back inside to the rest room, ripped off my shirt, washed my hands, face and hair in the sink with paper towels, still believing she had thrown acid on my face. As I looked at the paper that had made contact with the presumed acid I realized that the paper was just wet. What an evil bitch! I went back out, picked up the bottle and taking a chance put a drop of the liquid on my finger, it did not burn.

The woman behind the counter approached me, asking if I was okay.

"Yes I think so. Do you know this woman?"

"She comes into the store quite often and browses around for a while. If we ask her if she needs any help, she always answers, 'No thank you, I am waiting for my poet friend.' She claims her brother-in-law, Mr. Chambers, lives in the neighborhood." She rummaged on the desk behind the counter for a few moments, then said, "Here it is. I think this is her name, Catherine Chambers, and she lives in Queens."

"The name of my brother's wife is Catherine and they live in Queens; but that woman is *not* Catherine Chambers. That woman's name is Rachelle Richards and she has been stalking me."

The woman looked stunned, "Please don't come back to my store; it's not safe for either one of us."

As I left the store my inner-fear began to fracture with astonishing speed. It was as if I was shattering from the inside out; my face chilled. It felt as if my skin was cracking into millions of particles as it swept upwards to my scalp and escaped. It flipped to resolve in a split second as if fear's physical manifestation fell away.

As I walked along Prospect Park West towards home, I felt like a panther; all my senses were at high alert. She could be anywhere; she seemed to be getting stronger, and more aggressive. What if it had been acid? What if the bottle had been a knife or a gun? What if . . .

My feet were trembling in my shoes. There seemed to be no passage way out, no way to purify the dynamics. I alone had to move through my darkness and learn how to survive. Gelek Rinpoche had told me the only way through was to shatter her. I could not do that, I did not know how. I had to first shatter myself in order that I could shatter her. Coldness and tiredness overpowered me. I struggled to avoid slipping into the void.

Yet as I now walked in the late night on the cold cobble stones and tried to focus, I could only experience failure and panic. Through fatigue, fear gave illusion reality, leaving me naked in the expression of myself.

Where would this path take me? I had followed it as if in a procession; ahead, was the reality of death. I had to discard this way of thinking and reign in the controls of my life. I intended to live through and experience freedom; I wanted to experience my own shadow again. I knew if I knuckled down and weathered the storm, the doorway to my future would open.

Saturday, October 8, I set out for New Paltz, New York to spend a weekend at Ujjalla's bed and breakfast to participate in a purification and healing ceremony in a sweat lodge led by noted Native American Medicine Man, Charles Thom, Sr.

The ceremony was something I had never experienced before but only had read about as being a ritual for purification. I believed that the experience would somehow cleanse my energy field of all the obsessive toxins that were relentlessly assaulting my mind and body. I was committed to sustaining the discomfort for two days.

The rocks were heated in an open fire until they became white hot, then, placed inside the sweat lodge. We all sat around the rocks, naked in the darkness. Herbs and sweet grass were cast upon them followed by a splash of cold water. As I sat watching the ritual begin, I felt free and excited and began thinking it would be fun. Then the flap of the entrance to the sweat lodge was dropped closed and we were left in darkness.

As the steam filled the darkness, the Medicine Man chanted, calling on his ancestors, and I continued thinking how cool it was to meditate in a sweat lodge with a real Medicine Man. Suddenly I was overcome with fear; the air and steam were scalding hot, my nails and nostrils were burning. The chanting intensified; my breath and eyes burnt in the darkness. I was experiencing vicious scalding pain. "This is crazy," I thought. I needed to leave the lodge. This was insane.

The chant grew stronger, the sweet grass burned and the water continued to be splashed upon the rocks. I screamed out in the darkness to release the physical pain. It was savage in its intensity. Drumming fused with the steam as I tried to cling to my sanity; my body could not bear it any longer.

Suddenly there was daylight; we crawled on our hands and knees out into the sunlight only to be greeted by buckets of cold water poured on our bodies, putting us in total shock. Not really knowing why we wanted more, we again entered and sat in a circle, our bodies glistening as the impurities of our body seeped into the earth. The stones were silent in their heat – waiting – the Medicine Man began the drum beat – calling the spirits back. There was no laughter in the darkness, as the water exploded into steam upon the waiting rocks. The drumbeat quickened; the chant lifted. Yet now the scalding steam seemed more bearable.

We continued until nightfall; every thought had been washed away. Somehow I had arrived at a state where the scalding steam had no effect. The drumbeat sounded far away; the chant was all that was left. My brain was silent - no thoughts, nothing – no longer coherent. I was washed, cleansed by my own perspiration. At the end there were only six of us out of twenty who lasted and crawled out of the sweat lodge.

NINETEEN
Scared For His Life

As soon as I returned home Sunday night, Rachelle called asking to see me. I told her that was not possible.

"Damn it; you will see me. If you won't, I will kill you. I will stab you through the heart. I understand what is going on and will put an end to you and your being busy in the world. You don't set any time aside to see me. You treat me like a whore who is of no use but to fuck. If I can't have you, nobody will. I know how to get a gun. I will go after members of your family or friends close to you. I will not stop until I have succeeded. I am threatening you with your God damned life." She slammed down the phone before I could react.

I was shocked and numbed by the impact of her words. This was the most frightening of threats. It no longer was only about me; others were now in danger. Reality snapped me into action. I immediately called the 78th Precinct on Sixth Avenue between Dean and Bergen Street off Flatbush Avenue. I reported Rachelle's threat to my life, family and friends. The officer took down the information and stated there was nothing else she could do for the moment. I hung up feeling disappointed and frustrated. The dynamics had changed; I had to defuse the matter. The only solution was to go and see Rachelle. I phoned and told her I was coming. I left a hand-written note on the table including the name and address of where I was going and

Teresa's telephone number to contact in case something were to happen to me.

Walking to my car in the rain, my stomach churned and I felt nauseated. I was scared for my life. I drove over and sat in my car for a while to center myself. I repeated the Lord's Prayer, not knowing what waited for me at the top of the stairs. I entered the roach-infested hallway where the roaches just moved out of the way. Holding on to the wobbly banister, I slowly climbed the dirty creaky stairs, all the while telling myself I was crazy to go to her now. But I believed her threats to be real. Facing her was the only way I knew to attempt to dilute her built-up rage. She was waiting at the top of the stairs.

We entered the apartment and stood inside the door; there was silence. I felt insecure and vulnerable. Was there a knife, a gun - she was not stupid. What if she went into a rage? I was on heightened alert.

Finally she broke the silence, "Thanks for coming. Would you like a cup of tea, it must be cold and damp outside?"

"No!"

"What can I say?"

"Nothing!"

"Can I invite you in so we can talk?"

"No!"

"You frustrate me. I am at my wits end. I need you."

"Why do you want to kill me?"

"You have ignored me and left me empty. I am desperate for you to honor our connection. You ignore it and that drives me to want to stop you, and the only way to do that is to kill you."

Panic was racing through me. I was terrified and felt if I spent another second there, my life would be over.

"I hope you feel more peaceful now that I am here."

"I want a lot more. If I can't get a lot more, you know what I will do."

I opened the door and walked out all in one movement, as I said,

"We need to talk soon. I am glad you are okay. It's late. Will you be home tomorrow?"

"Yes."

"Okay, I will be in contact."

"But wait . . . "

"No, I have to go," I said as I headed down the stairs.

She began to scream. I was terrified not knowing if I would reach the downstairs hallway alive. Once on the street I made a sharp right and walked around the block before going to my car hoping she would think I walked home. As I came back around and got into my car, a police car pulled up next to me and asked if everything was okay?

"Yes," I replied. I did not know if their being there was a coincidence or not.

Desperate for help, I was finally able to reach Rachelle's analyst, Tuesday morning, when I phoned.

"It is very important that I talk with you about Rachelle Richards, one of your clients, who gave me your name and number."

"What is this all about?"

"It is about setting up an appointment for the three of us to meet."

"That is not possible. Who did you say you were?"

"Connell Chambers."

"Who are you talking about?"

"Rachelle Richards."

"I don't have a client by that name."

"You may have her under the name of Nicole Richards."

"Even if I have, why would I want to listen to you?"

"Because she stalks me ceaselessly day and night, disrupts me at my office, harasses me with phone calls, and rings my door bell through out the night; she vows to kill me."

"You must be that horrible man that is driving her crazy by denying your relationship with her. Why are you so cruel to her and sexually assaulting her?"

"None of that is true. We are not in any relationship and I have never assaulted her. That is why I need to talk with you and share what is really going on and how dangerous it has become."

"Let me tell you mister . . . whatever your name is, there will be no dialogue."

"It is very important; there is very little time before her threats become reality. It is possible that you are oblivious of her vicious and destructive nature."

"Listen mister, whoever you are, I do not discuss my clients with anyone."

"Why won't you listen to what I have to say? I am the person she imagines having an affair with and whose life she has threatened. I will give you the name of witnesses who will confirm what I am telling you."

"I am not interested in your story. She is in excellent emotional condition."

"Then why does she need psychotherapy?"

"She is a long way from home and is finding it hard to adjust to American society."

"Believe me; she is not in the least interested in adjusting to anything."

"There is one thing that I know for certain, she is a gentle and kind soul who is spending her life working for peace and the planet. She is deeply spiritual and is heartbroken by the way you have been treating her. She claims that you broke your promise to honor the connection you both agreed existed. You are in total denial of what you are doing to her."

"I never agreed to anything. There never was a promise or connection. This whole situation is very volatile and dangerous. She claims she can get a gun, and fully intends to kill me or members of my family or loved ones."

"I am not listening to you; I have clients waiting, so get off my phone."

"No, I will not. Your 'gentle and kind soul' client is crazy and is trying to destroy me. She has stated on numerous occasions that she intends to kill me. Why won't you at least look into it? *Please!*"

Nothing I said seemed to make a difference. She accused me of being a danger to society, especially to women, and that I was the liar and abuser. I begged her to please set up a meeting for the three of us.

"Listen Chambers, I have experienced you in the past few minutes and you continue to defy me. If you don't hang up I will charge you with harassment. Get yourself into treatment immediately and face the reality that you are in a relationship."

I desperately needed her to listen. I told her the police were aware of Rachelle's movements and that I was the one in danger. Rachelle had vowed to kill me, and stalked me daily.

"I am warning you to get off the phone immediately."

"No! Do you hear me? She wants to kill me; I can be shot at any second. Do you know what that is like? It's terrifying. I am exhausted and really frightened."

"How dare you call me and refuse to accept that I do not want to listen to you. No wonder she refers to you as the dictator. How dare you call me attacking my client's credibility? You are living in the dangerous world of illusion."

"What a sick mixture, a dangerously obsessive mentally disturbed client and a therapist who is in denial of the possibility of being wrong. Watch closely, one of us will die soon, maybe both. You make me sick. I ask you one more time to . . . . "

"Fuck off!" she shouted as she slammed the phone down.

I was stunned that she would not even listen: what a bitch. How could she not want to know? She was as sick as Rachelle. God only knew why I could not get this nightmare to stop.

After my frustrating experience with the analyst, while still in my office at 4:30 p.m., Rachelle called.

"How dare you call my analyst? That conversation is private; you have no right to infringe on it. What are you going to do about it?"

"That's none of your business."

"It is my business. We were to see my analyst together."

"That is right. I thought I could set up the meeting with her for the three of us but I was wrong. But since you made serious threats to my life and others, the situation has changed, leaving me no choice but to report them to the police."

I hung up the phone.

That night I attended Greta's show at Eighty-Eights. Listening and watching her on stage, I realized the danger she would be in if Rachelle knew about her. Though I wanted to share with Greta the trauma I was going through, I decided, right or wrong, to isolate her from the situation.

After the performance, as usual, a few of us went out for dinner. It was important for me to spend time with people I cared about and trusted. By the end of the evening I was more relaxed; we hugged, kissed and said our goodbyes. As I drove back to Brooklyn everything seemed surreal.

As soon as I put the key in the door the reality of the threats once again engulfed me. I slowly walked up the stairs wondering if I would have a good night's sleep.

On cue at 3:00 a.m. the phone rang.

"I want to know about you." Rachelle then proceeded to tell me about me.

"I perceive there may have been a major trauma in your life, which causes you to struggle in the dark. For the last two to three days I have been weeping periodically with a deep sense of pain for you and a sense of sadness. It may be with you, as my brother is with me. He was blond, very beautiful and looked like a cherub. You are a beautiful person and special human being. There is such a need for you and others who have all this kind of integrity. This is what I respect, admire and love about you. I would love to spend time with you to share healing thoughts and read poetry. Good night, Connell. I hope everything is all right with you. I will speak with you in a few days," she said as she hung up the phone. This definitely was not a conversation. If anything, I was expecting some sort of escalation of her prior threats but now I found the absence of it unsettling, as were the dysfunction of her thoughts.

The following night at 12:40 a.m., I was awakened once again by Rachelle, who proceeded to have a totally unrelated conversation,

"My mother was always running; she needed to make money. She continued to buy up houses. The greatest tragedy is that she never realized that all her creativity was in the same place as her pain. If I did not understand this I would have died a long time ago like my father. She acts out and recreates on the people very close to her the very pain she is experiencing. It becomes cruel. This is what happens to me. I ran from home at seven. She had inflicted intense pain on me and all the other children. I have to share something else. My story of studying with Stella Adler was a journey I had planned. It's as if God has been leading and I've been following. Buddhism gives me that structure for faith."

Her monologue was peppered with entrapment. I was tired of her scenarios and of all my wasted nights.

The following day she called again, this time, at the office.

"Good morning, Connell. There's something exciting I want to share with you. Saturn and Uranus come together at 9:30 Tuesday morning and is heart related as our hearts are at the center of the galaxies. Its energy is like a valve. Capricorn and Saturn have had bad publicity. You must meditate and be silent at that time. Uranus is very unpredictable and can instigate violent changes on the sea of life. Saturn will conquer in order to stop the violence and keep Uranus steady somehow. Tuesday is a real symbol of the time, a good opportunity to break through negative patterns and for people in conflict to come together to prevent unpredictable violence."

"Thank you, Rachelle; I'll try to meditate on Tuesday at 9:30. I've got to go."

TWENTY

Unseen Forces

On the morning of October 20, Rachelle called just as I was about to leave. I did not pick up the phone and let the machine record the message.

"Connell, you continue to separate yourself from me. I am so deeply threatened by your non-acceptance of me, and your refusal to listen. I lie here, bleeding and can't keep on going. This energy that is waiting to be released has to explode somewhere. I cannot handle being put off; it makes me feel impotent. Remember I have my rules and my structure."

At the end of the day I went home feeling tired, and went early to bed. I was jolted out of sleep at 2:00 a.m. by the ringing of the phone; I did not answer. Eight more calls followed one after the other. On the last call,

"Connell are you there? Can I talk to you? Are you - hello, are you there? Can you talk to me? Hello, Connell, are you there, are you at home . . . are you there yet? It is almost 2:30 in the morning. I don't understand." Just then the message cut off. Then, again,

"Hello, are you there yet? Whatever time you come in, call me. I am in a great deal of confusion and don't understand. Hello are you there, Connell?" she continued her old format. As I was listening to her voice the front door buzzer of my apartment building rang nine times. I was totally exasperated and incapable of extricating myself from this situation. This had to stop, but how?

The following night, the routine continued. At 12:10 a.m., again the phone. I did not answer.

"I only have had a few crumbs, it is very painful and you don't share with me. You are ignoring the unseen forces. What I feel on a deep level is a connection with you. For almost a year, it has not been honored. I have been crying and in pain by being blocked off by you. I can't be so near to you and not be close to you. It is a feeling of being banished. I would like us to connect at the source. It's all about surrender. All you really need is a catalyst like me. I want to ask you to come and find me."

As the machine continued recording she went on talking about her childhood. At thirteen she tried to stow away and got caught. They put her away. Her aunt thought her crazy for running away to go to the theatre. At the age of twenty-six, she wanted to be a Buddhist Nun, she spent time in Lebanon with a Jesuit priest, then came to New York to study with Stella Adler. Her values and actions threatened those around her and she felt she was being crucified daily by others. Meeting me allowed her to acknowledge a feeling of connecting.

"My feminine cycle is tied up with the moon. It is when it allows the seventh ray to come in when Herculean tasks are done. The sun moves into Scorpio tomorrow. It rules very dangerous forces. I am one who will be ruled by self-destructive forces in this next month. We must be careful not to self-destruct in our choices. We can be enticed to the darker extremes. There is a choice you must make during this time. Remember my sun is in Scorpio, my moon is in Aries."

It was now 2:35 a.m. Her intrusive phone calls through the night, and dogmatic lecturing were stressing me out. I needed my sleep as I had a busy day planned. I was looking forward to celebrate Natalia and Anderson's wedding later in the day.

In the afternoon I picked up Greta, whom I had invited as my date, and drove up the West Side Drive to the Riverside Church. After the service, as Anderson and Natalia stepped out of the chapel through the stone Gothic archway, they were touched by the soft sunlight and gentle breeze, which created magic. Natalia looked stunning and surreal. The reception was held at an intimate restaurant on West Ninth Street. The evening was filled with good conversation, laughter and music. It was refreshing to be out with Greta, celebrating and dancing. For a short time I was transported elsewhere.

It was a beautiful, crisp autumn night; the full moon was rising over the park casting silver shadows. As I strolled home along Prospect Park West, I reminisced about the wedding and how great it had been to get away from the tension that had been building in my life. Climbing up the familiar brownstone steps, I suddenly felt a chill of apprehension.

Blasted out of my deep sleep by the ringing of the phone, I automatically picked it up thinking it could be Greta or Anderson, who often called at night. I looked at the clock; it was 2:40 a.m.

"Hello, who is this?"

"It's Rachelle, who else were you expecting it to be at this hour? I'm feeling that you are determined to stay away. You intentionally never have time for me. You spend many hours doing other things. It's been a very long time since I've been able to get hold of you and you've been very busy causing everything to get a lot crazier."

She related that in Mexico, researchers on electro magnetic frequency and its patterns had found that crying was the strongest element that would change those patterns. Therefore, someone like me, who cared about humanity, had to surrender to the power of crying. She had been crying for two to three months, waiting, and that I had not responded to one tear. She then shifted and now wanted to read me something. I told her I could no longer stay awake.

"I'm going to read it anyhow." I felt I was caught up in a twister. I looked at the clock, it was 3:04 a.m., I did not respond. Instead I pressed the record button on my machine.

> *I feel your pain your anguish, for it has become my own*
> *For in the beginning, we felt we shared each other's thoughts*
> *We are now exchanging energies, which tear at our souls.*
> *Submerged fears surface, bringing tears of the unconscious*
> *And the threat of our communication when a channel is open*
> *Abuse it at the peril of your love. It is older than we.*

I must have dozed off for a few moments when suddenly I heard her say,

"I didn't realize it was so late, Connell, you must be tired. Thanks for listening to my poem."

I answered groggily, "It's okay."

"Connell, it's not really okay. Up until now it had always been about your poems, you know what I mean, *your* poems. Oh, well, it is late. I probably should go to sleep or probably, just go away, shouldn't I?" she said with a surge of sarcasm. "You know it is emotionally destructive if you keep on saying, 'I am not with you, don't have time for this.' "

She rambled on saying the reason I could not win, was because I had Saturn in Taurus, my eighth house in Taurus and three planets in Taurus that were polar opposites of my moon sign. These, being powerful links of sexual energy, also created tension and difficulties. The biggest hurdle to overcome was the difficulty of expressing closeness, which was sexually expressed.

"It begins by loving the person who is the closest to you, which is *me* in the *now*. By being decisive you will experience the beauty of love. Why don't you come to Australia with me?"

"It's sleep time, Rachelle. The session is over. It's 4:15 a.m., there is no charge." I gently put down the phone. Listening to Rachelle, it was obvious that she was quoting again.

TWENTY-ONE
Denial

"**C**onnell, good morning, this is Rachelle."

"So what is your problem now?" It was 11:20 a.m. on the 25th.

"I've been waiting since Thursday for one phone call. I don't want to keep waiting around. There is so much that needs to be spoken of. You have always made the choice to not spend quality time with me. I cannot bear it, yet you took time off for a wedding where you were possibly with a lot of women."

"Yes, of course I was with a lot of women. I was at a wedding, so what?"

"A person can only hang around for so long. My feeling is to first leave, as I cannot handle the pain anymore."

"Then, leave; I think that is a good idea."

"You are not really prepared to make any compromise."

"You are absolutely right, because your reality is fantasy theatre of the mind."

"You just expect me to be at your convenience. You insist upon it."

"I don't expect you to wait or insist on anything."

"I am connected with your life, and you are not giving me what I need, which is consideration."

"Rachelle, you are not connected with me. My life is not intertwined with yours. Please, accept it!"

"I want you to feel I am here like a voice in the wilderness. I would love if you could take time to be with me a few hours on Sunday. The point is you won't."

"Rachelle, you are absolutely right. Thank you for the call, but I am busy; I have to go."

After driving to the airport to pick up my mother and sister Jo, who had flown in from London for Geraldine's wedding, I returned to my office, and finished my evening out at Greta's show. I arrived home late hoping for a good night's sleep.

The sharp ringing of the phone awakened me.

"You're out late again, Connell," she said, "I called your office in the late afternoon. They told me you had left. I asked where you had gone and they said you went to the airport to pick up two women arriving from London." Her voice changed. "I am tired of how you worship them. I was at St. Francis Xavier Church tonight, and spoke with a priest to see from another perspective."

"Rachelle, first you talk about two women, and then you switch to St. Francis Xavier Church, a Catholic church. You don't make sense, what are you trying to say?"

"Imagine if we could come together, we could reach a healing, spiritual, and contemplative togetherness. I think it is really sad to do these things separately. I demand to know where you go on Sundays. Why is it always so secretive?"

"It is not secretive; where I go and what I do is simply none of your business. It is time for you to stop. You don't have a clue as to who I am. You have become a nuisance; you beg too much."

"You allow yourself to be in communion with others. Why can't we be intimate? The very act is in itself the love that God allows through us. I would have expected you to come to me by now. It would mean trusting yourself and giving yourself over to me."

"That will never happen."
When we finally got off the phone it was 2:05 a.m.

Rachelle imposed in so many ways that my exposure to phone calls was becoming stressful. As manager of the tele-marketing division of my company, I had four phones with four lines, sixteen possibilities for her to reach me. At least if I could not get her off the line, I had sixteen possibilities of putting her on hold.

On Saturday October 29, at 10:30 a.m., one of those possibilities occurred; Rachelle and my fears were realized. Whispering into the phone, as was her usual style, she asked if I was going to Geraldine's wedding and pleaded not to be excluded from my life. She was tired of begging and begging, and just sitting every day hurting and bleeding.

"I feel the deeper evil all the time. You have not made the slightest gesture towards me. You could look at the cap sitting on the bottle and never get inside the bottle and it wouldn't bother you. I must find a way to get in. Your outright refusal to come through is an indictment. It states that you don't trust me."

"That is a fact, I do not trust you."

"You are terrified to make a leap of faith. I understand; it must be dangerous. You just have to let me guide you. If you don't, you are setting up things that go against God's will. Now, and from here on it will only be between you, me, and God."

"How dare you assume how things will be, and include me in your triad with God? God is not on a mission with you regarding me. I do not need you for me to be in communication with Him. You know nothing about God or His will, period. It is not His will but your own will that you are trying to impose. Do you really think you are a gift from God to me? What's this, 'the coming of Rachelle' that I should 'bow in reverence or tremble in fear?' I have had enough of your analysis. I am tired of your lecturing; you have become dictatorial. This place of intimacy that you speak of will never happen."

"You don't have to take time for me because I'm not that important, but you could take quality time for yourself by being with me. Remember we were old from before. Why are you denying the connection of God's gift? I offer you something very major, a true, honest partnership. I have wanted this for a year. I need a decision."

"There is no decision to make, as there never will be a partnership."

"You did not make a correct decision. I do not accept your way of phrasing it. I only want us to be together."

She continued talking about her love for me and how very rare and special a person she was. She was unable to understand why I would not surrender to her or the essence from which she spoke, and instead choose to go against God's plan. This, she felt, left her no choice but to go to England and become a mistress.

"I don't know if I will ever see you again. I am getting very sick and deteriorating physically, mentally and emotionally; it won't be long before I disappear from this planet."

No matter how many times I tried cutting off her dialogue, she ignored me. If I hung up she would call back within five minutes. Other phone calls were continually coming in. I handled them as best I could while recording and listening to her on the speakerphone.

"Rachelle, it is 2:05 p.m. I must get off the phone."

Fifteen minutes later, she was on the line again.

"Rachelle here. This is all about revenge. I feel hurt and ignored. If a woman is hurt, she will become powerful. She will find a way to turn the sword. My natural tendency is to get that revenge. I have struggled not to get into this frame of reference capable of committing murder. But if I can't get my way, I am quite able of viciously turning against myself, as I don't have a lot to lose. I would warn you, your family, and friends that I am going to become very dangerous."

She accused me of drawing her into a cheap and sordid affair, making her feel like a whore. "You won't come near to discover me; you have always stayed away from me." This, she felt, gave her the right to do whatever she wanted. "I probably will kill my cat right now. If I am going to go and destroy the trees, I might as well go ahead and really do it. So what's wrong if I shoot up a few human beings? As much as I can love and care I can destroy. Medea killed her own children when her husband left. You have chosen to kill our connectedness. Connell, it could be very quick."

Though shaken by her words, I pretended to ignore her threats.

"Rachelle, these phone calls are always at your time. It's already 3:00 p.m. and I need my time."

"Okay, I'll ring off but I won't go away."

It was now 5:00 p.m. Once again it was Rachelle.

"I am in a terrible way and I do not want to do the horrible things I said earlier. I have difficulty in staying here and not seeing you enough. I don't want to go away."

I made another attempt to reason with her and told her I was not the answer to her problems, that she was the one solely responsible for her own problems. When I suggested she call her analyst, her answer was that my denying her a response she would drive me to hell. It was impossible to get through to her.

I put the phone down. I had become weary of her constant preaching, and phone calls. I believed I was protecting myself from her manipulative and threatening words by writing down what she was saying. My mind would shift to a safety zone once she opened her mouth. Any form of response made her feel stronger. Yet, no response brought out her anger and intensified her threats. My days were filled with tension, apprehension and stress; my performance at work was suffering. I had become vulnerable. She constantly invaded my phone. I did not know how much longer I could live with this insanity. The pressure was building and I was afraid of losing control. Her long discourses of thoughts, wishes, desires, obsessions, demands, and her declarations of love over eons and the constant threats to my life, were a conglomeration of fragmented dictatorial proclamations. I desperately wanted to scream at her to shut up, get off the phone, and get out of my life.

TWENTY-TWO

Decoded

Sunday morning Rachelle called me at the office saying she had listened in on my answering machine and erased a message left for me by my friend Pamela from California. When I confronted her saying I was pissed about her illegally breaking into my privacy, she defiantly answered,

"When you stifle me, I intrude. I can hear you in your apartment talking. I can play back your messages and write them all down. Your friend implies that she has had a part of you, and that she was really looking forward to seeing you and that 'everything is wonderful here where I am. Oh, I hope you have earmarked that bush for me very close to your house. We are going to make some wonderful love in that bush, bye.' Those are her words."

"If the words were there, deal with it. I would rather get a pleasant message on my machine, instead of your twenty-four pathetic intrusive messages demanding me to 'pick up - pick up - pick up'. As to who she is, that is none of your business."

Pamela, possibly thrilled that she was coming to New York, may have left a message in her usual vivid sense of playful and seductive humor.

"You work so hard to keep me out. I feel that there is a lot more going on in your life for the past year than meets the eye. I have been trying to catch you out on something for a long time because I have been feeling this deceit and this lie."

"I do not owe you an explanation. You have no right to intrude and bombard my life."

"I know," she replied, "But I believe you have evenings and you spend them doing things with other people."

"Of course I do."

"Yeah! Of course you do and you've been lying to me about it."

"I don't need to lie; it is none of your business."

"I will tell you something now I think you really should understand. I see how this woman that you have been seeing can give you the strength to deny the reality of me. This sounds as if you were dating her. I have tried desperately to understand the mind-set that you have, that we don't have a relationship. I called your sister because I wanted to find out more. Do you know she has invited me to call her back? She listens to me and knows what it is to really love someone."

"You don't love or feel or care about anyone. You just conjure up lies. My sister has no interest in speaking with you after your insulting behavior on Christmas. Why lie that you called her."

"I opened up to you on that level of creativity, the most fundamental way a woman can create on this planet. If repressed and squashed it becomes destructive. That is what you are forcing me into by your behavior. When you don't allow yourself to get close to me I begin to suspect that you are with another woman. I would love to touch you, and just feel you physically and relate to you on that level. I have been trying to compromise by not being as demanding as I certainly could be about time; you make no compromise. We are having an out and out war here, you and me."

Rachelle moved from love, touch, sharing, denial, compromise, to all out war in the matter of six sentences. There was nothing for me to say; I remained silent.

"Saturday night, after I spoke with you, I lay in bed wailing in agony, which came from the depths of my womb where my creation is. I literally just walked and walked, wept and wailed out loud all night." She suddenly stopped crying; her voice changed, "You can't afford to change because the minute you do you may just surrender a little bit of your love towards me. You are denying something that is given by God."

I was living a verbal nightmare.

"Well, Linda expects to speak to you later on Saturday night also," she said with sarcasm, having obtained another name from my phone machine.

"Linda is from Taiwan. What's your problem? You monitored fourteen of my phone calls so what confuses me is why you take only one or two and then you elaborate on them. I wish I did have all these flirtations I am supposed to have had, according to you."

"Well I certainly know you are not giving it to me. What is it about me that is so disgusting?"

"Nobody has said there is anything about you that is disgusting."

"Well, all right, there are only two or three things that it could be that make you stay away from me and deny me so much. One is that you really dislike me as a human being; another is that I am disgusting physically or in someway I am just grotesque. I believe you are sleeping with somebody. Are you going to see me soon?"

"No, because seeing you is not a good idea; it only gives you the wrong message. You have to accept the fact that we are not together, and I am not in love with you."

"I know that you just say that, but I don't think you mean it. I think you should come closer and let it be."

Later that day, Rachelle called again in a very angry mood.

"You have no reality."

"Look at your reality." I snapped back.

"My reality," her voice, now shrill and getting angrier, "my reality – was a reality with you, which you cheapened."

"Rachelle, you have lived with an illusion for the past seven months."

"No, I have not, and I am not finished. I am going to kill you and I am going to do it tomorrow," she said in a slow, low, threatening voice.

"Oh, yes?" I said, trying not to give it credence, yet worried.

"Yes, I am, I am going to come and kill you, and you better watch where you go because I am going to be right fucking there. I don't have anything to lose because I have believed in you, then I hear on your machine, a woman saying all this intimate stuff. You should have given me some. You are capable of fucking her, under a bush outside your God damned house. You probably have set up a whole vocabulary and a whole thing around this so that you can get to her bush. What about my bush problem?"

"Handle it. Rachelle. You can interpret the phone message which ever way you want."

"I am stating it word for word of what it is. It was the last few days before the weekend, and I know because you were with her."

"This conversation is ridiculous, the woman lives three thousand miles away. Your conclusions have nothing to do with me. This is a blatant breach of privacy and theft and because of this, I must go."

"I am not going to let you go, this is just too much, this is far too much."

"Goodbye." I slammed the phone down. I was so furious I couldn't wait to get out of the office and drive out to Farmingdale earlier than planned.

If I thought that hanging up the phone each time she called would eventually put an end to this situation, I would have done so. My instinct was to defuse the danger by answering her calls, and psychologically appease her anger. I also wanted to ward off her coming to my front door ringing the buzzer through out the night, as she often did, when she could not reach me by phone. I had to take her threats on my life and on those close to me seriously. I was frightened and constantly on the alert. I was dealing with an obsessive personality: a stalker mentality. There was no easy solution to this nightmare.

TWENTY-THREE
Harsh Realities

When I arrived I experienced the joy of my mother's serenity and her soft silver beauty as she sat in her quiet graceful presence. I was excited and looking forward to spend some intimate time with her before she returned to Canada. I knew there would not be much of a chance to do so at the wedding. I had brought some priceless photos from childhood to share, and surprised her with a beautiful photo of herself in her early twenties, which she believed she had lost in Ireland years ago. Looking at the photo opened up a treasure of memories. By this time Teresa, Jo and Geraldine also joined us and regaled in her stories.

We sat sipping tea together and continued our chat, just as we had done down through the years, a ritual we both cherished.

"How are you?" she would ask intermittently through the evening. "I feel you are troubled."

"Just life and what it throws at me," I replied. "So how is life on the farm in Canada?"

"I spend a lot of time alone. It is cold up there."

"And your health?"

"There are no cracks in the structure."

As the evening came to a close, we settled into a rare and intimate communion with each other. Time passed quickly; she wished me a safe journey home.

"Take good care. Stay close to God."

I walked outside with Teresa; the night felt cool and silent. We hugged without words.

I came home to Brooklyn hoping for a night without intrusion. Once settled in, I checked for phone messages. Six were indicated. I was apprehensive as I pressed the button to retrieve them.

"Hello, Connell, this is Rachelle, I thought you were going to phone me later. I misunderstood your meaning of later; I'm totally confused. I think I'm going to take some sleeping pills and go to bed," she said bursting into tears. "I can't go on, and you don't even care, and you're probably not even coming home now." Then like a switch in personality, "You probably are going straight off to your secret tryst on Sunday. I have been unable to do a single thing all day. I am going to be here, just in case you do come home, and remember to call me."

As I pressed the button to retrieve the second message, the front door buzzer rang. Right at that moment, I felt a sick feeling in my stomach. I looked out my bedroom window to see who was there and saw Rachelle standing against the tree, her hands in a praying position raising them up and then bowing down as if she was performing a ritual, the same as she had done at a previous time. She was getting spookier by the minute. I went back into my living room and spent a few moments looking out at the spectacular view from my window. To my right, I could see the skyline of lower Manhattan, and further right the elegance of the Twin Towers. I could glimpses the Bridges of Manhattan and the pearls of lights on the George Washington Bridge and to the left, Port Elizabeth, New Jersey. As I was relishing this view,

I was snapped back to the harsh reality of the sound of a buzzer once again. I proceeded to the next message.

"Hi, Connell, so here I go again, talking to a machine, stumbling to try to say something like, like I just feel - superfluous. I suppose that you might say like, in context of you and I, I don't know, like I just . . . it's hard to talk just into the air; it's frustrating, it makes me angry. I just feel as if I should just remove myself because you don't really care to have me around anyway, and-um-that's what I feel like. Maybe I'm wrong. I feel like-um."

All became quiet once more. This was a tragic situation. These messages disturbed me. The buzzer rang again; I became numb to its sound. I pressed the button once more.

"Connell, I really am in so much pain over everything. It's been over a year I've been living with this pain and I can't bare it." She was sobbing between every word, then suddenly, her voice changed and continued in a strong, emotionless, dramatic voice, "I just can't bear it any more . . . I can't play the game." The message finished.

At that moment, I perceived that her belief in a relationship with me was not real but that her obsession was real. This truth would mean that she had to face the reality. Rejection would authenticate the fact that she was not important. I wondered what she meant by 'I can't play the game." The buzzer rang once more. I pressed for the next message.

"So anyway, you might as well go ahead and put the last nail through my feet. I am ready for that now. So, keep on pushing that nail in there. Make sure I get hung up, good and proper. I would just take two or three days to die, then I will be out of the way."

During this period, Rachelle had informed me that she was attending Saint Francis Xavier's Church on Thursday evenings, claiming that she wanted to convert to Catholicism. Her references were taken dramatically to represent the "Christ being crucified yet being innocent." In this way, I would possibly become her Pontius Pilate, Judas and all things bad.

Rachelle, by now, believed that by backing out of having my poetry published, I had ignored a decision that was made by God. Therefore God now was working out his will through her, which strengthened her delusion that I was on the wrong spiritual path and that her mission was to bring me back. When Rachelle began to impregnate her "direct God connection," I found it hard to refrain from responding, especially when she stated, once again, "it will only be between you, me and God." While I was trying to interpret her message, the buzzer rang again. I could not let her in. She was unpredictable and could create a scene claiming she lived with me and as before insinuate we were in a relationship. I pressed the button on my machine for the next message.

"Connell, you know that I really wish you would kill me. Do it now, do it, please, please do kill me, get it over with," she said crying hysterically.

This could all be summed up by her dramatics and being an actress. She possibly could be acting out the scene in her living room. None-the-less, I was very distressed, and needed help to know how to handle this situation. I was at the end of my wits. The phone kept on ringing throughout the night.

The next morning, at 8:30, my phone rang in the office.

"This is Rachelle. With you, I bonded like with my mother; she severed it and you sever it. I believe that you have been with many women. I wish it were not so. My life force, my feelings, and my soul are connected with you. I become destructive if it cannot live. I want to kill, like Medea. You will become responsible for forcing me into doing that to you. I can't handle going two weeks without hearing your voice; I die a little all the time. If it is true that I am not one of the many, your defenses are so powerful they defend you from the fear of what exists, which is me and pure love."

"Rachelle, please let go obsessing on me and find peace and happiness with someone who returns your love."

There was no system in place to screen calls; I was entirely alone. A competitive company had just bought off the entire staff that manned these lines. Calls were coming into the tele-marketing department on all sixteen lines. It was now 11:15.

"Good morning, Chambers speaking, how may I help you?"

"It's too late to help me, this is Rachelle, and I am going to go away. You just had to keep hurting and hurting, because you just don't acknowledge your own hurt and pain."

"Rachelle, I don't know what you are talking about. I am not hurt nor am I in pain."

"I can't stay here with you carrying on like this. You have disrupted my entire life. I loved you from the very beginning. You are not aware that you caressed me with your words. Our dialogue brings about old pains. But it anguishes me that we can't be together. Where did you go last night?"

"This is an obsession that is eating you alive. Let it go. I am not in love with you," I said ignoring the question.

"Instead of seeing this as a relationship in process, you pull away and separate, creating fragmentation. Connell, nothing is ever over. Do you realize that I'm fighting with you for my life? Don't you understand that?"

"No, you are fighting with yourself for your life."

"You will never have anyone like me, Connell, who does not care if you are flawed. I want to spend time with you to share and create. I would like to be the one to inspire you to write. Come to me in humility and emptiness without expectation especially when I scream for you to try me on. Try me okay, please? By not wearing me, you are denying yourself something really nice. It's a gift that you give yourself. God is here speaking though me offering you this gift."

I could not respond to her constant regurgitations as other calls were continually coming in on the open lines and I had to conduct business. I put most of her calls on "record" listening to them later when I had a moment. I could not take her double talk anymore. She was sick and making me sick; I wished she could just shut up.

"Rachelle, I'm at work I can't continue these one way conversations. I've got to go."

"Tell me something before you go. Don't run away from me. I care about you and I'm talking about honoring a connection. If I'm excluded, I have no idea of what destructive act I may do."

Suddenly, the phone was silent. I thought she had hung up, but I could hear the sound of traffic as if the phone was left hanging in a phone booth. This made me very nervous, because it meant that she could be close by watching me, as she had done at other times.

I arrived home late, and checked my phone calls. First a message from my brother Victor in Texas, leaving me his new telephone number, followed by a call from Pamela in California. What a relief; no call from Rachelle.

How does one respond to an obsessive personality that threatens to kill you and your family if you do not fulfill their sexual demands and fantasies? Can one survive if one swims across the center of a whirlpool? How does one extract oneself from being sucked into the vortex of terror? Is there an answer?

TWENTY-FOUR
There Will Be Blood

After arriving early in the office, l left for the airport in the afternoon to pick up Natalia and Anderson who were returning from their honeymoon. I was glad to have them back; it would release me from the pressure of caring for their cats and fish. I was back in my office by late afternoon.

An hour before closing Rachelle called.

"Connell, admitting to having an affair will destroy your image. Since I am experiencing your sexuality, when I get close, you push me away. I need to deal with this very badly."

"What do you mean by experiencing my sexuality?"

"The whole thing is in the imagination, and that makes you dangerous. My life is an open book. You hide, hide, and hide! You push the wall up so far and you think you're invincible. You don't realize that I walk right through it. You may feel secretive and protective, but I believe everybody's business is everybody's business."

"No, it's not. Stop violating my privacy."

"To me it is not a felony to listen to someone's machine. It is imperative that I know what you are hiding. By the way, I left the messages on your machine after I checked them. You have quite an array of friends, but it is so much fun to let you know how I have applied my skills to penetrate your so called privacy."

"You are an intrusive bitch. How dare you intrude on any-body's privacy, especially mine?"

"Connell, there have been a lot of strange occurrences yet I have given you the benefit of the doubt."

"So you are now my analyst and judge as to how I live my life. Who are you to think you have a control over what I do?"

"The fact, that my relentless pressure on you for the truth pisses you off, makes perfect sense. You are a dangerous indi-vidual and you must be stopped no matter what it takes. To treat me like this is unforgivable. Should you attempt to come close, it would be an affirmation that I was right."

"Who made you a vigilante to pass judgment and classify me as dangerous? I don't have time for all this nonsense. If I don't hang up, I am going to be late."

"But, Connell, as I said, I need to deal with this very badly."

"Then, deal with it." I hung up the phone, left the office and drove down to the village, where Greta was performing at Eighty-Eight's.

I did not get home till after midnight. I glanced at my answering machine. Sixteen messages. I wondered how many of those were Rachelle's. I took a deep breath and said, "Here goes." I pressed number one.

"Connell! Are you there? Can you pick up the phone please? If you're not there I'll find you."

The following nine messages were all the same as the first, begging me to pick up the phone. Then, on the thirteenth,

"Well I'll just try and talk to your machine. I know you are mad at me right now and you have reason to be. I believe that any kind of adversity can be used constructively, and I would like to attempt it. I think there are just things to resolve."

Fourteen, "Hello, Connell, I do need to talk with you, could you please pick up the phone? Hello –hello - *Connell – would – you – pick up – the phone – please*?" She repeated the same things over and over. "You work very hard at keeping your life separate from everybody except for certain forays into other relationships. When I find out, who they are, and their particular interest in you, I will dismember them. I have been hurt. Still I forgive and try to move on because I care so much about you."

I was stunned by the casual way she used the word, dismember.

Fifteen, "Connell, It is urgent that I speak to you. *I really don't want to get crazy.* I do need to talk with you, please, please. I know you feel hurt because I won't buy your story. It's not just that, it's also just a need to talk, to connect."

As I was listening to all my messages, the door buzzer rang about twelve times. This was a pattern. Rachelle first filling up my machine with messages, and then proceeding to arrive in my neighborhood and either hide in the park across the street, or sit unobtrusively on one of the park benches, or hide under the stoop of a building until I got home, no matter what time it was. I later discovered she would call the garage where I parked my car and check with them as to when I arrived; in that way she was able to monitor my every move. Rachelle rang the buzzer every five to ten minutes possibly believing that I would become unnerved.

About 3:00 a.m. exhausted, I finally fell asleep to the sound of the buzzer.

Wednesday, I arrived in the office at 9:00 a.m. as usual. Around 9:30, the call came.

"I buzzed you numerous times through the night and here you are in your office at 9:30 answering the phone. All I am trying to ask is to give me just a little more of you. If you did, I would be relieved and grateful."

"Rachelle, in the past when I stepped forward, you took full advantage of me with your fabrications; it won't happen again."

"So don't go out of your way, do it in stride, you could make it very special. Your niece is getting married in a few days and you know what I am capable of if I am not invited. If you invited me, you would make me feel very, very special. I demand of you that you see me this evening and we spend time to discuss everything."

"I really don't have time. I have a very busy schedule for the next five days."

"Connell, I am saying this calmly to you, if you don't invite me, you won't be alive to get there. If you somehow slip through the cracks, as you are quite capable of doing, I will be in the vicinity of St. Killian and nobody's life will be spared. If I can't get you, I will eliminate each person until you and I come face to face."

Her words sent chills down my spine, as she accelerated her threats to encompass my whole family. What was to be a celebration would turn out to be a massacre; the slaughter of innocent people.

"Don't be so melodramatic. It's only a wedding," I responded, trying not to show any reaction.

"Connell, you are missing the whole point. You are in such denial. It's about me. It's about exclusion and it is your fear of presenting me as the woman with whom you are in a relationship."

"Rachelle, we are not in a relationship. Stop making that claim; you are lying to yourself. You are not part of the family and are not invited. Yes, I think it's about time we sat down and had a serious talk."

She had accelerated her threat to encompass my whole family. Feeling dangerously threatened. I felt it was urgent to defuse the situation as quickly as possible. I decided the best approach was to talk to her face to face. I told her I would be in the area of the New Prospect Café on Flatbush Avenue around nine o'clock that evening, and if she wished, she could meet me there. She informed me that she would be in the Spirit Path office and if it wasn't inconvenient, to pick her up. Understanding that I had to defuse all confrontation, I agreed. She was thrilled.

I arrived on Flatbush Avenue at eight o'clock with the sole purpose, to drop off a hand written note at the police precinct before my meeting with Rachelle. The note specified, whom to contact, in case something should happen to me, where I was going, why and with whom I was meeting. I addressed the note to officer Peggy Cannon, whom I already knew due to a break-in in my apartment a year prior and who had advised me to see her if I ever needed any help. I had been in touch with her more recently, asking how to deal with the harassment Rachelle was causing by incessantly ringing my doorbell.

I left the Precinct feeling that I was approaching this the right way. There was no other option left to me; I had to try to diffuse the situation. As I drove toward Spirit Path publishing office, I became nervous, realizing that this was the first time in quite a while I was going to see her face to face and for a moment wondered if my decision to meet her was right.

When I arrived, Rachelle was already standing at the curb waiting. Upon seeing her, a weird feeling churned in my solar plexus. It had just begun to rain and I had a déjà-vu of the first time I met her, offering her an umbrella. Boy, did I read her wrong. She now was a threat to the safety of my family. This awareness strengthened my resolve.

I stepped out of the car, went around to open the door for her; it was as if she was walking towards me in slow motion. Rachelle was wearing a long, taupe color coat with a shoulder bag to match. I automatically shifted into high alert and instinctively scanned her for any concealed weapon; her pocketbook seemed flat. As I held the door and watched her get into the car I checked for any irregularity in the flow of the fabric that would indicate anything hidden; everything seemed in order. It was a short trip to the restaurant. She was quiet and proper. As we pulled up, I opened the door and offered her my hand. This gesture, a natural one, allowed me the chance to glance at her wrists as well as her boots for any concealed weapon. I continued to observe as I helped with her coat. She was wearing a washed-out salmon colored one-piece dress, which I felt could not conceal anything. We sat down and exchanged cordial pleasantries; everything seemed orderly.

"You are in a good mood. Are you going to share what is making you feel so good?" I asked.

"Yes, I would love to. You will find what I will share with you most interesting. I know that you're aware I'm on a Journalist Visa and that it will expire very soon, which means I will have to leave. Now, that is all changed. Roger, the editor of Spirit Path has offered to be my sponsor for a Permanent Visa," she said smiling broadly. A chill crept up my spine.

"Well that's a positive step. What will it do for you?"

"I knew you would ask. It would help me to fully live my love relationship with the theatre."

"Congratulations!" She kept on smiling. I had never seen her in a really good mood.

"Let's order something, I am hungry."

"Do you know what you'd like?"

"I would like to get my Permanent Visa; in that way we would never be separated again."

Her answer hit me in the gut as I tried to not show any reaction.

"I wish you the best with your Permanent Visa," I responded dryly.

I had dropped my guard. I needed to have control of the rest of the evening.

The conversation moved back to the purpose of our initial contact, which was poetry, and the denials that developed in misinterpretation of choices surrounding that issue; the constant talk about the present pain that seems to impregnate all discourse. We touched upon her childhood history, her spiritual work. She discussed the purpose of confession, communion and informed me that in order to know me better she was now converting to Catholicism. Then finally, to her audaciousness in illegally downloading my phone messages and interpreting them as she saw fit.

At this subject, she bristled and said she had problems believing my stories. During the whole meal my eyes followed every movement of her hands, whether it was the knife, fork or spoon. Every time the waiter spoke, I made sure my contact was with him while he was standing behind or beside Rachelle, permitting me to keep all her movements in check.

When it came to ordering desert, I asked the waiter what he would recommend.

"The Pumpkin pie . . . it couldn't be any fresher; it's out of our own garden," he said.

"Okay, I'll have it."

Rachelle's eyes glanced quickly at his face and then shot to my eyes. She had a shocked contorted look on her face. I thought it weird. For a moment, I had taken my eyes off her hands, but as I glanced back at them, she was playing with the dinner knife in a dagger like fashion passing it from one hand to the other.

"Are you aware of what you are doing?" she said glaring at me.

"What am I doing?"

"You are proving to me that you are a pathological liar."

"Where did this come from?"

"When I offered you Pumpkin Pie at my home, you refused it."

"What's so dramatic about me selecting to eat a Pumpkin Pie now?"

"It means you are a liar. You are lying about everything and you must be stopped."

"Rachelle, it is not that important."

"It is so serious that I can kill you for it."

"Come on, there are bigger and more important things to kill someone for."

"Yes, you are right," she said as she placed the knife back on the table with her face cast downwards. Her eyebrows lifted, looked straight up into my eyes, "like not being invited to Geraldine's wedding, total exclusion from your family and absolute denial of our relationship."

"Rachelle, I don't send out the invitations. It's getting late now and I have to go."

She sat quietly at the table in a demure, sulking kind of way, while I paid the bill.

"Come on, let's go," I said.

"Oh, no, not yet, I forgot. I have something for you," she said as she took her small shoulder bag and placed it on the table. I watched her hand go into the bag as the words, "I've got something for you," kept playing over and over again. I was already standing up with my left arm into the sleeve of my jacket and my right arm behind me entering the other sleeve, leaving my chest open and vulnerable. Oh, shit I said to myself. It seemed like an eternity as her hand was coming up from out of her bag.

"This is for you," she said, as her hand reached towards me holding what seemed like a shiny blue metallic object. As she opened her hand two small ceramic light blue lovebirds were revealed, one with upswept wings and the other with wings drooped. She put them into my hand.

"Why are you giving them to me?"

"If we both can't fly together, we will die together."

165

We left the Café, walked towards the car; I opened the door for her.

"No, I don't need a ride. Thank you for a nice dinner. You forget so easily, I like to walk in the rain," she added, very melodramatically. I took her at her word. She came around to the window of the car and looked at me.

"I'll call you later . . . is that okay?"

I did not respond and drove off.

I arrived home and everything seemed quiet and normal. It was about midnight when I finally went to bed. As if on cue, the moment I was falling asleep, the phone rang once and stopped, almost like a signal. It was then I realized there was a message on the machine. I pressed the button.

"Connell, are you there? You know, I'm not going away, even though you think you controlled the evening. It's not that easy. I want you to definitely call me again. Not on Monday, Tuesday or Wednesday, but tonight. I demand it. So pick up the phone and talk to me."

Then another message came on, a little louder, "Connell, I know you are there, you just left me; talk to me. Can you hear me? I now have to take drastic measures, like calling up your brother and calling up your sister at 3:00 in the morning. So I think it would be a good idea to pick up the phone and talk with me, especially after a special evening of dining together. You are trying to bother me with this behavior. I know what it's all about. Just stop it okay, because I am going to get angry. I don't want to . . . " suddenly music was heard on the line.

I lay in bed, confused about this whole situation and, wondering how I was going to handle everything from this moment forward to the wedding. The next few days were going to be busy with family and relatives arriving from all over. I drifted in and out of sleep.

At 6:00 a.m. the ringing of the phone awakened me.

"Good morning, Connell. I just wanted to remind you to not forget to pick me up on the fifth for Geraldine's wedding. I forgot what you told me I should wear."

"Rachelle, stop pushing, you were never invited."

"Connell, I know that, but you still haven't told me what I should wear."

"I don't have time to get into this dialogue, I've got to get to work."

"If I am not invited you have to begin to forget about sleep. I will isolate you from everything you know."

"I've got to run."

"Isn't that your life, you're always running?"

"Yeah, I guess so, goodbye."

I arrived in my office and tried to concentrate on my work. At 10:35 a.m., I went across to the Munson Diner to get coffee and a toasted blueberry muffin. Returning to my desk, I eagerly took a first bite of my toasty muffin, which smelled great, when the phone rang.

"I don't believe your story," said the voice at the other end.

I stared down at my muffin and coffee and made a decision to go right ahead and eat it.

"Rachelle, I'm very busy at this moment."

"I will not allow you to push me around, you bastard. I do see the possibility of becoming more embittered towards you. Either you invite me to the wedding or I will arrive there on my own, and there will be blood."

"I can't get into this right now, I am busy. I've got to go."

"I realize you're busy, Connell and appreciate you're listening to me. Without your contact, things build up in me. When will you call? Four days without hearing from you will be too long. When can I see you again?"

I ended the conversation and hung up.

I was excited about spending time with my brothers and sisters, and yet disturbed about Rachelle's threats. However, the evening went nicely with no phone calls and I finally was able to get a goodnight's sleep.

TWENTY-FIVE

The Wedding

Friday, November 4th, the day before the wedding, the phone rang at 6:00 a.m.

"Good morning, Connell, I hope you had a good night's sleep. I was busy all night. I want to tell you that I went scouting in Farmingdale. I located your sister's home, found Saint Killian's Church, the reception hall, and studied the lay out in order to carry out my plan if I am not officially invited."

Though her words gave me chills, I responded in a manner of indifference.

"Why would you bother doing that?"

"Well, Connell, you've already forgotten that you 'invited me' so in case you forget me again, I now know how to get there and when I do arrive, there is something I intend to do that may surprise you."

"You are just dreaming dreams. I've got to go now."

I was troubled throughout the day as to how to handle and contain this volatile situation. I wrestled as to whether I should deal directly with the police or inform my family that they were in danger. I decided against informing my family, as I believed it would cause panic at the wedding and instead, informed the police.

I called the precinct and was advised to contact the State Police, who would then work with the local police. When I did so they informed me they would have to check her out. I told them the police officers in the sixth precinct in Brooklyn were aware of who she was and her threats. Feeling I had taken the right action, I tried to relax and focus on spending the evening at the Grand Hyatt Hotel with family.

At 6:15 p.m. I received another call from Rachelle, this time at the office.

"How are you? I guess you're looking forward to the wedding."

"Yes, I am meeting with my family this evening." I regretted saying it the instant it was out of my mouth.

She immediately asked, where, to which, trying to sound light, I replied, "It's a secret."

That brought up the subject again of my being secretive about my life, her insistence on knowing the truth, and demanding I give her more special time, not once a week, but many times a day.

"Connell, I'm just saying to you like God, come on in. God came into me, why not you? God has been demanding this of you for a year. You have refused to accept, which has drawn the wrath of God to you through me. We have come together by God's action and you refuse to accept my importance in God's plan. By your refusal to give me equal importance, you bring out the flip schizoid part of me, calling upon my terrible destructive powers."

"This is work you should be doing with your analyst."

"No, she doesn't understand that side of me. Good evening Connell, I know you are busy and I have to run."

Did I just touch a nerve with the word analyst?

I headed to the Grand Hyatt Hotel where family members agreed to meet before going to dinner at an Italian restaurant on Broadway and 85th Street. After dinner, before driving my niece and nephews back to the Hotel, I gave them a sightseeing tour of the city. It was now 2:15 a.m. and suddenly feeling tired and sleepy, I pulled over on 40th Street, reclined the seat and closed my eyes. I awoke at 3:45 a.m., continued my journey home and went directly to bed. I had some recall of my answering machine being activated and deactivated, but being so exhausted I never fully came out of my sleep. The phone rang at 5:00 a.m. and still groggy I picked it up; it was Rachelle. She started speaking as if in the middle of a thought; she may have believed it was the machine picking up. I remained quiet.

"I know the person who called lives in California and there is a bush across the street. Connell, I'm in a desperate way, I feel as if I'm drowning. You cannot save me unless you stop lying. I have been calling you all night from the telephone down the street. I did not mean to intrude on the wedding, but when you don't include me I feel discarded like filth. When I lie down I want you to touch me but you walk all over me. I am trying to understand who you are. There is the soul of the poet and then there is the seductive, deceptive liar. Our Saturn's are squared yet here you are reconciling with somebody else. You set this up without checking for approval of your independence. I feel incredibly betrayed by you. I am not allowed near the blood of your family, but I will get there."

What she was now demanding was a commitment for hours of open-ended time, given in a relaxed manner, to share my soul, through my poetry and voice. She accused me of always being the one who decides when, where and how long I would talk. "I have great compassion, love and feelings for you," she added, then, hung up the phone.

Around 7:00 a.m. the machine became very active. I found this fascinating to watch. It would ring twice, activate the tape, and while the tape was activated would ring again. This action would cause the ringing to override the machine. In this manner she could open up the speaker and hear me in my apartment. This action continued for another forty-five minutes. At approximately 8:00 the buzzer rang, first once, then every few minutes, and then in quick succession. Then the phone rang; it was Eli, my landlord, leaving a message on my machine stating there was a woman at the door by the name of Rachelle Richards, trying to get my attention. Within a few minutes, Eli knocked at my apartment. I remained quiet, and he left. If I answered, Rachelle would know I was there. The doorbell rang a few more times, then stopped. Approximately twenty-five minutes later, the phone, rung again. This time the phone and the machine went through a series of movements indicating someone had activated my machine in order to pick up and listen to my messages. This action continued without let up until 9:00 a.m. - then, Rachelle's voice,

"Connell, I really need to talk to you, please pick up the phone. I am really afraid, please pick up the phone. Please help me."

I could hear the sound of street traffic and the desperation in her voice, which she was always able to create, on cue, in a matter of seconds. All movements to and from my home, and my phone messages were being monitored. I was disturbed and felt trapped in my own home.

The wedding day had arrived and I had been looking forward to celebrating with my mom and family. Now, I was angry because I was sleep deprived. I had to make an exit plan in case Rachelle was stalking the building, aware that I would be leaving the apartment for the wedding.

I went to the window to check across in the park, where she usually hid, looked up and down the street; there was no sign of her. That of course did not mean she was not there. I was scheduled to leave for the wedding at 10:30 and knew Rachelle had copied Geraldine's phone message indicating the time of my departure; therefore I decided to leave earlier than planned assuming Rachelle would not be around my building that early.

I was looking in the mirror, combing my hair, and realized I had a slight smirk on my face believing I had outsmarted her. The phone rang shattering my smirk.

"This is Rachelle; you know how dangerous this game has become. If you don't talk to me now I will shift to the death mode. I am going to get ready to go out to St Killian's Church to confront you there. If you value your life and the love of your *protected* family, pick up the phone and talk to me *now*." Then with heavy breathing, accentuating each word, *"I – really – mean – this."* The last sound I heard was an angry scream.

I stood motionless and stunned. Panic surged through my body; I felt like crying. This was the first time Rachelle knew where I was going and all the protection I had built up around me collapsed. My family was in danger and she was aware of every move that was to take place. Now it was chess at the highest level. Do I stay home and hide or do I blatantly walk out the front door and go pick up my car and be ready for confrontation. My thoughts were interrupted as the phone rang three consecutive rings. My answering machine was activated, clicking back and forth. She was monitoring for any movement in the apartment. I stood transfixed watching the activity on the answering machine, getting angrier and angrier at this woman's obsession to get through to me. Then suddenly everything stopped. I froze, any move, any breath, a footstep the creaking of a floorboard could be detected through the voice speaker on the phone. I was trapped. Each moment felt like eternity. I looked at the clock; it was 9:15. I decided to checkmate. I realized I had the advantage; I knew where I was; I knew were she was; and I knew how quickly the level of her frustration would build. I knew she had to call again. Suddenly the phone rang. While she spoke, I was able to move around the apartment without being detected.

"Connell, if you think that I am not serious, then you should try me, although I prefer that you didn't because I happen to know that you are there and I think you know that. But I may be forced to do something even before you leave. If I succeed, there will be no wedding. I think it's really important that you speak with me now. Please don't make me angry, don't play these games, they are not nice. And when I am made to feel not nice, I do very bad things. So please pick up the phone and speak with me, okay?"

Message finished.

If Rachelle had just made this telephone call from her home on Garfield place, it would take her approximately fifteen minutes to walk to my home. I grabbed a black suit, black shirt, stuffed a pair of socks in my pocket, pulled on a jacket, threw the clothes over my arm, locked up my apartment, and ran down the stairs. Just as I was coming around the last banister in full view of the glass front door, I heard the front door buzzer. I was blown away. I quickly pulled back and cautiously peered over the banister, out of the line of vision from the door. There she was, standing at the door, all dressed up in a maxi length blue coat and hat ready to go to a wedding. As I realized the predicament I was in, I remembered the wooden ladder in the hall closet that would take me to the fire escape. While running back up the stairs, I became more resolute to arrive to the wedding on time.

I pulled open the two bolts on the door that led into a small closet-like space. There was a twelve-rung ladder that led up to a steel trap door secured by two more steel bolts that secured into a steel frame. I grabbed the bolts to slide them open only to realize they would not move; they were locked in place by two master-locks. I was trapped; another sinking feeling enveloped me. I sat on the steps of the ladder and wondered, what now? I was in total darkness, so I closed my eyes trying to think myself out of this situation. Then I remembered that as a child I learned to grope with my hands in the dark in order to find things. After all, this was a fire escape; there had to be a key somewhere. I searched in vain. No use sitting up here anymore, so I decided to go back down the steps and return to my apartment.

I was deeply saddened at not being able to get to the wedding. I was getting angrier at Rachelle's intensified entrapment and was livid at the theft of my privacy and peace. As I neared the bottom step, just before turning around to open the door, I realized I had left my suit on the top step of the ladder. I cautiously climbed back up the ladder and reached up for the suit with my right hand and with my left reached to grab hold of the lower rim of the trapdoor frame to give me support and balance. As my hand grasped the rim of the frame between the two bolts, to my surprise I had inadvertently discovered the keys that would open the master locks that would lead me out to the fire escape and to freedom. The chess game was still in progress.

I pushed up the steel trapdoor, climbed out onto the roof, closed the trapdoor behind me and stopped for a moment to take a deep breath. I sat against the chimneystack to clear my head and to plan my escape from the roof. If I went across the rooftop to my left and went down the fire escape, I would end up on Sixth Street a few yards from where Rachelle was standing at the doorway. If I went down my own fire escape I would end up in the backyard of my own building, where the only exit would bring me out under the steps and again where Rachelle was standing. My only option was to cross the rooftops of four adjacent brownstone buildings, crossing onto a small apartment building and climbing down the fire escape that would let me out on Fifth Street. This was my only chance; I took it and made it down to Fifth Street. Now I had to walk ten blocks to where my car was garaged.

As I was walking on Fifth Street towards Seventh Avenue, I was stunned at seeing my car parked on the side of the Street facing south. In all the commotion I forgot I had decided the night before not to put the car in the garage as it would confirm the fact to Rachelle that I was in my apartment. It was a gamble, as she would often search out my car in the streets. What a stroke of luck. I walk around the car to make sure the tires weren't flat and that the bolts were still in the wheels. It wasn't until I entered the Long Island Expressway from the Queens Expressway that I began to relax even though aware nothing is ever really over. I approached exit 46 leading me to the Holiday Inn where the family was first gathering, and, noticing, a State Trooper's car. No one knew what I had gone through to make it to the wedding. It was 1:00 p.m.; I was on schedule.

In the early part of the reception I was still on edge; everything seemed to move in slow motion. I watched friends and relatives who had not seen each other for a while exchange warm and enthusiastic greetings. I recalled Rachelle's threat that if I did not invite her, she would make it to the wedding on her own, bring her rifle and if she could not get me she would get another member of my family. Her words, "maybe then my anger will turn into joy realizing that at last I would be killing part of you, so, why not kill all of them, then you will *have* to kill me." My stomach churned; all the members of my family were gathered here in one room. I had to snap out of it quickly and get involved in the celebration.

I walked over to my nieces and nephews and tried to be light-hearted, joining them in their fun and games. I watched the beauty of Teresa and Tom dancing while realizing that if Rachelle made it to the wedding, they would be the first ones she would recognize of my family and her hunt would begin.

As I glanced away I was thrilled to see my mother and my three brothers, Daniel, Seamus and Victor sitting together at a table near me. My camera swung into action; I could not miss this great moment. Now with camera in hand I could inconspicuously scan the room for Rachelle. As the afternoon wore on, I became more relaxed and made an attempt at having fun mingling and chatting with other guests. At one point three women, obviously enjoying their stout, struck up a conversation with me. One of them asked why I was dressed in black.

At which I answered, "I like black."

Another responded,

"Sure you know where we come from you only wear black when someone dies."

"Where do you come from?" I asked.

"We come from County Mayo, Ireland. You know where that is?"

"And what brings you here?"

"We are Tom's relatives," another piped up, "Are you a Buddhist? They dress in black don't they?"

"No, they don't."

"Are you sure you're not one of those crazy people who connect with the dead, you know, like the ones we hear about back in the sod?" she asked with a smile.

"Maybe, who knows?" I answered.

"How would you know if you were? You are not alone here, are you?"

"Yes I am."

"You don't have a woman then?" she asked as she looked towards her friend and said, "Poor chap." Then looking back at me, "What about my friend Mary, you could have a fling tonight, you know!"

"No, I'm not interested at the moment. I've got to get back to my family right now."

I had been off guard. I was snapped back to the reality of where my life was. I quickly glanced around to see if my family was okay. I wondered if Rachelle was by now in some disguise, mingling with the guests as she stalked her prey. I remained on edge, but comforted, believing the State Troopers were out there.

I glanced over at my mom and sensed she was aware there was something amiss. Her eyes, always alert, caught mine and sent me a reassuring, comforting look. Looking into her eyes made me feel safe and realize I was not alone. The afternoon continued seemingly without any noticeable disturbance; however, I was preoccupied with the possibilities of what could happen. I wondered if things would have turned out differently if I had included my family in what was occurring in my life.

The wedding celebration was over. Rachelle had not revealed herself. This could be her moment to act at the moment of good-byes. I did not relax until the room emptied and I was back in my car. Not until I headed north on the Wantagh Expressway did I realize I had not thought of Rachelle for the past half hour. I felt energized as I drove through the heavy rainstorm.

There had been no signs of Rachelle anywhere. Where had she gone? Was she playing mind games? Were they all idle threats without foundation? So much tension had built up within me during the whole day. Now as I drove home, I was full of apprehension, knowing she would not give up without some sort of confrontation. Did she actually go out to Farmingdale . . . was she still out there? Did anything occur after I left? Did the police apprehend her? If not, had she set a trap for me in Brooklyn? As I got closer to Park Slope my stomach began to churn again with nervousness.

I arrived home after midnight. There was still no sign of her; there was an eerie quietness.

TWENTY-SIX
Insinuations

The next morning I phoned Teresa to make sure everybody was okay. Once reassured, I drove Victor and his family to Kennedy Airport and arrived back in my neighborhood in the late afternoon. I parked my car at my usual garage on Union Street and walked home, shopping along the way.

Though I had not heard from Rachelle all day I was still on the alert. Were her threats false, was she trying to throw me a curve or was she playing a perilous game? Had I become hostage to her games, or had I actually succeeded in diffusing some of her illusions? I tried to push these thoughts out of my mind as I settled for what I hoped to be a peaceful and uninterrupted night.

At 2:00 a.m., the phone rang. I hesitated to answer but thinking it could possibly be a family member, I picked up.

"Hello, Connell, I have a question for you. When does the woman from California arrive?"

"It has nothing to do with you."

"I find this very confusing. You will surely find time for her, but you'll never find time for me. It's a very odd message to have someone know a specific 'spot' that delights you."

"Stop harassing me. You have intruded on my privacy, stolen information and yet you talk as if you have the right to do so."

"Now, you listen. You have driven me closer to hell by your absolute refusal to include me with your family and the wedding, and that makes me boil. You are moving into dangerous territory."

"Refusal to include you? You weaseled an invitation to spend Christmas with my family, then, you attempted to belittle me in their presence, insult them, and insinuated that we were a couple. You showed no respect for me or for them. Now you have the audacity to tell me that I was obligated to take you to my niece's wedding? You will never be a part of my family."

She continued talking about the wonderful times we shared reading poetry and sipping tea together, sensing the beauty of our love and coming to know why I left her in other lives. She warned me that to insult anyone with Scorpio in their chart would be at their own peril. "I can be the angel of life or the angel of death," she said, adding that I had isolated her from everyone I knew because they would reveal to her, who I really was. I asked how she could talk about caring, loving, and inclusion and continue to insult, belittle, denigrate and threaten to kill my family and me. Her reference to 'dangerous territory' and 'driven to hell' because she was not invited to a wedding, was completely ludicrous. I told her, "Free yourself from me, get on with your life and find happiness and love with someone who will gladly reciprocate your feelings. I can not lie about mine." It was 3:35 a.m., another night lost. I was tired of these infuriating, endless conversations that went nowhere. It was senseless to answer her yet I could not hang up, if I did she would keep calling or come to the building and ring the doorbells, disturbing my landlord. I was dealing with a cunning and manipulating individual and trying to handle it the only way I knew how.

"I suspect you were with another woman tonight. Connell, what would your family, church and social group think if they really knew how sick you were? I now realize what my mission is. I will isolate you from your family, your friends, your social group and your church. I will sever you from society. If you decide to walk with me, I will show you the richness of Universal Law. You are such a beautiful human being and that is what makes all this really sad. You don't give me a chance to grow into you. I don't want to feel on my deathbed that I failed to save you and see your truth. Every choice that I made from when I first laid eyes on you was directly related to my moment of death. Now I am very capable of following through on my threats."

I was keenly aware that she could and was, indeed, capable of inflicting physical harm to my family and friends. I was furious, and did not know how much longer I could hold on. It was now 3:48 a.m. I needed to get her off the phone and to make her disappear from my life.

She continued, non-stop telling me, that it drove her crazy that I was constantly hooking up with people, and continually available for social encounters without ever desiring to see her. This made her obnoxious, which was her natural response to being ignored. She was pissed off, at being relegated to the rank of friend. She suspected that the person I picked up at the airport was a woman and stated that I was probably picking up women daily. The way I dressed, that she defined was European, was even brought to question, definitely proving, to her, of my two personalities, one spiritual; one playboy. What followed next, left me stunned.

"You have no real connection in this community in Park Slope. Most people here are in relationships. It is very unusual and strange to find someone like you living in this neighborhood. It's important that I let the community know who's wandering around in it. I can prove that you can turn a woman on. But whom in the neighborhood do you get sexual release from? I will make sure the authorities of this neighborhood will be aware that you defile those so young. I will prove you don't take women home. It is up to the county to find out, who you do take home. It's very easy, Connell, I tell them that we're in a relationship and you have never invited me into your home; they will understand my innocence. I will destroy you, when I tell them that you have left me open sexually and vulnerable to other men, making me a prostitute. Very strange pattern of events go on in your home, strange visitors. I have observed them. What type of business is going on in your apartment? I would advise you to leave the neighborhood quickly because things will begin crashing down around you soon. You have a perfect opportunity to seduce the community to fit your lifestyle. You have nothing cohesive at your home base here. Whatever you believe you have, I will destroy. For me to be in such close proximity with someone like you is horrifying."

I was so appalled at what she was insinuating that I went into shock. It took a few moments before I could catch my breath and fully grasp what she was saying. She intended to blackmail and destroy me if I did not succumb to her demands. She had crossed into an entirely new dangerous area, defamation of character, and was going ahead with her previous threats to isolate me from society in every way. I was trapped with no way to escape her vicious lies. I was frightened, sick to my stomach and felt I was going to throw up. I was face to face with evil. Whatever strength I had left, I used to restrain myself from responding.

"I know at this moment you are with another woman. I need a 'one on one' experience with you; I am still connected on a base connection. If, I can't have it, I will kill myself." The phone went dead.

I was now reeling in anger at this continual onslaught. Her accusations were vile and horrific and I was now convinced that she was deadly serious in her statement that, if she could not have me she would destroy me. How long could this go on; how could I free myself from being buried alive? How could I keep my sanity? How could I protect myself from her threatened slander? Who could I turn to? What legal channels were open to me? Would my neighbors, employer and friends be tricked into believing the poisonous venom pouring out of her mouth?

I looked at the clock; it was 4:39 a.m. I dozed off for about three hours. I woke up exhausted, showered and freshened myself as best I could. I had taken the morning off to drive to Farmingdale to have lunch and say goodbye to my mom and Jo before their flight back to London later that day.

It was early afternoon when I arrived at my office. The amount of pressure I was under was overbearing and the strain I was experiencing by not responding as Rachelle wanted, was causing me severe headaches. It was the cunning with which she was weaving her plan to discredit and defile me that solidified my resolve not to let her win.

Greta's shows on Tuesday nights were very important and had become a release valve for me. Tonight being there was surreal. I looked around at the people gathered in the room and wondered what each of them had left outside the door before they entered.

The evening went well and when I arrived home I felt relieved there were no messages on the machine. I fell asleep about midnight. Somewhere in the middle of a dream, I tried to answer a phone, but could not pick up the receiver. I woke up annoyed. My phone was actually ringing; I answered.

"Good morning, Connell, I'm very tired and have been working very hard through the night. I tried not to wake you."

"You just did, it's 4:15 a.m. . . . what do you want?"

"I'm very tired. I'm feeling the affects of the Moon, the Sun, Pluto and Mercury. They are all in conjunction with each other and the Moon is in Scorpio. I experience a lot of destructive and spiritual energy. It is all opposing your eighth house, which is in the Jupiter, Uranus, Saturn, and Taurus Conjunction. Connell, it's like a big magnetic interaction going on. I can feel the weight of all of these planets.

I have a right to my anger; Jesus taught me that in the Temple. It is because of these experiences in lives, that when you deny me my presence, when Jesus didn't, you upset me and get me very angry. I would like to have a meeting with you on Friday; can you squeeze me in?"

"Absolutely not."

"Connell, don't you understand, I come from a different place? You must learn how to speak and what to say to me. But the danger, Connell, is that you have sharp intellectual awareness and that makes it doubly bad for me. It's been a very long morning. It's time for you to go back to sleep; you have a lot to think about."

TWENTY-SEVEN
Sickness of Separation

I t was a calculated move on my part. I had to make one last attempt in the hopes of diffusing the destructive threats that permeated Rachelle's dialogue. I gambled that by spending some time in her presence, the elements of her rage would be diluted. I agreed to a prearranged meeting at her place, acutely aware of the danger this entailed.

Driving back to Brooklyn late Thursday night, I was deep in thought as to how I was going to deal with her. As soon as I arrived, without a moment's hesitation, she began discussing at length the present situation. I tried as best I could to create dialogue with regards to her place of spiritual righteousness and her inability to perceive any facts relating to my truth. It was very quickly evident that she had no intention of giving credence to anything I had to say. At one point she went off on a tangent and started reading astro-theology. It was clear that nothing would change and that I was wasting my time. The only thing acceptable would be my total submission to her demands. I, in turn stated that since all her dialogue ended up in abuse, sarcasm, and hatred, I thought it better to leave. Her hostility increased as I got up and started putting on my coat.

"You want me to beg you to stay?"

"No, I would never ask you to beg for anything."

As my hand turned the doorknob, my eyes quickly caught an object flying towards me. It missed my head by inches as it crashed against the door. Without missing a beat, I yanked open the door, slamming it shut behind me. I was out of there, yet had to walk down two roach infested flights of stairs all the time wondering if I would hear a shot ring out behind me. As I reached the sidewalk I could hear her horrific screams through her open window.

Fifteen minutes after arriving home, the phone rang.

"I feel a sense of great despair about all of this. When you listen to me, I love it. Then when you leave, I experience being discarded. This separation is terrible for me. I have never been able to release my desire for you on a soul level. Deep down I continue to feel the link and the potential for sharing and intimacy. I would love you to read me some of your poetry now while I work through this analytical conundrum."

"Rachelle, I am not a poet on call. It is 3:10 in the morning. Good night."

"Okay."

The following week of November 14th arriving home early, one of the messages on the machine was again from Rachelle.

"You bastard, I am really sick and disgusted by your total avoidance and rejection of me. You just put on your coat and shoes and leave. When I feel sick about a person, I have to destroy them. But if you force upon me the sickness of separation, I will release to you a full barrel load. Well, then . . . so be it. Beware!" The message ended.

I hesitated listening to the next one but I was relieved to hear the voice of Anderson Read. The following message, Rachelle, again. During the time I was listening to her ramble on, the downstairs buzzer rang six times. I ignored it. The buzzer rang once more, when her message finally ended. The next few messages were from Roseanne, Pamela, Anderson, Greta, then Rachelle, again,

"Hello Connell, are you there, can you talk to me please?" The buzzer went.

Rachelle's pronged assault on my privacy, her series of endless phone messages, the buzzing of my doorbell at all hours of the night and the escalation of her threats, all began making me feel extremely isolated in my own home. Switching the light on in my bedroom or study, which overlooked the front of the building, would immediately transmit I was at home as would making a phone call if she tried calling and found the signal busy. This caused me to hesitate using my phone. My level of worry and stress continued to rise. No matter what civil way I tried to dilute or stop these bombardments, it was to no avail. She was determined and relentless. I was becoming a hostage through intimidation and her ceaseless intrusion on my life.

The following Tuesday evening I invited my nephew James, who was still in New York, to Greta's show and arranged a blind date for him that night with Denise, a student at NYU who worked at Popolini's.

The very next day at my office at 10:00 a.m., Rachelle called.

"Where were you last night?"

"I was with my nephew James."

"You were not; you were with your friend from California. I know she is in New York. I know you were in your apartment because my spirit could hear you coughing."

"Rachelle, I have to go, I have to attend a meeting."

"You're always running someplace."

When I arrived home there were no messages on my answering machine. The phone rang at 2:30 a.m.

"Good morning. Who is this?" There was silence, then in a very soft voice,

"Hello, this is Rachelle." She started talking immediately about becoming a seer like in ancient times, and that my dark energy sparked in her things she loved and found exciting about me. "You are genuinely good and gentle, and I will settle for nothing less than you." It peeved her that I did not include her in my plans for Thanksgiving. "Who's Suzette? She must be new. I don't care if you sleep or have sex with her, but you create time for another person I have not heard of." I told her she sounded ridiculous.

She spoke of wanting to perform the physical acts of making love and the ultimate one of creating life to heal the wounds. Since I did not share, she had no choice but to intrude by manipulating my answering machine. In that way she could hear the sounds in my room and assimilate whom I talk with. Then returning to her darker voice, "I become ugly when I'm thrown away of no worth."

She hung up the phone . . . it was 4:55 in the morning.

All these nocturnal calls were taking a toll on me. I knew she was intentionally calling in the middle of the night to disturb my sleep. My nerves were fraying and I was angry and tense. I thought of changing my phone number but I knew doing so would only result in her positioning herself in front of my building, disrupting the lives of my landlord and the other tenant. I feared the constant ringing of the doorbell would result in my being evicted. I was further concerned about her showing up at my work place and creating a disturbance.

Once again I welcomed another Tuesday night at Greta's show to be with friends and enjoy a night of music.

TWENTY-EIGHT

Quagmire

Thanksgiving Day; I was anxious to get away from Park Slope and Rachelle's reach, and was looking forward to an early four o'clock dinner gathering at Greta's. The pressure applied by Rachelle enforced my commitment and resolve not to isolate myself from friends and social gatherings.

By the time I arrived at the Upper East Side apartment, most of the guests had already made their appearance and the party was in full swing. I immediately spotted Darine, stunning as usual, standing next to her tall and handsome brother, Peter. Darine, a vice president of a movie-advertising firm, and Peter, an etheric songwriter, guitar virtuoso, and deeply involved in the world of skiing, were both socially engaging and a lot of fun. Before mingling with the other guests, I greeted Greta's parents, Maya, a charming and beautiful lady, reminiscent of a time gone by, and Berg, a distinguished gentleman. It was a gathering of a lively, eclectic group of close friends: Leon Matrakis, antique dealer, who Greta loved and considered a trusted confident; Tom Gates, New York Editor for the Palm Beach Society Magazine, always regaling us with fascinating stories; Maroun Azouri, set designer and director; Stanley Zareff, director and acting coach, witty and smart; Mauricio Bustamante, actor, a spirited and colorful personality; Barbara King, film-casting director and her husband, Alex, rock band tour manager; Louise Tezel, always gregarious, and her husband Jerry, and Greta's cousin, Shoghère Markarian, tall and exotic, a pianist who had been a protégé of composer Alan Hovhaness. I loved being with all these interesting and diversified personalities; they energized me. Talk was stimulating as we indulged in the delectable food, drank, laughed, and danced; Stanley and Greta performed a mock tango. It was the kind of animated evening I needed to forget the reality and dangerous turn my life had taken. No one present had any knowledge of what I was going through but I managed to step up and join in the celebration. The festivities ended after midnight and I reluctantly headed back to Brooklyn.

At 3:45 a.m., the phone rang. This, by now, had become routine. I picked up.

"I love the art in myself, not myself in the art; so I had to come back to the center."

"Are you talking to me or to yourself?"

"It seems to me that you don't acknowledge someone from four hundred years ago; the human part fights it. I was always there before you knew me. Connell, you were so beautiful, now the beauty from your heart is not visible anymore. I want to experience you in my arms. Do you think it is possible to talk before Monday?"

"No, Rachelle, your dreams cannot be realized with me. I'll express one reality to you, it is now 4:43 a.m., and I need sleep. Goodnight." I hung up the phone.

Tuesday, 2:00 a.m., I pick up the phone.

"I'm having trouble sleeping. My mother's having problems in being reincarnated. I can understand that she was unable to deal with the death of her child. Instead of denying it, as my mother did, I had to survive in order not to become a victim of it. It began to destroy her. Lately you sound at the edge; you are in that place where my mother was. Connell, after a few days I start to miss you, I need that connection with you." It was 2:30 a.m.

A series of calls every few days kept coming to my office, and my home throughout the night. The dialogue was always the same. She was now my dictator, demanding intimacy and then threatening my life if I refused.

"Connell, what does the church think of your dishonesty? It must be scary to experience the truth of yourself as a human being. I potentially threaten your life."

"Both of us are going to have a breakdown if we don't get some sleep," I said as I put down the phone.

The next day, at the office:

"You cut me off last night. If I, goodness, am cut-off from you, you will have created evil. The result of my actions will be totally your responsibility, because I am like a child."

"Rachelle, I've got to go." I hung up.

In the evening Greta joined me at the Tibetan Center to meet and celebrate Gelek Rinpoche's visit to New York. Most of the people in attendance had participated in the Omega retreat.

On Monday, 2:45 a.m. Rachelle called, now referring to herself as the Angel of Understanding, and as usual, made no sense. Since she did not view the world as being solid, she possessed the tools to make spirit easily fly, moving in and out of it. All this build up of excitement and not getting a call from me made her feel vile and dirty. "Why is it that you just don't see me?"

"Thank you for sharing the revelation. Goodnight!"

Thursday 3:00 a.m.; I answered the phone.

"Rachelle, *please,* you have got to stop calling me in the middle of the night."

She went on as if she had not heard me. After first telling me I was the Angel she believed always travelled with her and was there, peacefully manifested, I was now an illness that had come over her making her feel dirty and diseased.

"You are fighting me with the viciousness of your power by using your free will and that is even sicker. You have chosen to be destructive, so now I will destroy everything in your path. After you walked out I smashed my fist through the window. I am very destructive and have no regard for the consequences. I may even split myself down the middle. I did put a knife to myself once in my chest, so it's not a new gamble. If God did not want me any more, I would tell God, from now on what I want is not necessarily what He wants. I will go screaming and yelling and take you with me. I can't live through another tragedy; I could, if you died. So let us make it final, let us go ahead with the destruction of each other. Or, let us go for a break through . . . the break through would be to be together physically. The relationship was for us to come together to create another temple for a soul. I will now go to the way of the dark past. This is all about my life, my thoughts, my feelings and me."

It was now 4:45.a.m. During her long disconnected ramblings instead of listening I had developed, in the past few months, the process of transcribing her words onto a ledger, all but verbatim. Since all these calls came in the middle of the night depriving me of hours of sleep, I felt at times I was somehow, in an alpha state as I lay on my side transcribing her rambling non-cohesive monologues. I was sleep deprived but my pen still had ink in it; even in my half sleep state, I was writing down every word she said.

"It makes me really wrong that I can't switch off. I am a sick person. My plants are smashed," she continued, bursting into tears, "So, let's kill animals and maybe a few birds. Or, pick up a few men and just walk away from them, or, go live with this man in London. I can be his mistress and act out that I love him; I will do it all the way as intensely as I do everything else."

"It is 5:00 a.m., enough is enough."

Friday, the 16th Rachelle called my office at 11:00 a.m. apologizing for the explosion. When I inquired, "What explosion?"

she was annoyed, and told me to seriously consider her words, that she had only started the finishing of things. Then she abruptly ended the call.

On Saturday, in my office, at 10:30 a.m., another call came through.

"I never had a Saturday or Sunday of your time, since you never return a call before Monday, I take that as your answer." She called again an hour later and continued speaking with viciousness and venom in her voice. I found it extremely hard to not respond. I just said I was very busy and had to go.

"You may go but I am here to stay forever. I will get revenge. I will sever you from your friends and family and destroy you in every aspect of your life, even if I die in the process. Good bye!"

I felt I was moving through a quagmire where at any moment the next step would be the wrong one. I was deeply troubled. I took a deep breath and proceeded with my business day. Phones were ringing all around me. I was completely stressed out.

On Sunday I was invited to Antonia's home for a dinner gathering. Instead of driving back to Brooklyn late at night, I accepted her invitation to stay overnight in her guest room. I awoke well rested and after a nice breakfast of hot porridge prepared by Antonia herself, I went off to work feeling revived. I was amazed at how effective "time out" could be.

Late at night, once more in Brooklyn, the phone rang. Just the simple sound of its ringing made my stomach churn. After hesitating for a moment, I decided to answer; there was a slur in her voice, "Are you okay?" I asked.

"No, I'm not. I have not heard from you. I have bruises all over my body. I think I blacked out. I have begun drinking alcohol and taking sleeping pills since you cut off from me and now I'm in trouble, and I'm going to do things to you, to hell with the consequences."

She constantly invoked the name of God and the Universe, demanding I totally submit and love her. Nothing I said would make a difference.

Tuesday morning right on cue she called the office at 10:18. She rambled on making no sense. I told her I was at work and had no time to talk. I. She begged me to call her right back. I put the phone down feeling relief that it was a short call. Two minutes later, she called again.

"Why the fuck are you keeping me waiting?"

"Why are you calling? I said I would call you later."

"You are denying me what is mine. You were given to me by the Universe; the same source that gave you your voice of poetry. I want you to accept me. Why are you contradicting your gifts? Prospect Park is our park, and you've never taken me there." She talked about trying to give us a framework. She claimed she already had one and had destroyed before, within it. But the energy in the framework could be changed if we worked towards the center with each other. "I have been coping this whole year without the closeness that Spirit had promised me and showed me last year when we celebrated together with your family."

"Spirit had nothing to do with it. Your actions were premeditated and there never was a 'we'." I told her she was preventing me from doing my work and I could no longer afford the loss of business. She said she intended to call me later in order for us to work in the framework. "The world is not going to run on your time clock any more. I am becoming that part of you that will destroy you," she added as I put the phone down. She was relentless, like a drug addict needing another fix.

In the evening I attended a reading of *Madame Bovary* by Sandra Lewis This was important and necessary to keep my sanity in check. Contact with close friends, art and music saved me from becoming a physical and emotional wreck.

TWENTY-NINE

Your Days Are Numbered

"Hi, Connell, I'm surprised you're home." It was 2:30 a.m. "Is there someone with you? I did not have time to connect with the two spirits that watch over you, so I hope you're all right. I just got in myself; I spent the evening with Paul." She paused a moment before continuing, "Damn it, can't you say something? You're worse than a bad stock. You can't even experience jealousy; your silence is cruel. The Paul that I spent the evening with was the Paul Winter Concert at the Cathedral of Saint John the Divine." She then suggested we build a framework and that since I had never invited her to my office she could come there and be introduced to my co-workers, "I bet you never told them we were lovers."

"Rachelle, stop it. We are not now nor have we ever been lovers."

"God damn it; this is an awful way to live. I find myself in a death trance. Maybe some night I will have you experience the coldness of death."

"Your calls are all endless monologues without substance that require a great deal of tolerance by the listener." As usual, completely ignoring my comment, she continued,

"You're trying, through your silence to hypnotize me into believing that fragmentation brings about oneness. If you tune into the full moon at 12:29 a.m. on Thursday you will actually feel a certain alignment of your energies. This energy only lasts for one month of the year. In that month, I would love to be right next to you." I looked at the clock; it was 3:35 a.m. "Rachelle, it is so late. I am really exhausted. I have got to sleep."

"If you're that tired why don't you come over and I'll take care of you, and if not, I'll come over there."

"Absolutely not!"

"You're nothing but a dictator," she screamed back at me, "Before dawn I'll be in your home or you'll be standing in the street with me."

"Goodnight!" I slammed the phone down. It was 3:45 in the morning. I dropped back to sleep.

When I arrived home the following night, sixteen calls were registered on my answering machine. I didn't have to guess who they were from. The first few messages were all the same,

"Connell, are you there . . . can you pick up the phone and talk to me, please?" The downstairs buzzer rang; I ignored it. Each new message was intensified with added threats and deadlines. "It's like I said to you last weekend that the first steps that I will take are to contact your relatives and friends and tell them of the games that are going on. There will be no holds barred unless you want to talk. I will give you one more chance."

Rachelle did not personally know my relatives and friends. She accumulated information on them by decoding my answering machine and taking down their messages.

"Okay! Well I'm just about to call your sister for starters and . . . um . . . I shall proceed with a course of action. You have no idea what you have started. I already know the end."

Next, with greater rage, "Connell, talk to me, I suppose you are there making love with someone else. Well, this may be the last time you have a chance to do that. It is really time to stop playing the games, so let's talk, shall we? I promise, if you don't talk to me I will come in to where you work tomorrow, I will call your family and friends and isolate you from everybody. I can become just as hard and as cold as you. I will assume that your silence will be your answer." It never seemed to occur to her that I might not be home to pick up the phone.

Next. Now in earnest, "So now it starts. You bastard, you seducer, I want you to know that I feel really sick about it, about the whole thing and about you. I feel sick about myself."

As I listened to my messages, between each one, as if on cue, the doorbell buzzer rang literally fifteen times; I was very concerned. My landlord was already annoyed because of the aggressiveness of the door buzzer at all hours of the night, especially since it was disturbing his children whose bedroom was directly below mine. He had questioned me about it and the constant phone ringing throughout the night. I was again afraid of being evicted. I had finally reached the last message.

"Connell, I am just around the corner. I've been ringing your doorbell all evening, trying to protect you because there is a very strong smell of gas outside your building. I am just about to make an emergency call to the Brooklyn Gas Company."

When I arrived home prior to listening to the messages, I had not detected any smell of gas. It was already well into the next day by the time I went to bed. The phone rang;

"Rachelle, what are you calling me about at 4:00 in the morning?"

"You have a smell of gas outside your house."

"How can you smell gas when you live fifteen blocks away? I assume you are in your home?"

"I'm calling you from a phone booth at the corner."

"What are you doing there?"

She told me her Masters had upped her responsibility in protecting me. They knew she loved me, but I had not made it easy and had turned everything into darkness. She felt insulted I had never taken her anyplace socially. Drinking was a disease she had, like her father. "Connell, you still can't smell the gas?" I told her to stop imagining things and hung up the phone. I was so pissed off, I felt energized. It was as if I was in a black comedy.

Twenty minutes later the phone rang.

"What is it now?"

"We lie in bed when talking on the phone; I am lying in bed and you're lying in bed. But if we were lying together we wouldn't have to use a telephone. That's why we have to sleep together. We talk all night as it is. I could lie next to you and continue talking. I really wanted to be with you on your birthday. For the first time in six years you made me come to understand the purity of self. It was out of working hard with my sexuality that I discovered the secret of my desire. I now have to work from that place, otherwise I will get physically ill. Making love in person brings about something special. We won't know it until we try it. The truth I keep looking for is on the psychic level. You denied other aspects, and you became someone else."

"The only aspect that I can deal with right now is that it's 5:20 a.m. and I have to get up at 7:00. What am I suppose to do?"

"Don't worry; there are not a lot of days left. Do you understand?"

THIRTY

Broken Ritual

My life was fraying. I was exhausted from parrying all of the convoluted statements that Rachelle fired at me. One moment she was saying "we have fear of intimacy" the next, accepting there was no intimacy, and then creating the possibility in order that she could fear it. She had to create this love "connection" fantasy so that she could have an identity and survive. I was irrelevant, but the fantasy had to exist above all. My refusal to turn a work situation into a romantic relationship stripped her of the tools needed to fulfill that fantasy. This brought on hostility, anger and threats of bodily harm. She warned me if she could not get me, she would go after my family and friends. No sooner was the verbal assault released it was followed up with her desire for closeness and intimacy. This duality was where the danger lay.

One evening Greta related a conversation she had at a recent dinner party with one of her dearest intimate friends, Lita, a beautiful person, and her husband Jack Chadrjian. Greta shared with them the little she knew of my being hounded and stalked by this woman called Rachelle, an actress from Australia. Jack, a lawyer, recalled a client of his who had come to see him utterly distressed, concerning a strangely similar story of being stalked by an actress who also was from Australia. The coincidence was extraordinary. However, though Jack could not recall the woman's name, he did not think the name sounded like Rachelle. At that time Greta was unaware that Rachelle was a stage name and that her real name was Nicole. Years later we speculated that the woman Jack was referring to and Rachelle could indeed have been one and the same person. This made me wonder if Rachelle had interacted in the same manner with other men. I recalled what she said about wanting to give us a framework and that if I did not allow us to work within it, she would destroy as she had destroyed before. I remembered the subtext of other instances where she used the word "destroy" or "ruin" in context with what happens to people who do not accept her plans for them. Her statements, "As much as I can love and care, I can destroy. Medea killed her own children," and then, her warning to me "I have the power to make the world love you or I could destroy you in a matter of seconds, as did Medea," all now took on an entirely different meaning. The total intrusion Rachelle had imposed in my life turned it into chaos. Nights of deprived sleep and the constant death threats impregnating my every move forced me to always be on high alert.

I was pleasantly surprised to receive a personal letter from Gelek Rinpoche sending me prayers, good wishes, and as an offering of spiritual support from his heart, a small miniature pendant of Buddha. I was moved by his inclusion of my presence in his life and carried his gift with me as a reminder of his words of wisdom. His teachings had strengthened my resolve to bring positive closure to my nightmare.

Christmas day was here again; what a difference a year made. Greta invited me over for dinner and I was looking forward to spending quality time with her and her family.

I remembered when I was a child how my brothers and sisters would still be working on finishing the home-made presents we created for each other right up to the Christmas dinner, and decided to follow this ritual. For both Darine and Peter, I selected a book and a quartz crystal from my own collection as well as a small crystal bird that I loved, as a surprise for Maya.

It was now ten in the morning and I had to kick into gear and create Greta's present. I had already chosen a beautiful hand made leather bound book with blank hand-rolled golden embossed marbleized parchment paper purchased years ago at a craft show in Vermont. I intended to fill each page with my own words of poetry. As I opened the book and prepared to write, I was at total peace and excited by the fact that I knew Greta in her wildest imagination had no idea that she would receive this present, along with a special quartz crystal from my home. The words began to flow upon the parchment . . . *At the sound of music . . . I cried, as my unfolding began . . .*

The phone blasted my creative moment.

"This is Rachelle; you better pick up the God damn phone. This is Christmas Day and you know you have a responsibility to take me to wherever you are having dinner. You cannot break this ritual. If you do, you will not see the New Year." I bristled in anger as her voice crackled over the voice machine.

"You better pick up your phone now. You will not do one of your escape acts on me again. You know I must be with you today. Call me, you bastard."

The phone went dead. I felt as if a cannon ball hit me.

"Damn it! I will complete this work. I will be at dinner with Greta and her family at three o'clock. I will not allow this woman to spoil this year's Christmas," I said to myself.

The nib of my fountain pen moved with speed as it scratched word after word in urgent creative expression across this special parchment. The phone rang, again. The pace quickened as I feverishly wrote words of love, peace, playfulness, and flirtation, and then, again, the phone. Rachelle's voice was now like a bad dream somewhere in the background. It was now 2:15.

The phone continued to ring; her voice continued to beg, cry, threaten and demand. I turned to the last page of my manuscript and signed my name, as a warrior would slash his sword in an expression of victory. I was fully satisfied that the gift I wanted to create in my home was completed in time. I walked out the door; there was no sign of Rachelle.

I arrived at Greta's home full of joy and anticipation. Presents were exchanged. Darine and Peter were excited with their gifts; Maya was overjoyed to receive the little crystal bird. Greta was thrilled at receiving the book of poetry and glancing through it, was stunned that every single page had an original poem written by me for her, "People usually write a dedication only on the front page of a book, but you also wrote a dedication on the last page." Berg, with his soft smile and gentle presence, sat in his armchair enjoying the excitement of the exchange. I watched him as he balanced his silver handle walking cane horizontally across his index finger with an expression of subtle satisfaction and great pride as he achieved perfect balance. Leon joined us later for dinner, as well as Shoghère, and a few neighbors. It was a beautiful Christmas, filled with laughter, good conversation and most of all love.

When I arrived home, I found a book left for me by Rachelle on the doorstep of my building, titled *The Listening Heart*. *Listening?* She never listened except to my answering machine. How quickly the bright lights and the tapestry of the evening were snatched away. Yet, as I ascended the steps to my apartment, I kept the experience of Berg and his walking cane as a point of reference. Balance, yes, I had to control it.

THIRTY-ONE
Smoke and Fire

The New Year arrived. The few days following Christmas went by without incident. I did not want to commit to anything. I needed time to think and plan my next move. Greta left for a twelve-day trip to Paris. Rachelle had not called; it was a strange dichotomy. I hated her intrusions and now the fact there were none worried me. I did not feel safe. Maybe she wanted to see if I would call. Life was getting back to normal as the New Year settled in. I hoped that the phone calls and intrusions from Rachelle would diminish as the last few days seemed to indicate. I went to sleep at a reasonable time without any of the usual phone intrusions.

I was shocked out of my sleep by a tremendous banging on the door of my apartment. The first thought was, "Oh my God, Rachelle has broken into the building; she is right outside my door. What do I do now?" I jumped out of my bed and pulled on my briefs. I thought of going through the breezeway into the living room and quietly opening that door. The five doors on the fourth floor landing all led into my apartment, giving the impression of being five separate apartments. The banging sounded as if someone was trying to smash down the door. My heart was pounding with the same intensity against my rib cage. If I responded I would give myself away; if not, maybe the intruder would leave. I thought of calling the police.

"Mr. Chambers! Are you there?" bellowed a male voice "There is a fire in your apartment."

Was this true? I could not smell any smoke – this had to be a trick. Maybe Rachelle had an accomplice. What if this were true? I had just jumped out of sleep and was still discombobulated.

"We will have to break down your door if you don't open it. There is smoke billowing out of your window."

I looked towards my window, nothing. I ran down the breezeway to the living room and kitchen, nothing. I ran back to the bedroom door, made the sign of the cross, grabbed the doorknob and, as I opened it, stepped to the left in case a shot was fired.

There filling the doorway was a massive fully dressed fire-fighter, helmet and all, with arms raised ready to smash open the door with his hatchet.

"What the hell are you doing?"

"We received an urgent call that there was smoke billowing out of your window."

"Where?" I asked.

"It's dark outside; there is no sign of it on Prospect Park West, but we need to enter to check out the rear."

"Who called in the fire?"

"A neighbor."

"Do you know who . . . a woman?"

"That's it."

"Where is she?"

"I don't know."

"She is trying to get access into my building and is using any means she can to get in or to flush me out into the street. She had the Brooklyn Gas Company here checking for a gas leak after calling them about the smell of gas." They walked through the apartment and confirmed there was no fire. They asked her name and I supplied all the relevant information. I hurriedly dressed to go down with them to make sure she had not entered the building. Everything seemed secure. As I turned to go up the stairs, Eli was in the hallway.

"What was this all about?"

"It's obvious, isn't it?" I walked up the stairs feeling very depressed. Nothing had changed. She was getting more desperate and dangerous.

THIRTY-TWO

Shattered

The following Saturday at 10:00 a.m. as threatened, Rachelle appeared in the show room. Nausea swept over me as she walked straight into my office, sat down at my desk and calmly advised me that a charge of rape, sodomy and abuse had been brought against me and I would be served a subpoena. I could not believe what I was hearing; the bottom dropped right out from underneath me. Was this what she meant when she said she could destroy me? How could I battle and protect myself from her vicious lies and accusations? Just at that moment before I could respond, my phone rang. I automatically reached to pick it up. "I need to take this call." I had to get control of myself, and not create a scene.

"Okay, I'll just walk around."

She walked about theatrically mingling casually with the sales staff while continually looking my way as if to communicate that she was talking about me; it was a horrible feeling; she returned as I finished the call.

Knowing her history, and sensing she was about to create a floorshow, I suggested we talk privately in an office off the showroom floor. As we sat at a desk I reminded her she was in a place of business and that personal conversations could not be carried out here. As politely as possible I asked her to please leave. Her response was that from now forward she would be the one dictating our future, and that I no longer had a voice as to what she could or could not do. Ignoring what I said, she continued,

"I have hired an excellent attorney and am going to spread your name across the newspapers with enough information to disgrace you among your friends and family."

"Go ahead and do whatever you wish. It makes no difference what I say; I can't deal with your sick mind anymore."

She would now have an open forum to voice her pain and illusions. I stated that since she had decided to go down that path, there would be no further communication on my part except through legal channels. She looked at me with a blank stare and walked back out onto the floor seemingly relaxed and glancing nonchalantly at the cars on display. I followed closely behind to make sure she was leaving when she suddenly approached the receptionist, pointed to Frank Costa the General Manager of the company sitting at his desk in the office, and in a tone of familiarity asked,

"Is that Frank in there?" not waiting for an answer, "Oh, Thanks."

Before I could stop her, she strode through the open glass sliding door into his office. Suddenly my life crashed before me; I felt powerless. I wanted to disappear.

With an air of confidence she walked straight up to his desk and said,

"Hi, Frank, don't you remember me, I'm Rachelle."

"Rachelle who?"

"I'm Connell's fiancée."

"Oh?"

"He doesn't talk about me any more? I guess he's still shy in public about his private life. May I sit down Frank?" she continued, smiling coyly at him.

"So what's this all about?"

"Well, we've had a falling out and he's not speaking to me, but that's okay."

"Then what are you here for?"

"I've never been able to talk to any of his male friends to try to understand how I can reason with him. He has told me there would be no more communication."

"What do you want to keep this guy for if he is not talking to you; what kind of relationship do you guys have anyway?"

"We read poetry everyday and constantly write love notes to each other and stay awake in bed most nights talking till dawn."

"There's no relationship there. Doesn't he even fuck you?"

"Yes, but now he's raping and sodomizing me, and I don't know what to do anymore. I'm beside myself." She was now sobbing. "Look at him out there, I'm afraid of him, he's like a predator."

"He looks okay to me."

"He gets frightening in the dark. He keeps sodomizing and sodomizing me and I'm hurting so bad."

"Why don't you ask him to stop?"

"It's gone past that; it is psychic sodomy."

"What the fuck is that?"

"He's raping my soul."

By this time a small group had gathered within hearing distance. Here was a woman crying in the General Manager's office using words like *rape*, and *sodomy* and mentioning my name. I was in a frozen rage. It was as if a bolt of lightning hit me. She was actually starting to make good her threats of destroying my life socially and at business and isolating me from friends and family.

Frank Costa was a cold and calculated man with whom, in the past, I had intense confrontations, fighting over business ethics. A sinking feeling came over me as I watched Rachelle and Frank converse, and, could not believe this was actually happening. Everything seemed to be moving in slow motion; I was in a trance. The sound of their voices faded in and out. I felt I was loosing control. She had changed the dynamics. I took my eyes off them and glanced to the right towards the other open glass door to the showroom behind where Rachelle was sitting and saw Tony Gulianni, a Sale's Manager and Frank's buddy, standing there listening to everything. My heart sank, I was sick to my stomach. As I caught his eyes looking at me, he put his finger over his lips as if to say, "don't say a word." Suddenly as if the volume turned up in my brain, I heard Frank saying,

"So you've seen his fucking prick a lot?"

"Yes, I have."

"Boy, you must have seen it from every fucking angle."

"Yes, of course, I have. He threatens me with it."

"How does he threaten you with it?"

"He makes me feel like a maiden as he rams it into me. I get so confused then, because he calls it his Excalibur."

"I didn't know fucking Chambers was like that. Rachelle, is that your name, Rachelle?" Frank asked as he reached across to touch her hand in a consoling way.

"Yes, professionally it's Rachelle, but I'm known as Nicole Ruth Richards."

"And Nicole, what do you do professionally?"

"I'm an international journalist working on a project here in New York."

"Nicole, what do you want me to do?"

"Just talk to him so that we can get back together again."

"I will talk to him and first thing I will tell him is that he must be fucked up in some way if he can't see how beautiful you are. If I can't convince him, then I'll go to any court you want me to, and I'll put him behind fucking bars." Rachelle immediately reenergized, her shoulders straightened.

"You would really do that for me? Why?"

"You are either a beautiful woman or a clever fucking whore, but whatever, I promise to help you. Do you know how long I've known Chambers?"

"No."

"I've known him for about three years. He buys me coffee in the morning, in late morning and in the early afternoon. He is into this British ritual, you know."

"What's that got to do with you helping me?"

"Those who drink together, piss together."

"I don't know where you're going with this."

"Nicole, just be quiet, I'm trying to help you."

"Go on, but I don't understand where you're going."

"We see each other's fucking pricks three times a day, every fucking day, for the last three fucking years."

"What does that have to do with you helping me?"

"I'm a Navy man, you know, I'm an old sailor, and when you're on the high seas for months without a woman you get interested in men's pricks, so you look at them, whether it's in the shower, in the bathroom, or when they're dressing or undressing, and I know a good prick when I see one. Chambers has a beautiful one. We both agree on that, don't we?"

"Yes, Frank."

"I just have two questions to ask you, then, I'll connect with my friends on the police force for you. What is the unusual mark half way up the back of his prick? Don't answer me until I ask you the second question. Remember he's an Irish Catholic guy, not a Jewish guy. Is he circumcised?"

Rachelle froze. Frank got up and moved from behind his desk with a look on his face of gentleness and concern as he said,

"I know it's an embarrassing question to ask such a beautiful lady."

Rachelle looked up at him, her eyes filled with tears. Frank put his right hand in back of her chair, bent over gently and said,

"Let me ask you the question in another way, would that be okay?"

"Yes, please."

"Okay, here's the question." Now suddenly raising his voice and challenging her, "Is he fucking circumcised or not? Answer the question."

Rachelle burst into tears and started shaking violently.

"I don't know."

"Well, then how the fuck can he be raping you and sodomizing you all this time?"

"He's been raping and sodomizing my psyche and my soul," she said dramatically, putting her head in her hands, bursting into tears as she lowered her head to her knees, sobbing,

"But he did it, he did it, he did it."

I saw Rachelle being shattered, by the man I considered indifferent and vulgar. I had hated his constant use of the four-letter word. Now he had used it like a surgical instrument with absolute precision. I was snapped back into attention with the bellowing of Frank's voice.

"You're nothing but a crazy woman, you're mentally sick, you're deranged. You asked me for help, I still will help you, Nicole, I will have you fucking locked up in a fucking institution. Get out, get out, get out, get out you crazy woman," he screamed at her with his arms flaring, as she backed away from him moving towards the exit door, which he by now had opened for her, verbally pushing her out, and closing the door behind her.

Rachelle slowly walked away from the door into the rain looking defeated in her long, faded lavender goose down coat.

I was still shaking as I watched her hail a cab and go north on Eleventh Avenue. I stood in my own stupor for a moment, caught between the feeling of relief and good riddance and the underlying feeling of pity for her. I was feeling extremely vulnerable as I realized everybody was now staring at me, and knowing that each had heard only snippets of the story. I focused in on Frank.

"Frank, do you want a cup of coffee?" A smirk came across his face, "So, we're peeing buddies, right Frank? Can I ask you one question before getting you coffee?"

"Yup."

"Frank, Do you know if I'm circumcised or not?"

"How the fuck would I know? What do you think I do, go around and look at men's pricks all day, did you believe me? I'm happy with Barbara. Go get me coffee Chambers."

"I'm going to get you an Oscar the shape of a big gold prick."

Anderson walked with me as I headed out to get the coffee. I opened the door outward with my left hand, as a customer I had an appointment with approached the door. Anderson stepped back to let the customer in as I stepped partially out. As the customer was passing me on her way in, I was suddenly punched in my right jaw. As I recoiled from the impact, I realized it was Rachelle, the look on her face wild and ferocious. I watched her hand pull back but did not see her left hand coming up which struck me squarely in the face. I made an attempt to move away from the customer and the glass door. As Rachelle's arms dropped to her side, I pushed the door open to my left, and moving my elbow to the right, allowed the customer to enter. Without warning, I felt a crushing blow to my lower right rib-cage and stomach. Rachelle had struck again. I was traumatized as I watched her drop the piece of wood she used as a weapon to strike me. My left hand went to my rib cage and my right, to my face, in an instinctual movement of protection as I heard her say in a dark, animal sounding voice,

"It will finish with your crucifixion." As I pushed the door away and stepped back into the show room, she disappeared.

Anderson, Frank Costa and the customer, all witnessed the assault. I felt numb and bruised. To everybody there it was a thirty-minute show. I had lived it, day-by-day for over a year and knew that this was the beginning of the end. Rachelle would not let up until it was finished. I first became wary when she used words like *guns* and *knives* in her threats. I had always been alert while in her presence for any sign of a concealed weapon. I had even done so today, while she was in the show-room. What shocked me was that her hands were her weapons. She looked so frail but her physical power caught me off guard. Feeling depleted I tried as best I could to avoid looking into the inquisitive eyes of those around me.

She knew how to play her game. I had to learn to be more vigilant.

THIRTY-THREE

The Assault

I had great difficulty concentrating on my work. I began answering the phone again with trepidation. So far, so good, then about an hour later,

"How does your face feel, darling? I didn't mean to hit you the second time, but I really didn't get the satisfaction that I thought I would out of the first. How does your nose and mouth feel, darling? I wasn't completely satisfied with that either. Do your ribs hurt? God damn it, that didn't satisfy me either. I guess I won't be satisfied until I have your heart in my hand, since you wouldn't give it to me freely. Now I will take it from you. It can be done you know. I know where you sleep. I will get in eventually. There is integrity, dignity, and decency at stake."

"No, there is not."

"Oh yes, there is."

"You have viciously assaulted me. There are witnesses who agreed to swear in court for me."

"Great, great, this is what I wanted to have happened," she said laughing, "Now we can take it to the courts."

"I guess you have done everything your attorney has told you to do."

"Yes, and more. I had three strikes for myself, and they will not be the last. I hope you don't hurt too much. Remember, I have just started. You will find your Calvary more brutal than

Christ's, but you will have nobody to help you. I am now directing and producing the final show, and I can do that so well. The next seed toward your destruction has already been planted. I've left my passport on the rug in the hallway outside your apartment door."

"How did your passport get outside my door?"

"Connell, because I was actually up there, uninvited."

"How did you get into my building?"

"Cats! Cats! Cats! Cats! Are you stupid? Your ground floor is a Vets office. Once in there I'm in your building. I should have thought of this before. Don't you think it's a little bit sick knowing someone for fourteen months and being emotionally, spiritually and intimately involved, while never being invited into their home?"

"Rachelle, I have not been involved with you over the last fourteen months."

"I have known you, loved you, and been intimate with you physically and emotionally for the past fourteen months. I have not been dreaming. Is the hurt in your ribs a dream? It's not, right? Is the hurt on your face a dream? It's not right? You are hurting. Where do you think the bruising and the damage and the depravation of my womb have come from? I opened on behalf of the Creator and you imbedded your evil in me."

"I have no part in your fantasies. All of this has been your creation, so stay with your creation. I'm asking you again, how did you get into my building?"

"I just got in, that's all."

"What do you mean by, that's all?"

"Please don't underestimate me, Connell; you really take me for someone very, very stupid."

"If I did not open the door for you, and neither did anybody else open the door, then you broke into the building."

"Dear me...ha, ha, ha, ha! You really can build a big case against me, can't you?"

"You left your passport outside of my door in order that you could say that you accidentally dropped it when you were leaving my apartment. It won't work, Rachelle, because all of your phone calls to my office are recorded as evidence since you assaulted me, and I have not been and neither have you been in my apartment today. So wake up to reality."

"Well Connell, actually I was not in your apartment but I did make it up to the fourth floor, where the top four apartments are. I assumed yours was the first one, since you did tell me it looked out over Prospect Park. Well I actually took some things out of my satchel in order to find some notepaper to write you a note letting you know I was there. I stacked the things up against the banister and since it was a little dark up there I must have dropped my passport."

"Rachelle, if you want your passport, I can get you your passport, that's easy."

"I want other satisfactions, too. It is either going to be one hundred percent negative or positive satisfaction. You, having my passport is not an accident."

"Rachelle, then why don't you take me to court?"

"It's the only way that some sort of justice can be brought."

"I accept the judgments of the courts."

"You mean having done what you did. The judicial system will destroy you."

"If the courts prove that I am wrong then that's the judicial system at work."

"I don't think that because of what you did, that you're going to allow the possibility that you were wrong several months ago. So I believe that you're going to sit on your misogynistic attitude forever."

"Rachelle, so what is the case in the courts that you're talking about? What is it based on?"

"It is based on assault. It is based on the integrity of what one does in a situation where understanding is denied. It is based on the shortness of the amount of time you have given our relationship. The seduction, as to how it took place. It is based on the people I know who are listening to this phone call. I know you've got it on the speaker. Really, ha, ha, there are lots of things you don't do, like you say you don't do, that you do. It is based strongly on the fact that all the while I've been trying to reason with the mentality of a rapist, and it is the psychology of a rapist that is happening to you. You know what you are doing."

"Listen . . ."

"You have the psychology of a rapist, that's why you're so hostile towards me."

"You're talking to me about the psychology of rapist and you broke into my building into my apartment?"

"No, Connell, I've never been in your apartment. Now wait a minute, Connell, you are misdiagnosing everything. Truth is now according to you."

"Rachelle, I will not speak with you; it is between our attorneys. If you want to talk with me, you must take me to court, or as you like to state, take me to the Supreme Court. Do whatever you wish to do to prove that you are right and I am wrong. I will run with you. I have no fear of going to court and I have no fear of being wrong."

"Yes, you do."

"Well then remember your first victory may be allowed, but it's the last day that tells the truth. You will have to test me in the courts of this land."

"I guess I'm going to have to."

"Then send the subpoena to me and I will follow it through word for word in order that you can be at peace with the proven reality of what you believe to be your truth. Goodbye."

I put the phone down. It was 2:00 p.m. I transcribed this conversation from my office phone speaker system.

Everything seemed to be spinning out of control. Rachelle was right in my face. Once, I had been assaulted, I realized the reality of her threats and that I was incapable of protecting myself.

"Where do I go, what do I do? Do I leave New York? Do I leave America and go back to Europe?" These thoughts played continually in my mind. Now I was thinking of running away in fear of my life and how could fear drive me away from the people I love?

I thought that for over a year I had learned how to handle this obsessive personality. In order to refocus, some form of protection was needed. I pondered my situation on and off for over an hour, then decided to call the local police. I was advised that the assault had to be reported to the police precinct where we both resided.

"What if I had been killed?" I asked.

"Then we would handle the case."

"But you just said it has to be handled by my local precinct, so what's the difference?"

"If you're dead you don't live there anymore, do you? You're just a body in our precinct."

After exchanging pertinent information, he advised me what precinct I should report the assault to, and informed me I could request an order of protection from the Court's Criminal System.

The rest of the afternoon was uneventful. As the hours went by, those who were witness to the trauma of the morning, having had no history of prior events, relegated it to just another incident of the day, eventually dismissing it as nothing of importance. Tonight I definitely needed sleep. I was aware that the dropping of the passport was a trap. I needed witness to it being there when I arrived home. I called the Police Precinct in my neighborhood requesting a police officer to accompany me to my apartment. My request was dashed when I was told by a police officer that if somebody drops something, remembers where it was dropped, and advises the person as to where they dropped it, it cannot constitute a warrant for police action. I explained to the officer that this was not accidental, that it was premeditated, that the person who owned the passport assaulted me in my office three times today and that I needed a police officer.

"What you need is a witness, someone you can trust who is socially coming to your home, who on arrival accidentally finds the passport; only then can you present them as witnesses."

As the business day wound to a close I shared with Anderson the conversation I had with the police. Without missing a beat he said, "Why don't we pick up something for dinner and have it in your apartment tonight?"

We arrived at my building and climbed up the oak stairway to my apartment. I wondered if the passport story was true and if so, had I been set up? Was she waiting in the dark for my arrival? I was so glad Anderson was with me because I desperately needed a witness. Before we reached the fourth floor, Anderson went on ahead. When he arrived on the landing it was pitch black since I turn off the ceiling light when leaving in the mornings. I pulled on the overhead cord that turned on the light, as Anderson looked down and said,

"What's that on the floor?"

"What are you talking about?"

"That! It looks like a passport."

"Passport, it couldn't be mine, mine is green and Irish."

"Well, whose is it then?" he asked as he picked it up.

"I don't know. Why don't you open it? "

"Well, the family name is Richards, R I C H A R D S; first name is Nicole, N I C O L E. She was born on the second of March 1946 and it says here she was born in Australia. Why is there a passport on the floor outside your apartment belonging to a person from Australia?"

"Why don't you hold on to it, because you're the one who found it?"

We both felt a little bit silly playing out this scenario, but we needed to follow the advice given by the police, and were pleased with ourselves that the scene was well done. As I went to put in the key to open the door of my apartment, I froze at seeing a white envelope taped to the door, and with apprehension opened it and read the note.

"CONNELL, IT IS IMPERATIVE THAT I SPEAK WITH YOU. IT IS ABOUT THE CHARGE OF RAPE BEING BROUGHT AGAINST YOU."

Anderson, evaluating the situation, insisted I leave with him.

"You're coming home with me tonight, you're not staying here."

Feeling depleted, no longer safe in my apartment and needing a good night's sleep, I did not argue.

After dinner Anderson, Natalia and I went over the claims Rachelle made in her résumé. She claimed to have been a stage director, actor, teacher and a fifteen-year veteran of the theatre. She also studied speech and drama at Trinity College in London for many years and at Stella Adler in New York City, and was founding director of the Actors' Theatre Studio, where she taught all aspects of the theatre and directed plays for children.

We then studied the passport in our possession. Finding no stamped entry into the USA we assumed she entered through Canada, since "Departed April 4, 1987 Toronto, Canada" was stamped in her passport. Anderson then dropped off the passport at our local police precinct. Finally, completely exhausted, I went to bed and immediately fell asleep.

I later learned that Eli had called the police that evening exasperated with the constant ringing, in his building, of all the doorbells for over an hour.

THIRTY-FOUR
Affirmation of Suspicion

O n Monday, when I went to file a request for the Order of Protection with the State of New York, I was advised I needed to give the reason for the request.

This led me to contact the office of Detective Dragonetti in Brooklyn. Detective Carl returned my call informing me they could only make an arrest if there was probable cause. I would need documentation, a recording of harassment or tape recording of a threat made over the phone.

Tuesday around eleven o'clock, I received a call from a Dennis Odel claiming to be from the firm of "Barnes and Archer", introducing himself as Rachelle Richards's solicitor. Odel requested I drop filing the Order of Protection stating that it was not a viable case. I asked him if he really knew what the case was about to which he answered, not exactly, but believed it to be related to an attempted rape.

"Let me tell you what this is really about. I have been threatened and harassed daily and physically assaulted outside my office with witnesses to that fact."

"What do you have to say about the attempted rape comment?"

"Rachelle claims her soul is being raped and bleeding daily," I replied.

"That doesn't make any sense to me."

"If you are a solicitor, do you think there is a court that would accept that possibility? If you want to know the facts, call Detective Dragonetti."

Each time the phone rang it increased my stress level. When I answered at 1:00 it was Rachelle,

"Darkness will befall you . . . I called Detective Dragonetti and convinced him you were a liar. Don't go home tonight unless you have someone to protect you; you have my passport."

"I do not have your passport. The person who found it in my building gave it to the police."

I left the office around 8:00 p.m. and headed home. I drove up Prospect Park West looking for a parking spot near the apartment and was irritated to see Rachelle sitting on a park bench across the street directly aligned to the front door; on the bench next to her was what looked like a rolled up army blanket. Instead of parking the car, I continued driving in the direction of the Midtown Tunnel, taking me back to the City. As I dropped my quarters in the tollbooth, I became acutely aware that it was no longer safe to go home.

I drove around the city aimlessly, wondering where I should go. As I waited at a traffic light, I felt extremely exhausted and finding a parking space on the west side of Second Avenue on 74th Street, decided to pull over. I sat in my car for over fifteen minutes transfixed watching the traffic lights change from Green to Amber to Red, over and over, and realized my life was stuck on Red. I sat quietly, and feeling a sense of great loss, confusion and sadness, began to cry. I was all alone, absolutely alone. I dropped asleep; when I woke up it was around 2:30 a.m. I proceeded to drive downtown. When I reached 51st Street and Second Avenue, I remembered that back when I was on a weekend leave from the United States Army, I stayed at a small hotel on 51st Street, The Pickwick Arms Hotel. I found the hotel and checked in.

The next morning in my office at 11:55, I received a call from a woman introducing herself as Wendy Thornton telling me Rachelle had just informed her about the break up of our *relationship* and was rapidly falling apart. The woman pleaded with me to speak with Rachelle. When I asked how she knew her, she claimed she was a friend of a friend of Rachelle's, and did not elaborate further. I informed her there never had been a *relationship*; it was all in Rachelle's imagination. I related the assault at my office, her threats on my life as well as those on my family,

"She is very dangerous and urgently needs psychiatric help; it is her analyst you should be calling, not me."

Wendy Thornton admitted she did not know Rachelle very well, but understood she was mentally and emotionally in serious trouble and had been diagnosed as being suicidal and more dangerous to herself than to anyone else. She felt I was the one with a greater grasp of Rachelle's situation.

"Rachelle's life situation is out of my hands," I said, ending the conversation.

Before getting off the line the woman left me her telephone number; the area code was in Pennsylvania. I pondered over who this friend she was referring to could be and came to the assumption that it had to be Rachelle's therapist. Who else would know all those details? That night, at 8:45 p.m., I booked myself back into the Pickwick Arms Hotel, where I continued to stay for an additional two nights.

Desperately needing to flee the city and Rachelle, on Friday afternoon, I drove directly to Woodstock. I was glad I had previously signed up for a weekend course in, *Total silence and Deep Meditation*, led by Bella Salerno. Sunday, returning to the city, still fearing for my life, and sensing it was not safe for me to return to Brooklyn, I went straight to the Pickwick Arms Hotel, which now became my refuge. A deep empty feeling permeated my being.

Wednesday, January 18, as requested, I listed the reasons I needed an Order of Protection issued; the physical assault at my place of business, in front of witnesses; ongoing death threats made on my life as well as the ones on my family; harassing me by placing false alarms to the Brooklyn Gas Company, and the fire department, in attempting to flush me out of my apartment; the involvement with the police; the ceaseless stalking day and night and phone calls threatening to kill me, making it dangerous now to live at home.

After submitting a statement consisting of two full pages, swearing that the statement, in its entirety was true, signed my name in front of an officer, and left after being advised to appear in court on January 24.

There had been a seismic shift in my life. I knew that I had to become as invisible as possible in every aspect until that day when the temporary Order of Protection would be issued by the Criminal Court, at which time a summons would be issued to Rachelle as to when to appear in court.

On Thursday Detective Dragonetti phoned and advised me of the proceedings and informed me that he, himself, would directly serve the summons and the Order of Protection to Rachelle Richards.

Tuesday, January 24th the Criminal Court issued a temporary Order of Protection by Judge Benjamin Whyler effective until February 9, on which day Rachelle Richards and I were required to appear at 9:00 a.m. After leaving the Court House in Brooklyn and returning to the office, I kept my appointment with my chiropractor as my back was reacting to the continuous stress I was under. Needing fresh clothes, that evening, I took a chance to sneak into my apartment.

There were five messages on my machine.

"Since it's impossible to talk to you in person, I will proceed to have a one-way conversation with your answering machine." She decided, for the moment, to throw down the gauntlet and to not proceed with the case. After making her usual vile accusation, she claimed the fact that I had denied we made love, convinced her that I was a seducer and manipulator only able to have short-term affairs. "The life that you think you have, is empty and meaningless, you are barren of emotions. You are a psychic vampire creating and finding pain in others and then making it your own to drink."

Second message; "I was put in your life to stop this cycle of behavior. If you continue to refuse to accept this fact, I will be the catalyst for your destruction. I will destroy you by my hands; they have tasted your fear."

Feeling more vulnerable than ever, sitting on my bed in the darkness, I wondered when she would strike. After packing the clothes needed, locking my doors, taking a deep breath to refocus, and gathering my wits, I headed for a speedy exit. No sooner had my foot reached the top step of the stairs, than the sound of the door buzzer piercing my brain caused me to loose my footing and slide down the three steps to the landing. Feeling trapped and sitting there in the dark, I decided to wait an hour. No buzzer, no sound, no phone call, could it be she had left? Finally deciding to continue down the stairs, the lyrics of *It's Now or Never* were running through my mind.

With whatever audacity and strength I could muster, I walked out the door; there was no sign of her. I made it to my car parked two blocks away and drove off. At the corner of Ninth Street, waiting at the traffic light, I was nervous, as the light seemed to take an eternity to change. As it turned Green, suddenly Rachelle was standing right in front of the car.

"Oh, shit, where did she come from?" She scared me. My heart sank. I was alone; the street was empty. What now? Did she have a gun – a weapon of some sort? Thinking fast, I pressed the blinking hazard warning lights, got out of the car, and walked to where she stood.

"Are you trying to get yourself killed?" She did not respond.

"Why are you standing in the cold without your coat?" She still did not answer.

Telling her to take my hand, I walked her onto the sidewalk. There was something strange about the expression on her face.

"Rachelle, talk to me."

"I'm not Rachelle, Rachelle has been sent away. She failed."

"Well, who are you then?"

"I'm Nicole, I need you to hold me, Rachelle hurt me, please hold me."

Feelings of fear mixed with compassion surfaced. I did not know what to do. I placed both my hands firmly on her shoulders, and asked her where Rachelle had gone.

"She left with Nicole," she answered in the voice of a child.

"Why are you standing here?"

"They told me not to move until they came back. Could you please hug me, I'm very cold?"

Was she playing out a part once again or was this, another personality? How did she calculate the timing to be right in front of my car when the light turned Green? All this frightened me.

"No, snap out of it and go home," I said firmly.

She reached both hands up to grasp my wrists. I was stunned by the strength of her hands. She continued to talk and whimper, like a little child. Taking my hands off her shoulders, thus releasing the grip of her hands from my wrists, I asked where Rachelle and Nicole had gone.

"I don't know, they're going away for longer periods of time now, they're fighting with each other."

"What will happen to you, whatever your name is, if they don't return?"

"I will die," she said looking straight into my eyes as their expression changed.

There was only a membrane between sanity and insanity. I was certain about one thing: I had to get away.

"Let me take care of you. First thing I am going to do is get my jacket out of the car for you; just stand there until I get back, okay?"

I got back into the car, and quickly drove away, taking one last glance at her and watching her explode into a rage, affirming my suspicions. About three blocks south on Ninth Street, I had to stop at a red light. Again, it felt like an eternity before changing to Green. She always had ways of covering distances that I could not understand; she either flew or had a hidden bicycle. Escaping over the Brooklyn Bridge to Manhattan, feet and hands trembling, I wondered what would be next.

The following day there was a message at work from Dragonetti informing me that Detectives Dragonetti and Yardly had served the summons to Rachelle Richards. While at the office I constantly looked over my shoulder ready to react quickly at any moment. I was surprised as to how I was able to continue functioning.

For the next few days I stayed at the Pickwick Arms Hotel. During this period it was crucially important for me to keep up social commitments. I drove up to Bella's in Nyack, connected with Judith Sainte Croix and attended her piano recital at Merce Cunningham Studios. On Sunday I went to Greta's opening night show of her new two-month run at Eighty-Eight's.

THIRTY-FIVE
Sanctuaries

On February 9, I arrived at the Court House as scheduled, and like everyone else, waited outside for the doors to open. Rachelle immediately approached,

"Do you really want to go ahead with this? Do you really want to do it?"

"Absolutely!" She watched as I processed through security.

The court opened with Judge Mariam Hudson issuing the temporary Order of Protection making it effective from February 9th to March 1st, emphasizing to Rachelle that the order also prohibited the making of telephone calls. Rachelle opposed the Order stating it was not acceptable. The judge responded by politely asking her how she made her teeth so bright. Rachelle answered there were teeth brighteners on the market. The judge then inquired how many toothbrushes she owned and she answered "three."

"And what tooth paste do you use to make them so bright?"

Rachelle's answer was vague; she said she didn't know.

"Do you have a large suitcase?" the Judge asked.

"As a matter of fact, yes I do."

"Well, I think the most important thing for you to do right now is to buy enough tooth paste and tooth brushes to last you for a long time because I am going to put you away."

The judge's words were music to my ears. At least the seriousness of my complaint was given recognition. Rachelle did not utter a word.

That evening at 5:00 p.m., I received a call from Ida Watson on behalf of Robert Delaney, court lawyer, advising me that Rachelle wanted to go to trial. As chance would have it, Antonia also phoned informing me she had to make a quick trip on the 15th of March, returning on the 19th, and wondered if I would come and stay at her home to take care of Cindy, her Westy, during that short period. Though she was aware I was in some type of trouble, she did not know the details. I gladly agreed as it gave me a safe place to stay.

Greta was performing once again and I was looking forward to going down to Eighty-Eight's to hear her and see Darine. I remember how freely I used to move around the city without experiencing fear. Now, every time I left the showroom, I felt the presence of danger lurking.

I drove to 49th Street and 11th Avenue and as usual checked to see if Rachelle was anywhere around. She had developed an acute sense as to where I was going. The light turned Green and I proceeded to cross Eleventh Avenue and go south. At that very same moment an old white American car accelerated from a parking spot, running through the Red light, missing me by inches. "Stupid idiot" I said aloud; it was a close call. As I turned south into my lane, I glance into my rear view mirror; the white car had turned onto the apron in front of the showroom. It was a white Dodge Dart and it looked like Rachelle behind the wheel. Had she been waiting at the curb for me to come out and attempt to ram my car? As the next traffic light changed, I saw the car pull out and follow me. I did not see the face of the driver but trusted my instincts. I could not continue in the direction of the club, which was located at 10th Street off Bleecker Street. I had to casually turn west and then head north.

"Nothing must seem rushed, take your time, Connell." I tried not to reveal any sign of awareness. There were approximately ten vehicles between us. I turned right on 42nd Street; she was still about one block behind. I knew she would see me turn, but then lose sight of me within a few moments. When I was about a hundred yards into 42nd Street, I made a quick U-turn and was now facing east as the light turned Red. She had just made the right turn onto 42nd Street; at that exact moment we caught each other's eye. It was definitely Rachelle. She was wearing a white straw hat and white-rimmed sunglasses. She was furious. I tried not to convey my nervousness as I waited at the Red light knowing she could not make a U-turn as she was in the inner lane of traffic going west. As my light went Green, I made a sharp right on Eleventh Avenue, accelerating south towards the next westbound street. The last sound I heard was the blasting of horns and the screeching of tires; she had succeeded in making the U-turn. The approaching light turned amber as I turned north accelerating at about sixty miles an hour catching every light on Green going up to 50th Street turned right on 96th Street with the intention of going east and then south. I was more relaxed now and felt I could make my way back south in time for Greta's show. The traffic light on West End Ave turned red this caused my pulse to quicken. Out of nowhere Rachelle's car pulled up to my left turning half way into my lane at the cross walk. Rolling down her window, she screamed.

"You will never get away from me, never, you bastard. Get out, now, I want to talk to you, you pathetic man. Now! I know how scared you are. I will hunt you down and kill you."

I partially rolled down my window keeping my finger on the button to quickly close it again.

"Okay, Rachelle, let's pull over at the corner on the right side."

I had to let her go first since she was blocking my lane. As soon as she cleared my lane, I slowly followed her to the curb. Just before stopping, I glanced in my rear view mirror and see-ing no traffic behind, I slammed the transmission into reverse and accelerated back about twenty yards, and then after slam-ming my foot on the brake, I immediately accelerated through a U-turn and sped toward the West Side Highway, all the while keeping one eye on the road and the other on my rear view mir-ror. As I entered going north, there was no sign of her. I was getting good at losing her but she was very quick to recover.

Now I was running out of time to get to the show. I exited at 125th Street and made a right to Riverside Drive. I was feel-ing more assured now passing 103rd Street and the Equity Library Theatre, where I frequently attended shows with Sandra Lewis. Photographing her during a hurricane seemed like so long ago.

Traffic was light as I approached 96th Street. At last I was on my way. I never missed one of Greta's performances but now I needed to protect her even if it meant missing the show. While thinking this, I was shocked back to the hunt. There waiting at the light at the right side was a white Dodge within one block where I had left it. Did she follow me or wait, gambling that I originally intended to go south? If I passed on Riverside Drive, she could pick up the chase; if I passed on the highway, she pos-sibly could spot me and enter from where she was parked. I had only a split second to decide. The traffic light went Yellow; I accelerated through it as she accelerated from where she was parked. I slammed on my brakes half way across the inter-section and made a hard left and left again, heading north on Riverside Drive.

I made a right going east and then south on Broadway and a left on 72nd Street to Central Park West, then a left on 65th Street through the park and south on Fifth Ave. I don't know how many Amber and Red lights I might have gone through. I felt my tension dissipate as I finally went west on 9th Street.

As I arrived on 10th Street close to the club, I sat in the car for a few minutes making sure she had really lost my trail then parked in the garage across the street from the club, which also happened to be next to a police precinct. I stood for a few moments before entering the club to make sure the coast was clear. I was now late and disappointed I had missed the beginning of the show. As I went in and up the stairs to the Cabaret Room, I was happy to see the face of Erv Raible the owner of the club, who greeted me and seated me where I had a clear view of the door.

By the end of the show, I was more relaxed but still apprehensive. Rachelle still could have outsmarted me and even now be patiently waiting downstairs at the piano bar or in the street.

When the show was over the audience slowly wandered down stairs, and as usual the intimate group of devoted friends hung in a bit longer with Greta to celebrate with another drink or two before calling it a night.

When ready to leave I went out to get the car and check out the surroundings. The coast seemed clear and as I drove Greta home, I wondered if she picked up my tension. The ride home was enjoyable as we chatted about the evening and the show. At a later date, Greta shared, that she had been aware I had arrived late, and sensed I had been in some sort of trouble.

I continued my drive home alone; Antonia had returned and I decided I had to make an attempt to reach my own bed tonight. I knew by now that my success in shaking Rachelle off was only temporary and would result in a *punishment* either by phone, at home or at my office. Or, that she would harass me by bombarding me throughout the night by continuously ringing my doorbell. I desperately needed to live in my reality not hers;

it was not easy doing so, but I was determined. Yet the more she outwitted me, the tighter her traps became on every level.

As luck would have it, a few days later my friend Joyce Vagasy called to say she was planning on being away for the next several months and asked if, from time to time, I would mind checking the cabin she and her husband had recently purchased upstate near Mahopac. She invited me to use it whenever I wished. In the beginning Joyce spent a lot of time at the cabin working on the landscape and decorating her cabin in the woods. However, her husband John, an architect, also had an office in San Francisco, causing them to constantly fly back and forth between the East and West Coasts. It was a tempting offer. A safe cabin in the woods was definitely a seductive invitation. The place was over sixty miles out of the city where, I believed, I had better control of my life. What if I went there and Rachelle found out, did the order of protection cover me there? Joyce was unaware that I really needed a sanctuary; the offer as an escape from the city came out of nowhere. I decided to keep it in mind as a safe haven and take advantage of it if need be. The instructions were to take the road to Mahopac. Why not check it out? To my surprise, it was secluded and charming. Now I had a place to go if things got tough: definitely, a seductive invitation.

THIRTY-SIX

Isolated

On the 28th, Anderson Read handed me a notarized statement for the courts.

For Whom It May Concern;

I, Anderson Read, was witness to seeing, first hand, Connell Chambers being assaulted (struck across the face and body) outside the entrance of our place of business on Eleventh Ave and 49th Street, by a woman who had previously spoken to him in his office. I was also witness to Mr. Chambers finding on the landing outside his apartment door, a Passport, and a note on his door, stating that he was being charged with rape. The person whose photograph is in the Passport, and the person who struck Connell Chambers, are one and the same. The name of the person in the Passport is Nicole Richards.

The above statement of facts is true. I agree this is a sworn statement of truth. Signed by Anderson Read; Notarized by Tony Gulianni.

On the first of March, I was once more in court. Judge Anthony Murray issued an extension of the Order of Protection that was requested by the office of the District Attorney. Council Lori Horowitz, answered a list of questions I had for the March 29, Jury 4, court date.

"Do I appoint an attorney for the court date?"

"No, the DA's office will handle this case."

"How will I know who is assigned the case?"

"You will have to call the number I give you, in approximately three to four days."

"What do I have to do for the DA's office?"

"You have to give the assigned attorney the electronic tapes needed as evidence."

"How do I follow through with the DA's office?"

"Call them. If you have any problems, call me."

On March 3, I called the office; it had not yet been assigned. I was advised to call back the beginning of the week.

A letter from Rachelle arrived postmarked, February 27th.

Connell, it may suit you to deny any responsibility for what you have done to me. Besides the enduring pain, which I suffer mentally, spiritually and emotionally, my body has also responded to the sudden assault on it by becoming permanent stigmata. My womb weeps blood almost continually. It would have been kinder of you to have killed me instead of seducing me.

At night I drove up to Bella's in Nyack, and on Sunday went down to Eighty-Eight's again, this time without incident. I spent a few nights at Anderson's taking care of the fish and cats while he and Natalia were away; then spent another few nights at the Pickwick Arms Hotel. On Monday, I made a quick stop at my home to pick up clothes. The trunk of my car had now become my traveling closet.

On Tuesday, the 14th, I was advised the case still was not on the computer. I was told the court had hundreds of cases and it would eventually be assigned; they could do nothing.

"My life is in danger. Could you please give me priority and advise me when it will be assigned?" I begged. The response, "There are no priorities in the DA's office. Call on Monday."

"What if nobody is assigned before the court date?"

"The case will be adjourned to a future date."

"My life is in danger; I need an answer now."

"Sir, you will just have to wait until someone is assigned."

"Can I speak to your superior?"

The same person I was speaking to answered pretending to be the superior. On Monday, the same dialogue was repeated. I again gave them my case number and requested information as to who was assigned the case.

"Forget about a computer, I urgently need an assigned person, don't you understand? I have received death threats on my phone, at work, through the mail. I am desperate."

"Call back later." Same result; nobody assigned.

At 2:00 p.m. on Thursday, I received another death threat on the phone while at the office,

"You are a dead person if you keep doing this, you know."

At 2:20, I called the DA's office. I was advised again that nobody was assigned and to call back. I refused to put the phone down. I demanded to speak to someone responsible for assigning DA lawyers. I eventually was able to get through to the person of Ellen Brown, who listened to the urgency of my problem. After checking as to why nobody was assigned to the case, she took down all the information and phone numbers I had been given then proceeded to speak to her superior; she promised to call me back that afternoon. At 3:00 p.m. she called and informed me,

"We cannot find your file; it is missing."

"What do you mean, it's missing? Is it miss-filed or is it lost? I need to know by 10:00 on Friday."

"Okay, I will research and call you back."

On Friday, about 10:00 a.m. Ellen Brown called back and asked where the case started. I told her it started at 346 Broadway," Are you positive?" she asked.

"Yes, I am positive."

"Then, Sir, the case summons has to be handled by you."

I was stunned, "What do you mean?"

"Since this case is not attached to an arrest, you have to handle your own case."

"Excuse me, I beg to differ; I have been advised by your office that the DA's office is prosecuting the case."

"This is a summons case. You have to get private council, and bring in witnesses and tapes to court."

In restrained explosive anger, "Who is responsible for this wrong advice? The courts never told me what you have just stated. The Order of Protection has already been issued."

"You should have been advised by victim's services at 346 Broadway regarding procedure."

"Since you must realize the predicament I am in and that I have been misadvised, what should I do?"

Ellen Brown advised I should, "Ask for 'A Stay' from the Judge, and state that you want the DA's office to handle the case and that you want the Judge to order them to do so."

Meanwhile Antonia had called, letting me know that she was going to be in Europe from the 24th of March to the 18th of April, and asked if it were at all possible for me to take care of her home and Cindy during that period. This to me was God sent.

On Wednesday, I appeared in court requesting 'A Stay.' The adjournment was denied. Judge Richard Strauss dismissed the Order of Protection in court, due to the DA's error in dating Docket number, which should have been March 27, instead of March 29. Because of this discrepancy of the court date made by the DA's office, the case was dismissed. From the Office of The District Attorney, a letter, dated April 3rd, arrived informing me as to how the criminal case in which I was involved had been concluded. The case had been dismissed.

An unsigned typed letter from Rachelle arrived, postmarked April 7, with the heading,

"THIS IS AN IMPORTANT MESSAGE. YOU ARE ADVISED TO TAKE IT VERY SERIOUSLY.

For the first time in four hundred and fifty-nine days, I felt some modicum of happiness on Wednesday, March 29th. Your vicious and hostile attempt to nail my hands and feet to the cross was thwarted. This is my life and I answer to the highest laws." She then accused me of being caught up in the blatant immorality that she believed existed in this country. She claimed, that knowing she had been celibate for six years, I treated her as a prostitute, and what was between us, as nothing more than a casual, sexually promiscuous debauchery.

"God has put me on a direct collision course with you and has given me the task of putting a stop to your evil ways and your sinful liaisons with other women. The day of reckoning is close at hand. Prepare yourself for some *extremely* disastrous consequences. The only way that I can experience separation is by death." She said she had nothing else to live for while this situation was in such a state of irresolution in the Universe, and prayed that I ask God to guide me on the true path of righteousness with His wisdom and love. "Surely you don't want to incur His wrath and anger any more – or do you? Put away false pride and stubbornness – it is death." She ended with, "WICKED MEN OFFEND AND ARE EASY TO BE OFFENDED."

THIRTY-SEVEN
Dead Pigeon

During this crisis period as I moved throughout the city, I selected choice locations and places that were sacred to me. One was the East-West Book Store known as the Himalayan Institute on Fifth Avenue and 14th Street, where I loved to browse. I felt safe there, as it was not on any direct path to anywhere. On Sunday, the 9th of April, a chilly spring day, while roaming through the bookshelves on Hinduism, Buddhism, Sufism, American Indian and Western Religions, I sensed Rachelle's presence close to me. I quickly turned around but nobody was there. Had it been my imagination? Then there she was again, appearing and disappearing between aisles of shelves. I moved to an open space area where CDs and cassettes were sold and browsed through them. As I picked up *The Answer is Silence* by Deuter, I heard a woman behind me say, "You will never find silence, never."

As I turned I saw a woman, whose face was partially covered by a rose-color scarf, move quickly towards the door and disappear.

"Hold it together, Connell, it's not her, cool it," I murmured to myself.

Everything was quiet; no sign of her. As I handed the cassette to the cashier, I was told someone had already paid for it. Believing it was Rachelle; I cancelled the purchase. I now realized all my actions were being observed. No way was I going to give her satisfaction.

As I was leaving I noticed a stack of *Spirit Path* magazines left of the door. I picked up an issue and as I pushed the door open to the street, the woman with the rose-color scarf slipped back in, lowered her scarf, and smiled,

"You know that you will never know silence again," she said disappearing into the labyrinth of books.

It was Rachelle. My stomach turned. I sat waiting in the car and watched the store until it closed; I never saw her leave. Was there a back door exit? Had she gone into the subway, or was she playing with me? Had she followed me or was it just a freaky coincidence?

The store promoted *Spirit Path,* which was displayed in the doorway; she could have just volunteered to deliver a bundle of the magazines. Why did I, instead of facing the reality of her game, always try to reason out a situation, looking for a possible coincidence? I knew I was in trouble. I could not collapse; otherwise she would win and nobody would ever know what happened. As I turned on the ignition, I felt confused and sapped of energy. Gloominess was overtaking me with the weight of imprisonment.

The following Thursday at the office, Murray signed for a package addressed to me, delivered by Eagle Messenger Service, located between 1st Street and Garfield Place, Brooklyn. I opened the box, filled with pink and white tissue paper, as Tony, Frank, and Anderson curiously looked on. A card resting on top of the tissues read, "You are a dead pigeon." I spread open the tissues, exposing a dead pigeon on its back. Tony looked at me and said,

"You know what that means Chambers? You're as good as dead. It won't be long now, before you are a dead pigeon." At that moment my phone rang, he picked it up and mimicking my voice said, "Chambers here," before handing it over to me.

"I am watching you as I speak. You'll never be out of my sight until I kill you. The pigeon is my first killing, you, my last. I won't go away quietly. I will bring a Civil Suit against you charging you with rape and the infliction of emotional and mental stress and asking for compensation of $75,000. Now everything is clear. You are a dead pigeon." She hung up the phone.

As I looked around the showroom Anderson, Phil, Alex and the rest of the crew all stood there transfixed. No one said a word. Finally Alex spoke up.

"Is that the woman you had been talking about? Boy, your instincts were right on." I did not say a word but immediately called the messenger service and spoke to Sam Silva; they confirmed the delivery.

"Who dropped it off?" I inquired.

"A young woman came in, said she lived in the neighborhood, at 107 Sterling Place, left her office number and stated she was leaving the country and would not be returning. I asked if she wanted to include a message, 'No, he'll get the message,' she answered."

I told him the package contained a dead pigeon, that this woman was involved in a criminal case, and asked if he would be a material witness. He agreed to identify her if necessary.

"She was a strange woman, in a hurry, and kept looking around, saying how important it was to get this package delivered." I called the Police Precinct at 524 West 42nd Street, between Tenth an Eleventh Avenues, to report this harassment. They informed me I had to call the precinct where the messenger service was and where I also lived.

I called Detective Dragonetti's office and spoke to Detective Carl who was familiar with Dragonetti's cases. He advised me to file an *Aggravated Harassment* charge, in case I reopened my request for Order of Protection, and added that I needed to keep the evidence.

"How does one keep a dead pigeon?" I asked, to which he replied,

"In the refrigerator, unless you have more than three witnesses who were present at the discovery."

Since there were three witnesses, I knew I did not need to keep the pigeon, but I did not know how to handle getting rid of it. I was so disgusted. Now I had to deal with the disposing of this poor creature that had possibly been killed just to frighten me. I said a prayer over the bird, placed the box into another plastic bag and, inwardly shaking, disposed of it in the garbage pail. This whole episode was harrowing.

Antonia returned on Wednesday the 19th and that evening I booked myself back into the Pickwick Arms Hotel. At the end of the next day, when I went to my car, I noticed the lid of the trunk seem to be unlatched. As I raised the lid I discovered that two of my bags were missing; one containing my clothes the other, music, poetry, meditative tapes and most important of all, the phone taped messages from Rachelle that the courts requested as physical evidence, some of which I had already transcribed. The realization of the tape losses was traumatic. I was so distraught by the loss that it took me a while before I could get over the shock and report the theft to the police.

I drove to Brooklyn and picked up my mail, which included another letter from Rachelle. I opened it with trepidation; it was hand printed and unsigned.

"YOU RAPED ME. ANYTHING I HAVE DONE TO YOU IS NOTHING COMPARED TO YOUR VIOLATION OF ME. I HAVE BEGGED AND PLEADED WITH YOU TO TURN IT INTO SOMETHING OF WORTH. YET, YOU HAVE CONTINUALLY REFUSED; THEREBY STRENGTHENING

THE EVIDENCE THAT IT WAS RAPE AND NOTHING MORE.

I WILL NOT SIT BY MEAKLY AND ALLOW A RAPE AND VIOLATION OF THE WORST SORT TO BE PERPETRATED AGAINST ME. I WILL NO LONGER TRY TO COMMUNICATE WITH YOU IN A REASONABLE MANNER. YOU OBVIOUSLY HAVE NO CAPACITY FOR THAT EITHER. HIDING BEHIND OTHERS WILL NOT KEEP YOU FROM EXPERIENCING ULTIMATE JUDGEMENT."

I was edging closer and closer into a place of no return. I was on overload. I needed to get away and decided to spend the weekend at Bella Salerno's Ashram, where she was conducting a retreat in Woodstock that including a discourse on the book, *A Course in Miracles* I checked out of Pickwick Arms in the morning and in early afternoon made a stressful exit out of the city, hoping Rachelle wasn't following me.

Returning to my office on Monday April 24, I was handed a folded form by Frank, "This is for you," he said, as he returned to his office. I turned it over to look at the front of the form.

Civil Court of the City Of New York, County of Kings, index number 690, 1989. Nicole Richards, Plaintiff versus Connell Chambers, Defendant.

Answer in person, May 19, 10:00 a.m.

My heart sank. This was not going to stop. My shock was replaced by immediate anger. I stormed into Frank's office.

"Who the hell gave you the right to accept a summons in my name?"

"Hey, the guy walked in, asked for you and when I said you were gone for the weekend, he handed me this envelope and said 'give this to him' and left."

I walked back to my office, numb. She was really going to do it. I didn't know which way to turn, what to do, whom to talk to, and what direction to take. Did I need a lawyer? I did not know a lawyer. How much was this going to cost me? My head was spinning. What worried me most was her capability to keep me continually on the defensive. One could never predict her next move. It did not take long before what I perceived to manifest itself.

On the twenty-seventh I received an article addressed to me in my office.

"Like Iseult, if a woman is ignored or hurt by a man, she will often find a way to turn his own sword against him, to wound him through his own power drive. But in an instant that a man wakes up to his own need, offers his love, and affirmatively relates to her, woman has an almost magical power to forgive. The feminine makes use of the sword of her antagonist; when he buries his sword and offers relatedness, she buries her sword in the same instant. This is one of the most noble and beautiful instincts in woman, one of the ways that she serves and transforms life. So, it is with Iseult. When Tristan convinces her that he offers relatedness and love, and that he values her and desires her in her own right, she lowers the sword. She, too, requires something of a man's time and effort. When he ignores her, she rises in wrath."

A few days later Rachelle called to see if I had received a message from Iseult. I answered I had not received anything and hung up.

On Tuesday, the second of May, I called Antonia to see if she could recommend a lawyer to represent me. Without knowing all the details, but aware I felt my life in danger and that it no longer was safe for me to go home, she generously offered me shelter in the use of her guest room whenever needed. We had a deep respect for one another and a loving friendship. I gratefully accepted the offer and spent that night in her guest room.

My body had been starved of a decent night's sleep. For the first time in a long while, I awoke in the morning and felt at peace. I had not realized how truly exhausted I had become. Antonia did not know the full story. She knew I had filed a request for an Order of Protection from the Criminal Court against Rachelle. However she did not know how bruised and stressed out I really was and how acute the danger. Antonia brewed coffee and prepared warm porridge for breakfast. I left for the office feeling invigorated. To the best of my knowledge Rachelle had no inkling of Antonia's home even though she had picked up her messages on my answering machine.

I walked to my car, slid behind the wheel and grasped the handle of the door to close it but a strong gust of wind yanked the door wide open and with my hand still on the handle, pulled my shoulders outward, while my knees remained trapped under the steering wheel. The awkward angle of my body in those few seconds pulled my lower back out. I succeeded in closing the door, but as I started the car and put my foot on the accelerator excruciating pain exploded up my spine. The pain stopped as instantly as it started.

"Could I move . . . was I paralyzed?" Everything went black as the pain struck again sending wicked pain up my spine. I was on the edge of panic. The frightening blasts continued for quite a while. Once more everything stopped; no pain. I didn't move for another fifteen minutes. Feeling better, I headed across Central Park. Suddenly the pain blasted my body once again. I could barely control the car as I continued and exited at 81st Street and made a left on Central Park West. I pulled over and opened the door to get out, but there was no muscle response. I tried to center myself and began to breathe deeply, directing the oxygen to the part of my spine that was not responding. Moments later some sense of balance returned; the pain was still excruciating but somehow more bearable. I made it to my office and called my chiropractor, trying to put what I had just experienced into perspective. Was it the manifestation of the heightened stress state I was living in or the coincidental gust of wind?

On Thursday I received a call from my niece Geraldine to let me know that Teresa had received a large envelope from Rachelle with a letter asking her to sign the separately typed statement claiming that she, Rachelle, had been at a family gathering with me at Teresa's home on Christmas Day, and to have it notarized and mailed back to her.

"Teresa, I wonder if you would be so kind as to sign one copy of the attached statement, have it notarized and return it to me. The second is for you to keep. I have enclosed a check for $1.00 to cover the cost of the Notary Public, and S.S.A.E. for your convenience. I never did get a chance to thank you properly for your hospitality. I have been traumatized for a long time by the events that subsequently transpired and have had great difficulty in functioning. It also never occurred to me that I would never be allowed to see any of you again — Connell had led me to believe that he and I would be together from that time on. Anyway, here is a belated thank you.

Rachelle Richards."

Enclosed also was a belated wedding card for Geraldine and Keith congratulating them on their wedding as well as a letter to Geraldine.

"Dear Geraldine, I am sorry this card is so late. I had wanted to give it to you at your wedding and wish you and Keith well for your life together. I liked you and your family when I met you all the Christmas before last. I was under the impression that I was in a relationship with Connell and was being introduced to the family. Although I was nervous at meeting so many new people at once, I felt very happy. I have been traumatized to discover that I was being used and tricked. I am a Catholic, and I do not indulge in casual affairs, so I am in great pain. This has been made worse

by being blocked from seeing or communicating with people that I met and liked and felt I would like to see again. I have felt shamed and compromised and I suffer daily. I felt very sad that I couldn't be at your wedding, having met all your in-laws as well as your husband.

Please excuse me going on but I have wanted to communicate with you for a long time, especially to extend my warm wishes to you and Keith.

Best Regards, Rachelle"

"If this is from that woman who came over on Christmas, she's one sick puppy. What shall I do with the envelope?" asked Geraldine.

"Send it to me."

When I received the package I was dumfounded at what Rachelle was trying to do and became acutely aware as to what lengths she intended to go to set me up in the Civil Court. She had the audacity to believe she could get my own sister as a witness on her behalf by getting her to support her claim that we were in a relationship and having that claim notarized.

"I, Teresa Faulner, sister of Connell Chambers, hereby state that my brother, Connell, brought Nicole (also known as Rachelle) Richards with him to a family gathering at my house in Farmingdale, Long Island, on Christmas day. They stayed for several hours and left together approximately at midnight."

Now, at least, I had documented proof in my hands; I had Rachelle's signature. I wondered to what lengths she intended to go to convince a jury that her fabrications were a reality. This was dangerous.

The situation had changed drastically. I was no longer protected by the court system and Rachelle was free to harass me in whatever way she chose. She had already told me she had compiled a list of names, telephone numbers and messages of people who had left them on my answering machine. She intended to inform each one that I had lost a case in the Criminal Court and had now been summoned to appear in Civil Court to answer a law suit she had started against me on the grounds that my action taken against her in the Criminal Court was done with the purpose to inflict personal and emotional stress and to also convince the jury that I raped and sodomized her, bringing in witnesses and written testimony to that fact. Her purpose was to isolate and cut me off from society. Messages, with the exception of a few close friends and family including Rachelle's monologues, had dwindled to a trickle.

I had promised Eli to take care of his cats for the next seven days. How stupid, what had I been thinking? My safety was compromised. Going home that first evening to attend to them, I was cautious approaching the building but did not see any sign of Rachelle. I went up to my apartment and without putting on the front bedroom lights, peered out the window, focusing for a few minutes on the areas in front of the building, across the street in front of the Park and the bench directly facing my window, where Rachelle often sat. I eventually caught sight of someone walking in the park behind the row of trees. At first I was not suspicious as people often stroll in the park even at night. But as I stayed focused, I noticed that the person suspiciously kept walking back and forth on the same path and periodically stopped and looked directly up towards my window. As suspected, it turned out to be Rachelle. Even though this was now May, she was still wearing her winter down coat, which she would need if she intended spending the night in the park. This ritual lasted for quite some time and proved to be the beginning of a week of nightly stalking.

Around noon on Tuesday I was surprised when I picked up the phone in my office to hear the voice of my brother Victor.

"Well, hello there, Connell, my beloved brother and best friend."

I was thrilled to hear Victor's deep resonant voice. "I hope I am finding you in good health. Are you okay?"

"Yes, I'm fine. What a pleasant surprise."

"Are you having a woman problem?"

"No. Why?" I answered as I felt the hair in back of my neck rise.

"I've been receiving messages in my office from a woman by the name of Nicole; do you know who she is?"

"What are the messages you are receiving . . . have you spoken to her?"

"Yes."

"What did she say?"

"She said I would be needed in New York as a witness in a Civil Law Suit against a man whose name is Connell Chambers, who has been charged with rape and sodomy."

"Did you tell her who you were?"

"No."

"Did she say anything besides that?"

"Yes. She said you were both in a relationship and that you were a very kind man and a very sensitive poet."

"Did you ask her why she was calling you?"

"She said when she shared with you that she was an outpatient at a psychiatric clinic and that it was a requirement she attend weekly, your personality changed; you became abusive to her and began to rape and sodomize her. Is this true?"

"You know it's not. Victor, let me tell you what's happening." I gave him a brief synopsis of what had taken place. There was silence at the other end of the phone.

"I want you to be my character witness in court."

"Connell, my brother, you know I love you. Trust the Universe. Open up the Tao book to page forty-eight and you will find the message."

"Victor, is that it?"

He was silent. I spluttered out,

"Is there anyway I can count on you?" I burst into tears.

"Why are you crying?"

"I am exhausted. Victor, I've been through hell; I am at the bottom. I need you to help me."

"If you really needed my help why didn't you call me?" His answer was even more bruising."

"So what's wrong with asking now?"

I have no memory of what I said to him after that, but I began to sob uncontrollably. What had happened to brotherly love?

"It's good to cry." were Victor's last words.

Phil Reinhart standing by the door of my office had a look of concern on his face,

"Are you alright?"

"Yes, okay," I said with tears streaming down my face.

"Did that woman make you cry?"

"No, my big brother did."

I went to the Munson Diner, checked around to make sure she wasn't there and asked José to get me a large cup of black coffee.

"Who's that for?" he piped.

"It's for me," I said as I sat down.

"You never drink black coffee."

"I know but I need it now."

That little bit of exchange with José snapped me back. I sat there brooding, sipping the horrible black coffee, wondering how many other people she contacted. The rest of my family and those close to me I believed would get in touch. Trying to analyze what had just occurred, I came to the shocking realization that through fear and judgment, I had become hostage to

Rachelle's threats and had isolated myself from everybody in order to protect them. I never shared being stalked or my life being in danger, for fear of the safety of those I loved. I took a last sip of the now cold black coffee and wondered, "What have I done?"

THIRTY-EIGHT
Plaintiff Versus Defendant

On the morning of May 18th I phoned the Civil Court stating the summons had not been served to me in person but was given to my manager by a messenger. I inquired how to proceed with the summons.

"As the defendant, you are required to appear on the 19th of May at 9:15 a.m. sharp, in front of the General Clerk of the court to either agree with the summons or if you deny the substance of the summons, then the court requires a hand written response and general denial of the truth of the statement of Plaintiff's alleged cause of action."

On Friday, May 19th, I appeared in Civil Court of The City of New York, Livingston Street, Brooklyn to answer the summons: "Nicole Richards Plaintiff versus Connell Chambers Defendant."

Nothing was written on the summons indicating what it was for. I assumed that it was based on what Rachelle had threatened doing in April: the charge of Sodomy and Rape and the intentional infliction of emotional and mental stress. I gave my statement denying Plaintiff's alleged cause of action.

"The plaintiff's statement is absolutely false and without cause. I knew plaintiff from approximately December 1987 to January 1988. Plaintiff began a systematic action to totally badger me and proceeded to assault my person. An order of protection was issued on January 1989. I have not lived in my home from January 10 to March 19 for fear of my life."

After listing a few more incidences of harassments and threats I ended the statement with, "The true fact is that there has never been a relationship between Nicole Richards and me." I signed The General Denial Form and gave it to the court, hoping it would put an end to the matter. I walked back to the parking lot all the while scanning the area, knowing Rachelle's M.O. When I reached my car both windshield wipers were lifted away from the windshield. I asked the garage attendant why my wipers were lifted up.

"Some young woman, about five minutes ago, did it."

I internally froze. "Shit! Where is she?" I looked towards the exit of the parking lot; there she was standing brazenly in full view, watching me. As we made eye contact, she sweetly smiled as she waved with her fingers, and then stepped out of sight. By the time I drove to the exit, she had disappeared.

I had a busy day ahead of me and was scheduled to leave for a weekend retreat at Bella Salerno's. The retreat was titled, "Make it Happen."

I no sooner arrived at my office that a telephone call from Rachelle came through.

"Hi, Connell, did you have fun in the Kings County General Clerks Office?

"How did you know I would be there?"

"I know everywhere you go. You are in there because of me, you bastard. Everything you wrote is a God damned fucking lie. You know you raped and sodomized me and you'll suffer and rot because of this. My soul is running out of life-blood, you bastard. Now watch out, I am really going to kill you. I'll drag you through the courts, before all the news media in every local paper. I will destroy you."

"How do you know what my response was to your summons?"

"I went to the clerk's office, showed my credentials as a reporter and demanded a copy of your response."

"You know Rachelle, you're worse than a disease."

"Yes, I am like the black death. I will impregnate every part of your life from now on. I will destroy you."

"You are sick. Why would you want to kill me; you're going through a court case and claim you will win?"

"Someone has to die for this nightmare to stop."

There were no more calls from her for the rest of the day. Just as I was about to leave for the weekend, my receptionist gave me a message that Rachelle's attorney had called; I returned the call. The attorney suggested we come to an agreement to settle out of court. I answered there was no substance to her claim, therefore nothing on which to settle an agreement. I put down the phone.

Driving up north I had the radio turned on to the news; the announcement came over the air that the Chinese military were attacking and killing the students in Beijing Square. For a moment my problems seemed small and insignificant. As I drove further north and away from the city, the tension in my body eased up as I looked forward to the weekend.

I returned to the city on Monday and had dinner with Greta.

By Friday morning, June 9, I realize going Pro Se, representing myself, would be suicidal. Watching television news I had caught an ad for the law firm of Weiss and Stein, "You pay no legal fees until the case is finalized," said the announcer. I dialed the number and made an appointment to see them at 1:30 p.m. at their office on 42nd Street, between Madison and Vanderbilt Avenues.

I was assigned an attorney who upon hearing my case stated they would have to stake out the area in which this woman lived to verify the story. In order for them to go ahead I was requested to sign a form agreeing to use their services. Prior to signing, I noticed hand written inserts on the form, which I took time to review.

A minimum retainer fee of $1500 would be immediately required. Reviewing all the additional expense I would have to incur, it would possibly exceed $10,000. I inquired as to how soon they could give me an appointment to discuss my case, and was told it would be six weeks. There would also be a consultation fee of $25. This was not the answer to my predicament, I thanked them for their time, paid the $25 fee and left. What deceptive advertising.

Saturday morning at 11:30, my receptionist informed me that a woman giving her name as Greta was on the phone asking for me. I picked up the phone.

"This is Rachelle. Are you sure you want to go all the way to court with this?"

"I have nothing to say to you, goodbye." I answered and hung up.

How clever, I thought, she must have realized that I had instructed the receptionist not to put through any calls from Rachelle.

On Monday the 12th I received a call from a Dr. Cannaught identifying himself as a court psychiatrist requesting my permission to subpoena the Criminal Court records relating to the Order Of Protection. I asked why he needed records to which he answered it was to verify statements made by me in answer at the court regarding the Plaintiff's statement. He needed this information prior to the Civil Court hearing on June 22. On Tuesday, June 13, I received a call from the office of a Judge Donald Gross requiring me to attend a Civil Court hearing in Room 306 at 10:00 a.m. on June 22. That night and the next I stayed at Antonia's home to take care of Cindy.

On Wednesday, I received a letter from Joyce, who was still in California, giving me some useful information concerning her "Squirrel House" as she called it. John had turned off the hot water heater and she wanted to make sure I would find the instructions as to how to turn it back on. She included the names and telephones of her neighbors, should I need them, and a detailed drawing as to how to reach her house in case I had forgotten the instructions.

I was reminded once more of this place of shelter to where I could escape.

On Thursday the 15th I attended Greta's cocktail party. When I arrived, she greeted me with her usual warmth and love. Greta enjoyed sharing and introducing her friends to one another. She had the gift of inviting just the right mixture of interesting personalities. Again it was a very eclectic gathering of people that included her dear friend Bill Possidento, Leon, and Joan, a playwright, and her husband Clifford Forster, and the usual group of close-knit friends. Jim Ritchie, the sculptor was visiting her from France, her good friend Princess Donatella Colonna, had just arrived from Italy, and Sabine Cassel brought French movie star Stéphane Audran. Of course, the party would not be complete without Maya, Berg, Darine and Peter. Being back in the social scene gave me the grounding and energizing I sorely needed. It was a party where everyone left their life and worries outside the door; one of those magical evenings, safe for me to dance. I was functioning in a contradictory reality.

On Thursday, June 22, I arrived at Civil Court on time for the hearing. I had not as yet been advised of its purpose. I glanced around observing people and checking if Rachelle was present. She was nowhere in sight. I felt relieved but knowing her, I was sure she knew I was there. Always having a pad and pen with me, as was my habit as a poet, I began writing to try to distract myself. I was apprehensive, not knowing what to expect. The benches were in narrow rows with little or no leg-room. Each time I felt someone's hand brush against my back as they entered or left the aisle, I stiffened. It could be Rachelle with the intent to stab or somehow attack me. I was abruptly brought back to reality when I heard the Court Clerk announce, "This is the last call for hearing number 16697." I looked around to see who the person was, not paying attention. I closed my notebook, and staring back at me was, Hearing Number 16697, only to realize I was the one not paying attention.

"Oh, shit, that's me." I jumped up with my hand in the air, like a kid in the classroom and yelled, "I'm 16697". Pounding the mallet down, the judge sternly admonished, "There will be order in my court room." I sat back down feeling like a stupid idiot with everybody's eyes on me. The Court Clerk called out once more, "16697, approach the bench."

I approached the bench, identified myself and was directed to go to Room 306 for my hearing. Room 306 was a small bleak courtroom with three visible chairs. One to the left as I entered, the other to the right slightly more forward and the third still further forward, next to the desk. I closed the door behind me.

"Anybody here?" I called out.

A weak, male voice responded coming from another room off to the left.

"Take a seat; I'll be with you in a moment."

A short, anemic looking man, shuffled in and sat down behind the desk, and asked me to identify myself by name and social security number, where I lived and the address where I worked and what days I did not work. I gave him all the infor-mation except for my social security number, as it had never been requested of me before. He insisted I give it to him. I asked for a pen and wrote it down. He asked me why, and I answered small rooms like these have ears. There did not seem to be a problem.

He opened up his tattered looking legal binder and from where I was sitting I recognized the Civil Court summons. He lifted it up and showed it to me.

"Have you seen this?"

"Yes."

"When?"

"Approximately, around the 24th of April."

"What day was that?"

"Monday."

"Do you know what this is?"

"Yes."

"Do you know what your rights are if this was not served to you in person?"

"No."

"If it was not served to you in person, you don't have to answer any questions and you can walk right out of here. Was it served to you in person?"

"No."

I was aware I could walk away legally, yet if I did so, a new summons would be issued and I would be in the same place a few weeks hence being asked the same questions. I decided since I was already there, to proceed.

"What day of the week do you say you don't work?"

"Thursday."

"Well that will put you in the office on Friday, right?"

"Normally yes, but on that particular weekend I was away Friday, Saturday and Sunday."

"Where were you?"

"That's not important, but if it is a requirement, you will have it in writing."

"Who issued you the summons?"

"Nobody issued me this summons."

"Somebody must have issued you this summons, otherwise you wouldn't have answered it and you wouldn't be here. Who handed you the summons?"

"Nobody handed me the summons. Frank Costa received the envelope from a messenger marked to my attention on April 21, at 2:00 p.m. I found it on my desk, in my office with my regular morning mail on the 24th of April. The reason why I am here, irrespective as to how I received this summons, is that it has no authenticity as to why it was issued. Whether I have to respond today or two weeks from now makes no difference. There are no facts that substantiate this summons and such will be recognized by the courts."

"How is it that Frank Costa remembers the exact time and date that he received the envelope from the messenger?"

"I don't know. I have a question; why wasn't I notified as to what this hearing was about?"

"It makes things easier since you cannot prepare answers beforehand."

As the judge reviewed my responses to his questions, I felt uneasy. I heard another door open on the right side but nobody came out. At that moment the judge called me to his desk and told me to raise my right hand and swear that every answer I gave was the truth. I felt relieved that this hearing was over. He told me to go back and take my seat. As I sat down I heard him say,

"Procurer, please come out."

The word meant nothing to me therefore I had no reflex response, until the procurer was sworn in after stating his name, his job title within the Civil Court.

"My name is Philippe Prudeau and my job title is procurer."

"In layman's terms what is the responsibility of a procurer?"

"I issue summonses for the Civil Court to defendants."

"In this case, whom did you issue this summons to?"

"Connell Chambers."

"Where was it issued?"

"At his place of business."

"What date and time?"

"April 21 at 2:00 p.m."

"Can you remember what day it was?"

"It was a Friday."

"Did you give it to Mr. Chambers or Mr. Frank Costa?"

"Mr. Chambers."

"Had you seen Mr. Chambers before?"

"No."

"Would you recognize Mr. Chambers if you met him again?"

"Yes."

"Is he present in this room?"

"Yes."

"Could you point him out to me?"

"That's Mr. Chambers; this is the man I handed the summons to," he said pointing at me.

I looked at him. He was tall with a little grey in his hair and beard, and in spite of a strong masculine presence, his voice was weak and spoke without conviction.

"Your Honor, I have never seen this man before nor was I in the office that day." Just then I realized there was someone sitting to my right. It was Rachelle Richards. I was shocked and instantly knew I had been set up.

"Mr. Chambers, you know we have a problem here. Someone is not telling the truth."

"Well I am telling you the truth and I can prove where I was that day."

"Where were you?"

I looked at Rachelle and her face was full of anticipation waiting for me to reveal where I had been.

"I will inform you as to my whereabouts and it will be issued to you in a written statement."

There was an immediate outburst by Rachelle,

"Your Honor, he's a God-damn fucking liar. Can't you see he's sucking you into the vicious games that he plays? You heard the Procurer under oath identify him as Mr. Chambers. What more do you want?"

"I want respect here. I want no more outbursts or profane language."

"I have lived with his lying and game playing for years and can't take it any more. I'm sorry about my outburst, your Honor."

"What is the truth?" asked the judge again.

"As the defendant, don't I have the right to ask questions?"

Rachelle instantly responded, "The defendant can only answer questions."

"I have the right to ask questions," I replied.

Rachelle got up from her chair walked over to the judge and in her soft Australia accent,

"Correct me if I'm wrong, please."

"Please, Miss. Richards, take your seat."

As she started back to her chair, she stopped after a few steps, and turned around,

"Can I ask you just one question?"

"Yes."

Rachelle took out a folded piece of paper from her bag, handed it to the judge and asked the judge to read the name written on it.

"Chambers."

"What is the word directly under his name?"

"Defendant."

"What are the three words under defendant?"

"Answer in person."

She walked back to her chair with a smug look of victory on her face. I was seething with anger. The judge said he had pointed questions that he wanted me to answer.

"Do you have a double breasted pin striped suit?"

"No."

"Do you wear reading glasses?"

"No."

"Do you always wear a toupee?"

"No. Never."

"How many cigarettes do you smoke in a day?"

"None."

"When you were handed the summons, what did you do with it?"

"I was never handed the summons, as I stated before. I was upstate with friends when the summons was issued."

Rachelle interrupted,

"Every time he has sodomized, and raped me, his answer has always been, 'I have been upstate meditating.' Your Honor, how long are you going to sit here listening to this Goddamn liar? Your proof is right here." She said as she pointed to Philippe Prudeau. He has no investment with anybody in this room. He has no reason to lie. His job is to issue a summons, and he issued one to this gentleman over here which he has identified as being the same person, case over, your Honor."

It seemed every response I gave the Judge was cross-examined and contradicted by Rachelle. The judge said he had final questions for the Procurer; it wasn't over yet.

"When you issued the summons to Mr. Chambers, how was he dressed?"

"He was wearing a grey double breasted pin-striped suit, light blue shirt and blue tie."

"Was he wearing a toupee?"

"Yes!"

"Was he or was he not smoking?"

"He was smoking."

"How do you remember he was smoking?"

"I am a reformed smoker therefore I quickly remember one who smokes."

"What type of glasses was he wearing?"

"He was wearing half glasses."

"When you handed him the summons tell me exactly what he did?"

"He took the summons, looked at it and said 'What the fuck is this?' It is a summons for you to appear in Civil Court to answer the charge."

"What did Mr. Chambers do next?"

"He freaked out. He threw the summons on the floor, stamped on it with tremendous anger, wiped his feet on it and spat on it. Picked it up threw it at him and said, 'Get the fuck out of here and don't let me ever fucking see you again,' and he verbally threw me out."

"What was the last thing you said to him?"

"My job is done, I have delivered the summons."

"If this summons was treated in the manner just described it would in no way look as clean as it does here," I said, feeling comfortable because the person described wasn't me. Then suddenly Rachelle piped up again, this time speaking in a sweet, innocent voice,

"Your Honor, may I just add something that may help you decide?"

"Go ahead, make it quick."

"In conclusion I wish to make a statement for the records that would contradict Connell Chambers' statement. Many times when we were out together, either for dinner or with social friends or relatives, he would be dressed in double breasted suits, some were solid colors and at times pin-striped.

He actually liked pin stripes especially the grey one. As for half glasses, he would occasionally use them for reading a menu or reviewing some of our poetry projects together. I have never seen him smoke, but then again he is very secretive about things, especially addictions. I've never seen him wearing blue in either shirt or tie; however, he has many times made reference to how he considers blue an important color when we discuss the subject of healing. Thank you, your Honor." She said all this in feigned innocence.

I looked at her in stunned disbelief.

"All of you just sit here, and wait for my decision." The judge left the room.

A chilling silence enveloped the room only to be broken by Rachelle,

"Connell, you better find Christ very quickly because I just nailed you to the fucking cross."

The judge re-entered. We stood up and sat back down.

"There are three conclusions. Number one, Nicole Richards the plaintiff, issued a request for the summons through the Civil Court on the grounds stated. The Civil Court issued the summons correctly to the defendant in his office on April 21 at 2:00 p.m. as stated. The person he handed it to and the defendant Connell Chambers, sitting here, are one and the same."

I was flabbergasted.

"Your Honor, I don't own a pin-striped suit. I don't own a blue shirt or blue tie. I don't smoke, I don't wear a toupee, and I have never seen this man. This is totally unfair. If you take time to check the history recorded in the Criminal Court, you will know who this woman is."

"My responsibility is solely to analyze, determine and advise the Civil Courts as to whether the summons was issued to the plaintiff, and I'm satisfied that it was. This hearing is closed. You are both scheduled to appear in court on September

21, 1989 in room 509. The trial will proceed on the plaintiff's behalf. The Civil Court can now proceed with the trial against Connell Chambers."

The judge left the room followed by Rachelle, who was now gloating in her glory. I turned to Philippe Prudeau and looking him straight in the eyes, said,

"I cannot believe that you can sit in court, raise your right hand to God, swear, look at me and lie. You know the truth. Is the dollar more important than the truth? Are you that desperate? I am stunned as to how you could so blatantly believe your own lies. You know that you never met me before. I was upstate New York in Woodstock on the day you served the Summons. It saddens me that people like you exist. You are a pathetic son of a bitch."

As I walked back out into the street everything around me seemed surreal. Was this really happening to me? "What do I do now? How do I handle this?" I realized that in no way could this case conclude in my favor by going Pro Se. I had to get an attorney to represent me. Rachelle had all the time to research and become aware of the parameters wherein she could work in order to successfully present her case. She had nothing else to do with her life other than to clearly formulate a destructive plan of attack on all fronts in and out of court. I wouldn't even know where to start. I had naively thought, that since I was innocent, no one could prove me guilty.

When I arrived back in my office one of the telephone messages left on my pad was one from Rachelle saying,

"Please call me. It's very important." I crumbled the slip and threw it away. The next one was from my sister Teresa; I immediately returned the call.

"How did the hearing go?"

I informed her of what had happened.

"Rachelle had the judge very well psychoanalyzed and the decision was to move forward with the case."

"Why don't you speak with a psychologist to understand her game plan?"

"What I really need now is an attorney."

"Why don't you call our psychologist, Dr. David Skiller and his attorney Frank Reed, who lives in Mineola? He does not take on new clients so you must say, referred by David Skiller. He will listen and may be able to refer someone to you." She gave me their telephone numbers.

"Good, what I really want is legal advice."

"Connell, there comes a time when God gives these people the brains to do what we can't."

THIRTY-NINE
A Knitting Needle

The indifference and disrespect expressed by Judge Gross shocked and disturbed me. I realized it would be suicidal to go Pro Se; it was of the utmost importance to hire a lawyer.

Rachelle continued to control the dynamics causing me to stumble at a time when there was no room to err. Knowing her predatory personality, I would have to minimize trips to the apartment. It was too dangerous to even think of spending any-time there, especially now that she had taken to prowling in the park directly opposite my building. Each time I went home, there was always the fear that she would be waiting for me. It took all my courage to walk up the steps and put the key in the lock. I had to keep my eyes on the glass panels of the door to catch the flash of a gun or rifle in order to duck before a bullet hit.

Her psychological victory in the court certainly would have empowered her. I still had to work out a way to pick up my mail and a change of clothes among the few that were left after the theft. It was very important that I should interact with Eli each time I was in my apartment. I was crucially aware that the lack of my presence as his tenant, and the fear of the disturbances caused by Rachelle, would give him grounds to ask me to leave.

I was walking a tightrope, not knowing when or where I would miscalculate and fall. I was positive she was planning her next attack; Rachelle's silence was even deadlier. Through the coincidental offerings from both Antonia and Joyce, I had comfort in knowing I had a few safe places to go. There was always Bella, the Pickwick Arms and as a last resort, my car to sleep in.

On July 7th, Greta left for France, and at midnight I drove up to the cabin. The following morning I left early to drive out to Antonia's, in the Hamptons, for the weekend. On Monday I left at four in the morning to avoid the heavy traffic going into the city and headed directly to my chiropractor before going to the office.

I continued driving back and forth from the city to the cabin over the next few days, and when there, I felt safe. Eventually, that became my routine for July and August: Antonia, Bella and the cabin.

During this nomadic experience, I was challenged to find diverse places to have my evening meals, and was pleasantly surprised in my search to discover quite a few intimate cafés. I often went to Popolini's where many students and professors from New York University hung out and where at times Anderson and Natalia joined me. With my pad and pen in hand I continued writing poetry even while dining, yet there was always an undercurrent of apprehension that Rachelle could appear at any moment.

My urgent need to retain a lawyer to represent me was a frustrating search. It proved difficult to find one who specialized in sexual harassment cases.

On Wednesday, August 16, while pondering this situation, I recalled a client of mine, Armand Panetta, a corporate lawyer with whom I had a good rapport. I decided to give him a call and ask for advice.

"If you go Pro Se or with a male lawyer, you will get slaughtered." He immediately gave me the name and number of Sophia Algoni, a well-respected lawyer who handles sexual harassment and criminal cases and he suggested I get in touch with her as soon as possible. Without wasting any time I made contact and filled her in with all the pertinent information. We scheduled an appointment for the 18th of September.

Sophia Algoni and I finally met at the Munson Diner. I brought her up to speed on Rachelle Richards and the Criminal and Civil Court cases.

"The preponderance of evidence is on Rachelle. She must prove that you had the desire to bring and the intent to cause emotional and mental distress and she must prove her emotional distress by bringing in a doctor to substantiate her claim. She has to also prove that you were aware of and knew about her mental condition. I want to see everything in person that you have about this case, then if it goes to trial I can wipe her out."

I told her the detectives and police officers in the Seventy-Eight Precinct were witnesses to Rachelle's interaction with me as well as Anderson Read, who was a first hand witness to the assault in January. Sophia thought Anderson Read would probably be a strong witness.

"Who else knows you and is aware of the situation?"

"Eli Brockman, my landlord has known me for seven years and has firsthand experience of Rachelle's actions. Eli and his family have become friends. Detective Michael Dragonetti, who has in-depth knowledge of the facts surrounding the Order of Protection, has already expressed I could count on him if ever I needed a witness."

"I also need character witnesses to establish that you are a person of trust and honesty, that you are non-violent, and that you conduct yourself as a gentleman in social gatherings."

"My ex-wife, Ingrid, would certainly testify as a character witness, as would Antonia Avery, a close and dear friend who opened her home to me without question, when it was too dangerous for me to go to my home."

"Since the summons was non-specific and was 'frail as to what is at issue' Anderson should be on call one hour ahead of time to appear if necessary on that day. He would be questioned as to your honesty as a person, his opinion as to how you conduct your life, and as to how you interact with your community. He will also be asked the names and phone numbers of other people he had conversed with directly relating as to the summons at hand. I will call him on Tuesday evening."

"So what do I have to do?"

"Here's the schedule. I need to be ready with witnesses no later than Thursday. Make sure you call these people. If this goes to a jury trial, they must have to agree beforehand that it's okay for them to be called."

"Will you be in court with me on the 21st?"

"No, not officially; I will be in the room, not as your lawyer but as an independent legal observer. We must develop a theory of defense. I have to prepare a brief."

"What do I do then when I go to court?"

"When you're called, you will take the stand."

"They will ask you, your name, place of birth, employer, amount of time in the US, if you've served in any branch of US Forces, and if you've ever been married and for how long. It is important that when they ask you the length of time in the service, you answer two years, during Vietnam, Honorable Discharge. When asked how long you were married, say twelve years. Give former wife's name. They will ask you if you know Nicole Rachelle Richards. Just answer a simple yes. When did you meet her? December 1987, for a brief time. What was the nature of the relationship? Business! Your main goal is to postpone this meeting."

"How do I do that?"

"You must ask the judge if you can approach the desk alone. If the judge says 'agreed,' then proceed straight up to the judge. Do not look at Rachelle. Tell him you have hired an attorney and that 'this is not a good date for the attorney who just received the case and needs to prepare a theory of defense.' Let me give you a list of good early dates."

Sophia then gave me eight days in December and three days in January that would work for her. I asked why we had to drag it out so long.

"By his answer I will be able to interpret where the case is at according to the date he selects. I will be within fifteen minutes of the court, should you need me. Remember what I told you to say. If he gives you a date, thank him, leave the court room immediately and don't look at Rachelle."

"I'll do my best."

"You're very strong-willed. It's hard to prep you," she commented with a smile.

So went my first meeting with Sophia Algoni.

As I walked out of the Munson Diner onto Eleventh Avenue, I realized how ironic it was that the meeting was at the same diner Rachelle had phoned from to harass me.

The next day Armand Panetta called inquiring about my meeting with Sophia.

"It went quite well. What I had trouble with is that she didn't need any verbal input by me about the case but advised me about the court system."

"The court system is not about innocent or guilty. In your case it's about acquittal."

"But I'm innocent doesn't that have to be validated?"

I arrived at the Court House Thursday morning at 8:30. There were about twenty of us waiting for the doors to open at 9:00 a.m., defendants and plaintiffs standing together outside, without any protection from each other. I was very apprehensive, anxious and feared for my safety. It was ten to nine; no sign of Rachelle. According to her, this was to be her victory day. By five to nine I believed that she must have backed out of going through with it. In that case, it would all be over. It was almost nine o'clock; could it end in such a neutral context? It was the deflation of anticipation and the release of tension. The doors opened. I quickly glanced around me, up and down and across the street; no Rachelle. I was next in line to enter the metal detectors, when the man ahead of me who had already entered was requested to step back; the delay irritated me, I needed to get through. I took another quick glance at the people waiting behind me and felt more at ease that Rachelle had not joined the group. I glanced at my watch; it was exactly nine o'clock.

"We can end it before 9:00 a.m." It was Rachelle's voice in my ear. Oh shit! Again, I felt the bottom slowly fall away from underneath me; I was ice cold.

"It's your choice, say yes right now it will be quick; say no, it still will happen. You knew it would come to this."

Was I going to die or was I going to win. I took a deep breath, walked through the metal detector without looking at her. Every conceivable electronic detector system was activated and I was asked to go back through the metal detector again bringing me face to face with Rachelle. I made an about turn, stepped once more through the detector again reactivating the alarm systems. I was ordered to stand against the wall where two security men, moving their metal sensors around my body, caused them to immediately activate. I was surprised, and confused. As I glanced at the opposite side of the detector I saw Rachelle's face gleaming with victory. I looked toward the metal detector system, and realized all three officials were checking out the electronic connections to the alarm system detectors along with the hand held detectors. After a few minutes, they requested that I walk back through the system one more time. As I came back, I glanced at Rachelle's face; she was not smiling. The result was the same. The alarms once again became activated. The senior officer called me to the side and stated. "You have no metal on you and we can't find anything to activate the alarm system. What are you wearing that we can't seem to detect?" I was quiet for a moment, glanced back to where Rachelle was still standing, her face blank of expression, and suddenly realized I was not really alone at this moment. I walked back to the officer and told him I was wearing a 'Greta Electronic Belt,' it wasn't visible but its purpose was to protect me from that woman over there; I pointed directly to Rachelle. He then asked, "What's a 'Greta Belt'?"

"What you have experienced is an electronic realization of the power of the mind to manifest an invisible protective belt around oneself." He looked at me and told me to go on in. I knew he thought I was a kook. I walked towards the stairs, sensing something really good had happened, and felt I was walking through a rotunda. I recalled Greta telling me how to call for and visualize spiritual protection. "Thank you, Greta," I said to myself. Behind my words was the feeling that millions of tears were about to burst out on my face. As I reached the top of the stairs, not knowing what was to happen, I knew absolutely that I was not alone. I had forgotten that this metaphysical stuff really works.

On arrival in the courtroom everybody was milling about: plaintiffs, defendants, lawyers, clerks, security guards. It was quite interesting to watch the different elements of the judicial system come alive like a well-oiled machine. I needed the court hearing to be over with so that I could share the excitement of what I had named the "Greta Belt" with Greta herself.

I selected a seat in the center of the benches because I felt it important to surround myself with people, thus creating a safety buffer from any close proximity of Rachelle's presence. As I settled down and was reviewing Sophia's instruction I could not get rid of Rachelle's words, whispered into my ear, "We can end this right now, say yes and it will be quick." I was extremely uncomfortable. I glanced at my watch; it was nine-twenty and the doors were closed. I stood up, as if to stretch my legs, and looked around to see if I could spot Rachelle; she was nowhere in sight. My mind flashed to the first time I watched the British Fox Hunt on PBS; neither the horsemen nor the hounds could find the fox. But the cameraman had the fox in his sight. Am I the fox? I needed to find the lens of the camera and find Rachelle because she was just as cunning as the fox. Before sitting down again, I made sure that at least the three rows behind me were full of people and as I sat down, I checked my left, right and front; all seats were full. The courtroom came to order, the roll call took place, and everybody settled down to a waiting game. I continued to check out the room, as I knew Rachelle was a game player. I had to continually suppress my sense of closure.

Finally, the case was called. Just before standing up to proceed to the bench a hand rested on my shoulder and I heard Rachelle's voice saying, "So you have chosen your time and weapon; I have already selected mine and you won't reach the bench alive. Please take this note, I want you to read it, and when they find it in your hand when you have fallen they cannot convict me of murder because I will have saved so many people from being raped and sodomized. I have mailed a documented report of what you have done to me and other women to all the news media. I also observed those women within the proximity of where you are sitting, and can tell which ones you have selected to stalk, rape, sodomize." Then with a squeeze of her hand on my neck said,

"Let the final game begin."

She walked to the end of the benches and made her way to the judge's bench. As I watched her walk up, I scanned her as I had done many times before, trying to detect if she was carrying a concealed weapon. Suddenly a terrifying thought hit me; who really knew where I was? Greta, Sophia, Antonia, Anderson, Natalia and Dragonetti were the only ones who knew I was here. My whole body went numb as my thoughts raced as to how and at what moment she was going to kill me. Was she going to spin around and shoot me as I walked toward the judge? Was she going to lunge at me and stab me? These were all possibilities; however, the building seemed to have an effective metal detector system. My mind was racing; I knew she must have something on her that could be as fatal as a weapon. Like a bolt of lightning I remembered something she had shared. As a child she would kill rabbits and rats with her mother's stainless steel knitting needles. One plain, one purl, one slipstitch over the knit stitch, such was the rhythm of madness. Nobody became aware of her doing it, so she continued doing it wherever she lived, if a problem of rodents existed. I recalled her saying that she always kept her mother's stainless steel knitting needles close to her at all times.

"It's very effective in any city if somebody tries to mug you."

I moved toward the bench in slow motion, observing her. Her handbag was too small, her shoes, too open and too small, to conceal a weapon. Was I missing something?

"Will the defendant please approach the bench?"

"Yes, your Honor."

I stepped right up to the bench and as I turned towards the judge, I felt vulnerable. Rachelle's hands had moved up to her hair, which was gathered in a bun and held in place with what appeared to be a long hair stick going through it.

"Oh, shit. I missed it."

Despair, panic, fear and stillness came over me all at once.

Before the judge could ask a question I said,

"I have just hired an attorney at this moment, your Honor. It is imperative that this is not shared with the plaintiff. My attorney has not completed the theory of defense and needs to reschedule as quickly has possible." There was absolute silence. The judge looked down, turned to the clerk sitting to his left, and exchanged words.

"Will the plaintiff please approach the bench?" As Rachelle approached my eyes were transfixed on her hair.

"This is it." I thought, "She has her audience."

The judge called for the attention of both the plaintiff and defendant and stated that due to new information he had received, the trial date had been rescheduled and moved to November 27th at 9:00 a.m.

"But your honor, it's not possible for me on the 27th, I am ready now," Rachelle protested.

The judge closed his files, stood up, and left the courtroom without saying a word.

Rachelle stood dumfounded.

"I don't know what game you're playing or what you have just pulled off, but I promise you that by November 27th you will not be here. You will not be alive. You have created so much destruction in this and past lifetimes and as I have told you, my purpose in this lifetime is solely to stop you now and in future lives. You have no idea what you have done over time. It is over. There will not be a November 27th."

She turned around and as she walked out of the court I realized that her dark hair had fallen over her shoulders. Where was the hair needle?

I walked out towards the parking lot my heart still pumping wondering what next.

When I arrived at my office the receptionist told me I had an important phone call. Knowing Rachelle's MO, I took the call. When I picked up the phone, it was Sophia Algoni.

"I'm glad it's you."

"Was that really *her*?"

"Yes."

"I read everything you gave me. The fact that she lost it with the judge indicates we should be able to get this dismissed as quickly as possible. Oh, by the way, I was impressed by your abbreviated version of my instructions. I told you, you were tough to work with, but you were right on track. We must get together to fine-tune everything for the 27th of November. Don't go to your home or be with anyone with whom she knows you associate. You have to be invisible until you appear in court. This plaintiff is dangerous."

"What did you think of her?"

"Based on what you have told me, she has a psychological complex, believes who she is, and that if anybody contradicts that belief, she is capable of destroying them in order to survive."

"Thank you."

A series of meetings in preparation of the trial in November began. I called all the witnesses selected.

"Just give me the date and time and I will be there. If you request Natalia, she will be there also," Anderson said. When I next spoke with Dragonetti, he said, absolutely and to just let him know the date.

Antonia wanted to be a witness; however, she would not be in New York at that time, but if the trial date were to move forward she said she most certainly would be available as a witness. Ingrid, being a psychotherapist, did not feel comfortable testifying. I was stunned. I then called Eli; he said he would be a witness but not in person. He would give a signed notarized statement for the court, and if the court needed him in the future he would then consult his attorney about how he could be of assistance to me while still safeguarding his family.

"I feel too vulnerable," he said. "She has access to my office, can walk in anytime and blow my head off. I have my wife and children to protect."

His fears were well grounded, since Rachelle had already visited the clinic with a cat, and while Eli was checking out the animal, she discovered the stairway that led into the front lobby of the building giving her access to the rest of the apartments when she planted her passport. Eli had already called the police about her and knew that she was trouble. The dye was now cast for November 27.

I related all this to Sophia; when I said that Ingrid would not be a witness, Sophia, like me was surprised,

"However, she has her priorities, which is probably the reason and not her profession. It's not important if she considers it not important. Let it go."

When I told her Anderson was on board, as well as Natalia if needed, she commented,

"As expected, I got his sincerity. Keep in touch and update me with Antonia. As for Dragonetti, I already spoke with him and he filled me in with information I needed; he is on board. As for Eli Brockman, from reviewing all the information you gave me, he is the prime witness in this case, as he was also the subject of her harassment and cannot be left out. He needs to take the stand. Convince him immediately."

Sophia, on reviewing my report was quick to make me aware that most of my witnesses were men. This was unacceptable based on the subject of the summons.

"What do I do?"

"It is important that you have at least three women as witnesses, and let me know as soon as possible."

I prepared a list and came up with ten names of women who could be possible character witnesses. My sisters Teresa and Jo, my mother, my niece, Geraldine, Greta, her daughter,

Darine, Joyce Vagasy, Pamela Whidden, Bella Salerno and Anne Morris. I was surprised at how quickly I came up with ten women witnesses; I felt more relaxed. This was not hard to do.

Teresa was on board immediately, as was Geraldine, who was excited at the opportunity to put a stop to this woman who was being abusive to her uncle. Jo, a nun, lived in London, was a possibility and would be a good witness, but the expense of getting her here would be an issue; if necessary I could request a notarized statement for the court. My mother had just moved to Canada from London and was approaching her eighty-seventh year, but I knew without reservation that she would be available if I needed her. Pamela was very helpful and protective of me during this period; she was very knowledgeable about the danger of Rachelle's personality, having worked with women and children within her profession. I knew Pamela would take the next plane to be my witness. However, Pamela's telephone calls to me were tapped by Rachelle, who in her twisted way of interpreting the messages, saw Pamela as a sexual threat to her, making me fear for Pamela's safety. If necessary, I would review other avenues for her statement. The complexity of bringing up Joyce, who gave me access to her summer cottage upstate for my use while she was living in California, was that Rachelle relentlessly tried to discover where my hideouts were. By having Joyce as a witness, it would expose the location of the cabin. It was imperative that I did not reveal the places or sources that gave me sanctuary.

Then there was my friend Anne, who had been mugged, viciously and brutally beaten. I had been there for her during the healing process, emotionally and spiritually. I knew she would gladly be a witness, but I didn't want to put her in a stressful situation facing Rachelle in court. If absolutely necessary, I would contact her. Bella was aware that I had a single purpose in attending her Ashram but never questioned me and we developed a mutual respect and enjoyed each other. Though I selected her, in hindsight, it would be wrong, as Rachelle's obsession to discover where I went on those Friday evenings and sometimes three-day weekends would expose her and the group. Rachelle had stated that she would scour all sources available to her and by the process of elimination would eventually discover where I went. From earlier conversations, she knew that I was active in different awareness groups.

Last, there was Greta, Darine and Peter. But Peter was another man and I needed women.

When it came to Darine, I knew she would be a strong defender of my character and was aware of my sensitivity to other peoples needs. She had once stated that she would be extremely upset if she discovered I was in trouble and excluded her as a source of help. Would putting her on the stand expose her to danger? What was I doing? How could I handle this?

Greta, I knew, like her daughter Darine, would be a fearless witness; yet because of her exposure on stage when performing, she would be vulnerable as an easy target for Rachelle to attack. I needed to protect her. Rachelle had emphasized that if she could not get me, she would get someone close to me. If anything was to happen to Greta, I would be devastated. I had made a decision very early on to exclude her from most of what was going on, although I realized now it was a very serious omission. Also I knew Rachelle had already shown her awareness of Greta by using her name to get through to my receptionist, who had been instructed to screen my calls.

Now I was left in a quandary; should I search further or would I be right back where I started? Was I gambling with the life of my friends? Was I being too protective of those I loved?

Was I right by not sharing all of what I was going through? If Rachelle did kill me, who would know why?

I remembered Sophia emphasizing I should make an all-out effort to get Eli Brockman to testify in person. I tried once again to convince him but he would not budge. He said he was too afraid. I reviewed some more names and decided that for the moment I would stay with Anderson and Dragonetti. I notified Sophia Algoni of my decision.

Through this ordeal my sanity was being tested. I once had heard that enlightenment was easy. All one had to do was to surrender oneself to a higher power. I tried but in no way could I apply this to what Rachelle was putting me through. It was imperative that I held on to reality. In the beginning, I did not put much focus on the incremental contradictions that I had noticed since I had no investment in the dynamics other than the poetry project. This limited perception caused me to be unaware of her strange patterns of behavior. I gave little attention to small incidental things while she was giving importance to the subtle differences. As I tried to play catch up, I became more critical of my loss of control and protection. My stubbornness to accept this new reality left me vulnerable. All that defined me was losing cohesiveness. Friendship fibers were fraying; truth and trust were being challenged and my laughter had diminished. Relentless daily intrusion in my work environment resulted in affecting my performance. The inability to go home and socialize freely and the encumbrance of needing to escape daily were exhausting. Without my own roof over my head, exposed to the elements under duress, and starved of my needs, I was depleted. All that reflected love was no longer reality.

Was my emptiness caused, by depending only, upon my will to survive? I wondered if the pain of emptiness went beyond pain and that the Absolute was in companionship with

Death. Was it possible to become one with Divine Spirit? Even with my belief in the power of prayer, I still experienced only emptiness. Would the true test of my belief in prayer only then begin?

Saturday morning a call from Rachelle got through to me at my office.

"Your words mean nothing . . . " I did not let her finish and hung up. On the same day I received a letter from Joyce.

"It's been a month since I spoke with you! So my spirits need lifting, my intellect needs filling and some friend of mine said he was going to send me a book to do both of what I need. Did it get lost out there somewhere? I didn't even write the name of the book down because you said you would send it. Well darling, ole Joyce is being truly tested and can use all the help she can get. I will come east to visit for a week in October. Hope to see you."

On Sunday, October 1, another call came through from Rachelle while I was sitting with a client in my office.

"I will not allow you to leave me like this. I want satisfaction. It is either going to be negative or positive satisfaction. I have been dealing with the mentality of a rapist and it is the psychology of a rapist that is affecting you."

I gently placed the phone back on its cradle.

The next evening Greta invited me to her home for an intimate dinner gathering with a few friends.

I spent the night sleeping in my car.

Pamela was due in from California on Tuesday and I was looking forward to her visit.

We arranged to have lunch together in Manhattan at a small café on the west side near 10th street. She was down to earth and a lot of fun. I brought her up to date with what was going on with Rachelle and we laughed as I shared how the episode of "love in the bushes" drove Rachelle crazy after listening to the message Pamela had left on my answering machine.

I thanked her once more for her healing package. She emphasized how dangerous she sensed the situation to be and warned me to be very cautious as to how I responded to Rachelle and to be fully aware of how evil this person was, and to protect myself at all times. Before we parted she slipped off the amethyst necklace she was wearing and slipped it into my hand saying,

"Hold on to this; it will protect you."

As I watched her disappear into the subway station, I felt a loss and a wave of sadness at seeing her go. For a brief moment I had released the stress I was under and now, alone again, the reality of danger intensely returned, sending shivers throughout my body. I no longer knew if I was capable of handling it any more. How could I defend and protect myself? I was exhausted and needed the quietness of the cabin and to immerse myself in the sanctuary of nature.

FORTY

Riptide

T he air was chilled as I sat upon my favorite rock above the cabin. What a priceless gift to be here while so much raged around me. I listened to the pages of my journal ruffling in the breeze, glanced at the darkened evening sky, joyed by the tranquil beauty of the moon, and pondered for a moment and began to write.

Does Moonlight know the power of its silver shadows as the spirits of night takes up their dance? Faces chiseled in the silver, as I all but paid no attention; profiles in the night. Their lips move in silent words as the wind touches the surface of the lake without sound. Trees in the waning moments of autumn gently release their curling leaves to the wind.

In the cloak of darkness my privacy has been intruded upon claiming my favorite chair as if owning the right to claim my throne. I have learned to step as carefully as a firewalker to prevent the birthing of another's dream.

Naked I must walk from the dark night of my soul and claim my moonlight. Tribal movements establish blockages. I must lift my wings and drink in the milk of moonlight to experience the child of self once again. I was told that I was born under the silver moon. So was the beginning of my earthly journey, pure in its launching; now to grasp its joy and meaning. Teach me my movements and in its sanctuary guide me even if it is all over. The candle flickers in its limited caretaking of the darkness. It is very lonely to be lonely alone. Yet the dreams of life walk like smiles waiting to burst into reality. The predator has become intoxicated by the power of love and the realization that it cannot be, becoming desperate as self identity dissolves never to experience self in the passion of life.

Dawn will slowly win, and in its onslaught upon the moonlight, is unaware of the importance of the night and shadows. The gentle canopy that has held me in place until now is removed.

The initial thoughts of creation dwell in the mind. I am living on the razor's sharp edge surviving in the presence of now; hoping that the creator looks upon me as we look upon a pearl and is teaching me the secrets of my soul. How beautiful it would be to be free of all of this stress and share time in friendship and romance. The time has not arrived and the river is dark and muddy. I will swim as long as I have breath until I reach the sea that I love. I wish to know the vastness of all and move seamlessly with the wise ones. I know that they know me and that the invisible realm of silence has sound. I need to intensely listen. I love to celebrate life in simplicity and wander knee deep in its complexity and lift my glass to celebrate love. There is a lady that moves within and wanders the deep interior of my heart and soul whom I protect with a great urgency yet she knows not of the dangerous currents I move within. Love is a trickster.

In the beginning it had been exciting to think of the possibilities that a year of exposure within a monthly magazine could produce. The meetings with Rachelle were supposed to be brief and focused. The history of our lives was not important with the exception of direct relationship to my work and a brief history of me as a poet. There never had been any intention to labor the project in selecting poetry that would be suitable for *Spirit Path*.

Why was my soul's voice quiet? Was it aware and willing to experience what was about to unfold. What was of such great importance to my soul's journey? Why enter the battlefield of subversive life?

In the accumulation of sunsets, I had learned the power of instinctual survival. I did not know the answers. Who really cared if I lost the fight, as few were privy to its contest? Still there were those who I held dear who I knew would care. I had not involved them or called them to the battle. There was one most precious for whom I created a manuscript as a gift from my soul. She had to be protected at all costs as her art form brought her upon the stage, intensifying her presence as a target. "If I can't get you, I will get those closest to you until there will be nobody left but you." That was the mantra of the predator.

In the constant silence, as I passed through the days and nights as if they were one, where I no longer knew deep sleep, where fatigue was a constant companion, I felt creation teaching me every moment, speaking in a language that did not need translation. So often in the silence of my tears, I hungered to know the reason why.

The court date was approaching and I was by now anxious for it to be over. I showed Sophia a typed notification I received from Rachelle, who tried passing it off as official, dated November 7, 1989, having to do with the deposition of a witness; Sophia gave it no heed. During one of our final meetings, Sophia emphasized once again to stress in court that we did not want to go to trial.

"Connell, Rachelle wants a jury trial. She has already put in place and signed all the necessary forms required for the courts to proceed, but we will stress to the judge that you do not want one and that we want it to go on record."

"But if she is going Pro Se, how does she know to do this and how do I counteract it?"

"You have to refer again back to the criminal case and stress the gravity of the harassment with emphases on written proof."

Was Sophia Algoni playing a game; did she know what she was doing? I left the meeting frustrated. The longer this was stretched out, the more vulnerable I would become, and the greater the chance of Rachelle succeeding in taking my life. I had to make a decision; I had to insist she be there. I went back to the office not knowing what to do. In the late afternoon I called Sophia and told her it was imperative that we meet the next day, before the trial, to which she agreed.

About twenty minutes after I spoke with her, the reception-ist gave me a call and told me my attorney was on the line. Being off guard, I said, "Put her through."

"You bastard! Do you think I'm a fool? I know you are play-ing a deadly game. Things have to stop right now. What hap-pened with the metal detectors last time we met?"

As was my pattern, I didn't answer, nor was she expecting me to.

"Do you have an attorney?" she continued.

"No, why would you think I have an attorney?" I answered as nonchalant as possible.

"Somebody is checking me out in the courts."

"What do they have to check out, Rachelle?"

"They wanted to find out if I had filed the necessary papers for a jury trial."

"You had advised me that you wanted a jury trial so I called the court to find out my options. They requested the case num-ber and confirmed that the papers were filed."

Without skipping a breath I added, "We have done well together on a Pro Se basis. Why would I need to change it? Rachelle, how are you holding up?"

"I can't go on with this."

"You're going through a lot; take care of yourself, goodbye."

By this time Rachelle was following me everywhere and seemed to have picked up my pattern and this worried me. She let me know she had access to a car, which was at her beck and call. How long could I endure this? She had to be stopped. About 7:00 p.m. Sophia called to confirm the meeting.

I met with her on the 24th and told her I felt it was the end of the game with Rachelle and that everything had to conclude on the 27th. It either had to be dismissed for lack of evidence or it was going to go to trial. I needed to know, and I needed her there. Time was running out. She told me they had served a motion to show Cause of Action on Rachelle. I asked what that meant. She said it was to specifically state what the grounds were for her to file a Civil Court summons; "However, we were not able to serve the motion. When we went to stake out her building, she wasn't there; she had moved. They pointed out her apartment and it looked as if it had been in a fire.

What do you believe is her reason for the civil court action charging rape? If you state that you both were sexually involved, it would defuse her claim of rape. If the records would show that you stated to me that 'we were not sexually involved' as an answer to three different questions in our court preparation, there is no way I can prevent a trial from proceeding."

"I will not follow that line of thinking, since that would not be the truth. So where do we go from here?"

"I will request that an EBT (examination before trial) will be served on her tomorrow. You must stay calm. There cannot be any confrontation."

"What do you think our chances are?"

"I think this whole thing has been brought on by her to create a show to draw your anger, to try to belittle you in the eyes of people, and for her to have control over you for that hour. If she goes Pro Se it is my responsibility to establish your character to show that you do not abuse women and that there is a criminal case for aggravated harassment on file against her. No matter what happens in the courtroom remember, I am your voice. The case may go to trial."

I felt better prepared after our meeting and returned to my office, finished my work, and at 6:00 o'clock left for Nyack to attend Bella Salerno's usual Friday evening meditations. I always felt safe with Bella and her group. After the meeting Bella, Andreas, Susan, and I stopped at an ice cream parlor. It was drizzling outside, but feeling peaceful, I ordered a rum raisin ice cream and thought how ironic life was as I observed the trio eagerly licking their ice cream cones. None of them knew the danger I was in or what would take place Monday morning. After watching them drive away I drove to the corner of the parking lot and parked under an old oak tree and prepared my car for sleep. I could not return to Brooklyn to sleep in my bed, the cabin was too far away, I hadn't reserved a room at the Pickwick Arms, and Antonia's son was using the guest room for the weekend. It was the only vestige left for me to hold onto: a last resort to protect my need for sleep.

The most stressful nights were when I made attempts to go home, to pick up mail, fresh clothing and then to take a chance sleeping in my own bed. Within less than thirty minutes of arrival, the phone would ring or the doorbell would buzz, cancelling any possibility of curling up in the warmth of my blankets.

I would immediately plan an escape route; once back in my car and feeling safe, I would not know where to go. I eventually discovered secluded locations in Prospect Park West where maintenance trucks parked overnight. It was crucial that my car not be visible from the road as Rachelle often slept and prowled in the Park area directly opposite my building, day and night, monitoring my every move. Some nights, needing to hold on to my sanity, I was compelled to get out of the car and walk deeper into the park. Though it was not safe, I felt protected by the darkness and the elements, yet I could never completely relax for fear of attack. My life was full of imminent danger; my thoughts were running rampant. What if Rachelle discovered this secluded area, saw a car resembling mine and recognized my license plates? She could come upon me while I slept. I would be a sitting duck, one shot: *Man Found Dead in Prospect Park Secluded Parking Lot.*

Chills ran through my body as I realized how vulnerable and paranoid I had become. How could I prevent this from happening? I remembered I had a set of cancelled license plates in the trunk of my car and would install them over my regular plates to throw her off the scent. This plan did not always work as, at times, exhausted, I would wake up in a panic realizing that I had forgotten to camouflage my plates. Life had become a day-by-day survival, and I was aware that there was no special time or place where it all could end. If I were asleep it would be quick. Panic would waft over me like a chilling wind.

For this night in Nyack, I felt safe under the oak tree.

FORTY-ONE
Walking Death

November 27th had finally arrived. I woke up about 6:00 o'clock in the morning and felt ready. I arrived at my office around 7:00 o'clock, freshened up and headed to the court in Brooklyn.

It was early and since there was a good chance Rachelle would be preparing to go to court, I took a gamble that she would not be around the area and pulled up in front of my home, which I desperately missed. I was able to shower, shave and put on fresh clothes; I felt great. I took the opportunity to gather some additional clothes, things I needed and left.

I decided not to park in the usual parking lot near the Court House. I parked three or four blocks away near Clinton Street. I did not want Rachelle to be aware I was already there. I arrived in the courtroom and sat down, carefully choosing my seat in the center of the row, positioning myself as I had the last time. The room quickly filled up and the normal preparatory buzz had by now become familiar to me. As usual, I periodically scanned the room. Right up until the roll call, I could not spot Rachelle. I remembered how peaceful I felt in the car under the tree in the parking lot in Nyack, and said to myself, "Stray not beyond self" and wrote it down.

Another fifteen minutes went by; still no sign of Rachelle or Sophia. I became restless. I remembered Sophia talking about a fire and the inability to serve the motion to show cause, and believing Rachelle had moved. I wondered if it was possible Rachelle was no longer around. Since I was not accessible by phone, was the trial date still on the calendar? Maybe it was all over and nobody was able to contact me.

I looked down at what I had scribbled, "Stray not beyond self." The words hit me like a Mantra and I realized both these women played mind games. It was possible both were somewhere in the room. I looked around once more but could not find either one of them. I relaxed back into my seat.

The person to my right, a dark haired, heavy set woman with a fine line of a moustache over her lip, wearing dark horned rim glasses, offered me potato chips, which I politely declined.

"When does this God-damned session get going? I've got places to go and things to do, what about you?" she asked.

I didn't bother answering.

"Do you got any gum?"

"No, ma'am, I don't chew gum."

"You're kind of polite, aren't you?"

"No ma'am, I'm actually impatient. I'm wondering like you when this session is going to get going."

"What are you in for?"

"No one in this room is in for anything."

"That doesn't make sense. Are you all alone?"

"No, I'm waiting for someone."

She was quiet for a few moments, then, asked, "Man or woman?"

"Woman." She looked at me and smiled,

"You look like a man who would have a woman problem," she said as she fumbled with her big plastic bag.

We both drifted back into our own thoughts. I had strayed beyond myself again.

As they began calling the cases, I became nervous. "What if the case were called and Rachelle had not yet arrived, what was the court procedure in that case; what if Rachelle were here and Sophia had not shown up? I needed Sophia with me. I felt thoroughly let down. How quickly the feeling of peacefulness disappeared. I no longer felt freshly dressed.

I looked at the woman next to me and realized how uncoordinated her clothes were, as if she just grabbed anything. While thinking this, she turned to me and in a very quiet voice said,

"Do you realize that people are talking about the feeling of evil in the room today?"

"No, no one has made that comment to me." She was silent again, and then said,

"I have spread the word as to who you are and why you are here."

I watched her move some things from under her jacket into the plastic bag. At that moment she looked like the cross of a weirdo and a bag lady. She moved her hands to the right side of her body as if toying with a sash. As I watched her hand, I realized she was wrapping the sash around one hand all the while looking towards me with her head slightly down. I suddenly felt the hair in the back of my neck rise.

"Do you realize that I'm the only woman sitting near you?" Her voice sounded like one of a heavy smoker.

"What is it you said before about passing the word as to who I am?"

"I told them," she said as she stood up and pulled off her black wig, "that you are a rapist and a sodomite."

I was frozen in terror as her voice began to rise and out of the clothes of this heavy dressed woman Rachelle emerged, her voice continuing to rise,

"You will be in handcuffs and be put away before the day is over. This is your judgment day."

Now lowering her voice and speaking in a theatrical manner, as if on stage,

"Such joy, such absolute joy." Her voice now rising again,

"I have wanted to destroy you for so long for what you had done to me. Now I have you in my rat trap, you bastard."

It all happened so quickly that by the time I gathered myself she had already moved out into the aisle and disappeared. I felt everybody's eyes on me. I felt stupid and angry. How could she have successfully pulled off something like this? Where was Sophia?

I was stunned by how close she had been to me. The fear that I had lived with about the possibility of a quick assault was replaced by the shock that she had been sitting next to me. The suddenness of her revealing herself and the quick disappearance left me bereft of emotion. I could only feel rage. I had to take a hold of myself as the case could be called at any moment. I had not expected to be in this position.

The case number was called and Rachelle arrived within seconds; perfect timing much to my chagrin. She walked directly to the bench with attitude and, as if on stage, clicked immediately into character. She reappeared, now wearing a dark costume and white blouse, ready to play the part. She stood alone for a few moments, her expression slightly deflated, and theatrically turning towards me beckoned me with her hand to approach the bench. I ignored the gesture and stayed seated. Now with an expression of controlled anger and impatience, she raised her hand and with her fingers again motioned me to come forward. Sophia, unbeknownst to me, was in the courtroom observing her theatrics.

The judge called for the defendant; I stood up as if I was about to approach the bench, but when Rachelle looked back at me, she observed me sitting back down. Once again with her fingers waving in the air she motioned me to come up. At that same moment Sophia, unnoticed by Rachelle, approached the bench,

"I am the defense lawyer for Connell Chambers."

Rachelle had a look of absolute shock and, looking back at me, her face was livid. She turned back to face the judge and in an angry tone spouted,

"This is supposed to be Pro Se. I am the plaintiff and it's what I want. Dismiss this woman at once." She looked as if she was about to snap; I sat frozen.

"We had an agreement to go Pro Se," she continued as her voice rose, slowly loosing her composure.

Sophia would have no way of knowing the ferocity in which Rachelle would now seek revenge. My heart was pumping heavily and yet I remained seated as per Sophia's instructions,

"Remain seated no matter what happens. Remember I am your voice." What an oxymoron.

"Your Honor, this is the law. This was an agreement. He cannot change the game. When something is set it is set. That is Universal Law – he knows that. That is where all this comes from."

Her words were released at rapid speed as she became emotionally disheveled. My eyes were glued to her, as her whole Shakespearean tragedy was fragmenting. The words of Gelek Rinpoche exploded in my brain:

"You must shatter her."

I gripped the edge of the bench to quiet my nerves.

"What is the order of the court?" Sophia asked in an unemotional tone.

"Rachelle Nicole Richards versus Connell Chambers is ready to go to trial today."

I knew that Sophia, who was standing close to Rachelle, was in danger; Rachelle could flip within seconds. What if she decided that upon this stage she would select her Macbeth-ian moment? I clung to the edge of my seat. There was nothing I could do except shout or scream if I had to.

Sophia's voice came through as if on another frequency,

"As the defense lawyer for Connell Chambers, I request a new trial date."

"Your Honor, she can't do that. It cannot change. The date was set; it cannot change, it cannot change," she repeated as her voice became weaker.

I watched her as her confidence melted away, yet the danger level was reaching boiling point. Sophia's monotone voice came through.

"I need to subpoena Nicole Richards' psychiatrist to the court. I have informed her but she sees no purpose."

"This is not acceptable; the trial must proceed." Rachelle piped up.

Sophia again spoke to the judge, this time not audibly; the judge called a recess for ten minutes. Sophia and the judge both left together to the judge's chambers. The security guard smoothly moved to Rachelle's side.

My life was flying by so fast I had to take a few deep breaths. I knew it would only be a matter of time. Rachelle was trapped in her own game. I could feel the destruction build. Rachelle's eyes were transfixed on me.

Sophia and the judge returned; court was adjourned. The judge addressed the Court Clerk and requested him to enter December 7th, 1989 as the trial date. Rachelle and Sophia were called to the bench. Rachelle held her composure for the moment as they were ordered to appear on that date at 9:00 a.m. Whew! What now? I released my breath; her grand finale was just solidified.

When Rachelle realized what the judge had just announced, her face paled; she had a shocked and vacant look. As she walked towards me her mouth stretched open as if she was screaming so loud, it was not audible. Her pace slowed as she passed me and without stopping said in a low, dark, threatening voice,

"This is universal war, one you will never win. You will not make it to court on the 7th to prance in with your bitch lawyer and belittle me again. Now you really are walking death."

Rachelle was finally able to get through to my line at the office on Wednesday.

"You will not make it to the court on December 7th. I am the judge, and the jury has found you guilty as charged, and the sentence is $75,000 for damages, and death.

I have discovered where your hideouts are upstate and I am closing in on you. I am not alone in wanting you destroyed. My close group of friends has come together to work with me, and have put together a network of every move you make. I now have a thorough list of all of your special friends. If you decide to move forward with this lawyer bitch, I have set up who will be the first of your friends to be attacked. It will intensify, you bastard. You are trapped at work, on the phone, in your car, in restaurants, in churches, on the streets, and, where you shop. The traps are set for the final blow. In selecting you I had to closely observe you. You played your role beyond expectation. All great tragedies have a final moment and a good playwright knows how the timing must be. You are so vile and despicable that you even smell of death. It must be very sad to know that you soon will be killed and nobody will really know the story. I know you have written most of our story, I hear the pen on paper at work when I call you; do you realize I will never let you write our story – never. You will die and you will be a short-term mystery. Why are you so quiet?"

"Rachelle, I have nothing to say. Do you realize how many hours, day and night, you have spoken without response? It is too late for any cordial dialogue; you have brought both of us to this moment. It seemed to have been your show from the beginning. I do believe and understand your dangerous theatrics. One of us will be standing and that is in the hands of God."

Friday evening, I left for Nyack and Bella Salerno. Rachelle was obsessed in her attempts to discover what particular group I was affiliated with. She scoured New York City and State to locate it. Bella's Meditation Group, however, grew through word of mouth, never promoted in any New Age magazines.

Bella, as usual, instructed that when we meditate, we should let go of our thoughts and be open to whatever flows in. At the end of the session, each of us described what we visualized. As I shared my experience, one member of the group interrupted me in a tone of annoyance and asked,

"Why is it that you always see things?"

"I don't really know. When you close your eyes, don't you see something?"

"No, never," she snapped.

"I wouldn't think it is unusual for Connell, when he closes his eyes to see things, he's a poet," said Bella. While she was speaking, I glanced around the room wondering if someone else was going to comment and noticed there was a new member in the group who was looking at me with curiosity. There was something about seeing her that made me feel uncomfortable. I could not easily see her face in the candlelight. She certainly was not present at the beginning of the meditation. I surmised she must have come in quietly and taken her place in the back of the group. I felt relief when the session was over and the regular room lights were turned back on. My God, I hoped I was not becoming paranoid. I proceeded to get my jacket off the coat rack; the woman was standing right next to me.

"So you're a poet who sees things? That must be exciting. Susan told me that you were a good poet and that in 1987 you had a workshop in Park Slope. What a coincidence, I live in Park

Slope." She put out her hand and introduced herself. "I'm Lena Strauss."

"You must have arrived after the session started. I hadn't noticed."

"I wanted to be here on time, but we just employed a new assistant editor for our newspaper and I had to show her the ropes. It took longer than expected."

"Doesn't she have experience?"

"Yeah, she was the assistant editor for a similar monthly magazine, and was recommended to us by Sidney Cohen, an actor, who was the ex-boyfriend of my friend Sandra Lewis, who is also an actress."

"I know Sandra very well. And the name of your magazine is what?"

"*Light Beam!*"

"And what magazine did she work for?"

"*Spirit Path!*"

I froze. This could not be happening. This could not be coincidental.

"Why did she leave the other magazine?"

"Because she had been going through a Civil Court case and was absent a lot. But she won the case plus was awarded one hundred seventy five thousand dollars." Cold sweat crept upon my scalp.

"What was her name?"

"Rachelle Richards."

I felt I was instantly disintegrating in front of her. My voice quivered as I said under my breath, "Time is running out." As she grabbed her jacket off the coat rack, my eyes were transfixed by the gentle movement of the coat hanger, as if, I was looking at the pendulum of a grandfather clock that was slowing, coming to a stop in front of my eyes. Trying to center myself and focus on the meaning of the moment, I said to her,

"Time is running out."

"I guess we've all got to get home, it's late."

We walked out together and having somewhat regained my composure, and trying to sound casual, I asked,

"Did you tell your new *Light Beam* employee where you were going?"

"Yeah, she was going to join me tonight but she was very tired. I asked her to come next week but she said she would be in Civil Court on Thursday. But she'll come on the fourteenth."

I said goodnight. As I walked towards my car in the rain, I was trembling; everything was crashing down around me. Nothing seemed right anymore. I needed to think and must have stood in the freezing rain for fifteen or twenty minutes trying to absorb the realization that I could no longer escape the inevitable. There was something numbing and comforting in the rawness of the cold and the rain on my face. As the rain subsided, I continued walking and was left alone with my own soggy footsteps.

FORTY-TWO

Turbulance

My life had frayed so dangerously that I wanted to disappear. I mused over my predicament. If I left New York City to go to any place in the United States, she would eventually find me. Ireland, where I was born, was an excellent choice. I knew the people, its culture and the land. How would I get there? I could not go directly; she would find me through the process of elimination. She had the tenacity and the time. I could fly to one of the Nordic countries, possibly Norway, where there were a lot of fishing companies who export to the British Isles and Ireland. I could get part time work on a fishing boat and eventually jump ship on to the mainland of Ireland. From there I could make my way inland and try to work as a laborer on a remote farm where no questions are asked as long as you do your day's work. There would be no record of me with the government, no entry or customs records.

This would not pose a problem as I have an Irish passport. I felt that everything had heated up to the boiling point. It was not possible to just keep going. She had never retracted any of her threats. Every moment was the same, to intensify the fear factor, to always be so close and on top of every action in my life; I felt the sensation of suffocation, yet somehow I had been able to sustain the core of my reality no matter how compressed it had become.

What if I succeeded to escape from it all, arrived in another country and she was incapable of finding me? What would she do? By my disappearance, who would become the target to be sacrificed? Her anger and rage would become so fierce that in order for her to survive, she would target a family member or someone who had left messages without leaving phone numbers, but who, by their tone alone, expressed closeness, fondness or love. This stopped me in my tracks. I had protected those closest to me, especially Greta. My God what was I thinking? I could feel the blood rush to my head, my body temperature rise like hot damp waves. My mind and heart were in the same place. I felt so alive, so isolated, so fearful, so scared, and so close to the edge of another's madness determined to destroy me. Was I going crazy?

"I cannot leave, I have to stay here. I still had some control of this. I might not live, but those I love would. I must tighten all the masts of my ship and believe beyond doubt that it must complete its course immediately and that I will still be breathing."

It was beyond imagination how my life had become suffused with the ceaseless pressure of the twisted mind of one who had lost touch with reality.

My muscles hurt deep inside, my spine pained me, and my sciatica constantly sent flashes of severe pain throughout my body and brain. Sometimes it was so severe that it felt like a sharp needle being pushed into my brain; I was drained of body strength. Was this what my life was to become? Everything had to stop; I had to push deeper into my belief that my cries were heard and that "right action" would carry me through. I had not had a peaceful night's sleep for more than a year. Sometimes I felt like a stray animal dressed in a pressed suit. Could I survive? I wondered how far my safety net had been stretched.

Rachelle had expressed on the phone that not only had she followed me closely in the city and Brooklyn but also on the highways. She had managed to convince her employer to give the use of a car for at least another two weeks because she was working on a very exciting story about an individual deeply involved in the "New Age Movement." Now she could trail me and observe patterns that would lead her to my "Secret Hideaway." She knew that it was somewhere near Carmel, and would find out where it was from all the phone numbers she had collected. She reminded me that her spirits would deliver me to her as they did on that rainy night in Park Slope.

"It will possibly be on a dark country road upstate where you feel safe far away from me. It may look like a deer or a drunk driver on the wrong side of the highway speeding towards you. The last thing that you will see is the white car, a flash of gunfire and my face. You are coming to the truth of your purpose, to bring me eternal relief by me taking your life. We will then be dammed together for eternity. What great joy, we will go out together. I always wanted to go out with you. It all seems so close. I am very excited."

Living with this infusion of such intensity in my advanced state of exhaustion, I was not fully aware that the toxins in my body were having an affect on me. Her voice would actually become audible as if she were in the car with me. When I tried to sleep, her words invaded my senses. This was of serious concern while I was driving exhausted on the dark country roads late at night on the road to Mahopac. I knew I was experiencing slight hallucinations. What if she were on the road following at a safe distance behind or in front and suddenly stopped? What if she moved up next to me on the right side, gun blasts? I had become paranoid and used all my power of concentration to prevent illusion from overtaking me. I tried to stop thinking of what could happen and concentrate instead on the court date ahead of me, December 7.

FORTY-THREE
Mental Collapse

For close to an hour I tried to shake off a white Dodge Dart following me at every turn. I had a suspicion the car was driven by Rachelle. I drove around a few blocks to see if it would follow. Each time I turned a corner and reached mid-block, the car also turned. Perhaps it was just someone looking for a parking spot. I made a quick turn from Central Park West as the light turned from amber to red and believed I had broken free. If it were Rachelle, she must have realized that I was aware of the car and probably believed she had succeeded in freaking me out. I drove around for a while to check if the car would reappear. Feeling comfortable that the path was now clear, I proceeded to head north towards Mahopac.

Waiting at the traffic light on Broadway, feeling tired, I decided to go to The Holy Trinity Church on 82nd Street. I came to know this church during this trial period as a sanctuary, a place of worship and meditation. I felt an urgent need to go in and rest in its tranquil environment to pray for protection, and to re-center myself, before leaving for the country. I turned onto 82nd Street, and found a perfect parking spot opposite the church entrance.

As I proceeded to back up into the space, traffic maneuvered around me to pass. A car, blasted its horn as if pissed off for some reason; I wondered why and glanced back. The driver, a woman with blond hair resembling Carol Channing, was probably unable to pass. However, as she was not looking towards my car, I paid no heed and backed into my space. I glanced into my side view mirror; the white car had not moved. The woman was placing something that looked like a long box of flowers on the dashboard. I got out of the car and as I walked around the front of the car to the sidewalk, cast a quick glance towards her. The blond hair had disappeared; she no longer looked like Carol Channing, "Oh shit, it's Rachelle!" Her arms reached for the object on the dashboard and quickly pulled it towards her.

"Oh my God, it's possibly a rifle." Everything seemed to move in slow motion.

I walked past the car on her right side and glancing sideways realized if it were a rifle, she would not have the space to turn it around quick enough to get a shot off. As long as I moved to her right and rear, she could not get a good shot at me without getting out of the car. I did not want to reveal that I recognized her or transmit any sign of panic. I walked to the telephone booth at the corner and pretended to dial. This gave me a few seconds to think. I waited a few moments then casually walked back to my car. How could I escape her trap? It would not be smart for her to shoot at me through the windshield, or to get out of the car where it would be witnessed. It would be more advantageous for her to follow me as soon as I drove off, and shoot me through an open window when we stopped at a traffic light.

The traffic light on Amsterdam Avenue was green. I calculated my movement on the timing of the light. If I moved out too fast, I would send a signal; if too slow, I would be in trouble. How could I manage this? I observed the traffic lights for a few moments. I had to hit the light the second it changed from Amber to Red; this would bring her to the light on Red. I was counting on her not running the light. The hunt was on.

I seemed to be getting better at handling myself as her predatory hunts intensified. I now was aware that she knew what direction I always took when leaving the city. It had been easier when she did not have access to a car. She was good at upping the ante, but it was taking a toll on me. Her ceaseless pressure was a challenge that pushed beyond my known limits to survive. Had I really broken loose of her trail?

I entered the Hutchinson Parkway around midnight feeling more relaxed, yet apprehensive. Rain began to fall on the dark parkway, making it harder to see. I experienced waves of exhaustion; my eyelids were feeling heavy. I imagined folding back the warm blankets and lying down upon fresh sheets. It was such a beautiful feeling.

"My God what are you doing Connell? You are driving at sixty miles per hour on a parkway; pull yourself together, you could get killed," I said to myself, as I snapped back from my reverie in panic and tried to gasp for breath; I was in trouble. The waves of strain and fear had become more frequent. A few moments later everything began to feel clearer; I felt I could now drive all the way to the cabin. Why not, I had navigated this highway many times before under tremendous strain.

As I continued to pierce the wet darkness, my thoughts drifted once again towards Rachelle. She had woven her web very cleverly over a long period of time, and possibly by now was waiting for me to collapse. I wondered if she had driven back to Brooklyn or was somewhere behind or in front of me? This had become a deadly game of cat and mouse; the stakes were high. How long did I have?

The blast of a car horn startled me. I suddenly realized I had left the highway and was traveling along the shoulder at about sixty miles per hour. "STOP – CONNELL - STOP!" I screamed out loud, while steering the car back onto the road, feeling more frightened than ever. Good God, I realized I must have nodded off.

"Connell, this is crazy, you will kill yourself." I was loosing it; I needed to get off the parkway as quickly as possible; this was suicidal. The compression of the moment was vice-like, leaving me with no strength to force it back. I mustered all the power I had to reach the next exit, get off and try to get some sleep. I rolled all the windows down, turned off the heat and put on the air conditioner. Music, yes! I thought if I played loud music it would annoy me, but it would keep me awake. At last I saw the sign for the next exit, four miles. Good, now I had a point of reference. I felt invigorated by the cold, annoyed by the music and thankful that in approximately twenty minutes I would be able to recline in the seat, close my eyes and rectify the problem. The music was horrible but it kept me agitated and awake. I stretched my hand out the window to catch the rain and then, with dampened fingers, attempted to cool my eyelids in a desperate effort not to sleep. I struggled to keep my eyes open but was becoming disorientated and no longer sure of where I was. There was a truck on my right side and as I turned to the left, I saw another truck passing me on that side; I wondered where they had come from. I did not remember seeing their lights approaching from behind. I concluded I must have drifted off for a few seconds. Thanks to the cool rain I kept dabbing onto my eyes, I believed I was alert. I proceeded to alternately ease off the accelerator to let the trucks pass, and then accelerate, to get ahead of them. I did not feel comfortable driving at the same speed in such close proximity; I felt I could reach out and touch them. "Yes, I must accelerate ahead," I thought, "because if I drop back I will be caught in their water sprays." I was pleasantly surprised to realize how alert I had suddenly become. Oh! But something seemed out of place; what were trucks doing on the Hutchinson Parkway? Trucks were not allowed on parkways, something was wrong.

I decided it was better to slow down and pull over onto the shoulder until they disappeared. I glanced at the speedometer to see how fast we were all going; the needle was at zero.

"Shit, now it's broken, damn it! The dashboard light is off. It must be an electrical failure." Panic hit with surgical accuracy as I realized I was traveling between two trucks, with no headlights, at sixty miles an hour.

Suddenly everything was silent; no road noise, no engine noise, even the trucks were traveling in silence. I must have been dreaming that I was awake. "Oh, God! Wake up! Wake up!" I now screamed. "I am on the parkway, I am asleep, Connell wake up, for God's sake, wake up. You are going to get killed, Connell, wake up! WAKE UP CONNELL, YOU ARE GOING TO DIE! But I am awake, I must be."

I glanced at my transmission to see what gear I was in; to my shock it was in PARK, I WAS STOPPED; everything was stopped. Yes, I was awake, I could move yet nothing else could. Where was I? I slowly took stock of everything around me. It took a few moments to orientate myself and realize that I was in a parking lot and parked at the rear of a commercial building with only a sole light at the end of the lot. Panic hit me like a hunter's spear.

"How did I get here? Am I going mad? Am I asleep or awake?" There was no separation left between sleep and a wakeful state. I had crossed over to somewhere else. I thought I was going crazy.

It was impossible to be here, I had no recall from the moment I reached out for the rainwater until now. No memory of selecting an exit from the parkway. Had I caused an accident, killed someone and then run in panic and found this hiding place? My mind was blank. I got out of the car, examined it for damage, blood, anything, then touched the trucks that were in the same weird spot I was now in. I was freezing and desperately alone.

The walls had fallen down. I was scared. As I walked, the rain hitting me was so intense, as if telling me something, reminding me of something; rain, rain and more rain.

It was raining when my path first crossed Rachelle's. Now here I was at my wits end trying to work out the final puzzle, alone, hurting physically, emotionally and spiritually in the rain again. I wondered if there were rain spirits, guides or whatever that care for us in their mysterious ways. I got back into the car, grabbed some napkins, dried my face and hair, tried to center myself, and decided to meditate. I once learned that a good meditation could revive the mind and body and keep one alert for at least three hours. That is what I needed to do now to get to the cabin.

I woke up feeling a little better. I backed up the car; my lights worked.

As I made my way back to the highway, I took note of every inch along the way and was perplexed as to why and how this mysterious event had occurred. Entering the parkway, I lowered the window, turned on some soft classical music, kept the heat off and focused on arriving "home." I had to trust and get to the cabin. I glanced in the rear view mirror to check if there were any traffic behind me and realized I was shedding tears.

Home, a strange word to use, since my real home and bed were back in Brooklyn, and for so long having been invaded by Rachelle, were now in dangerous territory. I always had to scour the neighborhood to make sure it was safe for me to attempt to enter my building. While inserting the key in the door, I would simultaneously hold my breath while watching in the glass for the reflection of a flash from a rifle, ready to duck at any second. What a drastic change had come upon my life. Everything that was me that I could touch was moving further and further away. Sadness had become my deep companion.

The darkness was comforting as I drove north. I was sick to my stomach and nervous. How could I have navigated my way along the parkway, stayed in lane and not hit anything, selected the exit, stopped at a stop sign, turned right, and driven about two miles until I found a safe and secure place to park so perfectly between the trucks, and turned the engine off. This was hard to comprehend. How was it possible to do everything right without any memory? This frightened yet emboldened me. Frightened because this was a dangerous trip to make and feeling protected was a foolish presumption.

It was difficult to concentrate on the road. I decided that I would drive from one exit to the next depending on how alert I felt as I approached each one. Yet, I was afraid I would believe I was alert, yet not be. I could not trust myself as the line blurred between alertness, drowsiness and delusion. Quick tremors and spasms passed through my body as I drove.

Did I want it all to stop? No! It could not end this way, I loved being alive in all its challenges and gifts; there was so much love in me I wanted to share. What would have happened if I had approached her car on 82nd Street from the driver's side where I would have been right in her sight; would she have fired? It seemed like a long time since I escaped from the city.

The music was therapeutic; I no longer felt exhausted. Maybe the last leg of the drive was a wake-up call. I was even scared to go to sleep though all I had to do was leave the highway and rest. When I would think of eventually lying down to sleep, my concern was that I would believe that I was actually dropping asleep behind the wheel. The music seemed to drift away; thoughts were shifting so fast that at one moment I thought I was asleep yet having no problem driving.

"Connell, are you there? Pick up the phone. Connell, I know that you are there. I am getting very mad Connell. Pick up the phone NOW!" I practically jumped out of my seat. Her voice

was as clear as day. I thought it was coming through the radio speakers. I grasped the steering wheel so tightly thinking that I had just nodded off again, but I had not, I was wide-awake. This frightened me. The music seeped back; the voice was gone. The parkway was void of any traffic, just me in this time warp trying to go to bed.

"You will see the white car, my face and you will feel the heat of the bullet." I was experiencing a powerful sucking force pulling me into a death trap. I slapped my face hard with my hand to feel the sting assuring me that I was still here and alert. *"Keep it together Connell you are loosing it, hold on with everything you have; there will be a tremendous impact. It is as powerful as a tornado right in your path. Pray harder than you ever have, for you will not get through to the other side alone."* The music seeped back. Had it stopped as her voice came on so forceful and clear? Thoughts and fears were playing havoc with my sanity. Was I wide-awake or dreaming? How could I hear her voice so clearly? I was fully awake, aware that I was driving yet her voice, her words, would not stop. Suddenly I thought the car was filling with water and I could not escape. I could not turn off the sounds of her threats or her madness. Was there a force beyond my comprehension breaking through into my psyche at will?

Just as suddenly all quieted down, the car was holding steady, her voice stopped. I glanced down at the carpet by the front seats. It looked bone dry; no water anywhere. It all felt surreal as I picked up speed. Without warning the steering wheel began to feel heavy and stiff as if it had lost its power-steering; it could not turn left or right. Ahead the parkway curved in a wide long arc.

If the steering wheel did not respond quickly I would crash into the curved divider. I applied my full strength to turn the wheel hard to the right to avoid a collision.

"This evil bitch won't give up, damn her, she cannot win," I yelled out as I sped towards the concrete divider. I slammed on the brakes; they failed to work.

"Oh God, please help me! Help me, please, help me stop the car, do something," I screamed. Life was splintering into millions of simultaneous seconds.

"You thought it was all a game, your game Connell. It never was . . . it was always mine. I was always in control. You always knew that I wanted to 'go out with you,' now it is about to happen and you have lost control. Checkmate!"

Time froze; I screamed as I tried to expel her voice, once again from my mind. I kept slamming my foot on the break pedal while desperately trying to force the wheel to turn the car away from the divider. Her blood curling laughter exploded within the car.

"You cannot do anything. You are already dead, dead, Connell. Do you hear me? You are dead. I never was alive!!! You never met me."

This cannot be, traveling at sixty miles per hour with the power steering lost, brakes gone. The voice of madness permeated everything. Then, just as suddenly, my steering and brakes were functioning as I exited the parkway; there was an eerie silence. The soft sound of classical music again filled the car. My whole body was freezing and violently trembling. I was stranded in a time and reality warp. At the stop sign, I made a left turn, drove until I saw a small diner, and pulled into its parking lot. I was in the middle of a real nightmare that I could not wake up from because I was already wide-awake.

I entered the dimly lit diner. A few drunks were trying to sober up, possibly for their next drink. The waitress had deep dark shadows around her eyes, a leathery and sagging skin and a drooping jaw. They all looked like something from the walking dead. I ordered a large hot chocolate. I had shifted into a bazaar twilight zone. On the way out, I looked into the mirror to make sure that I still had a reflection; movies told us the living dead had none. I confirmed the reflection was mine and felt a smirk cross my face. At least I knew I was still here in flesh and blood. I felt intoxicated by the hot chocolate in my stomach. I reclined the seat in the car as far back as I could, and wrapped my Scottish blanket around me, feeling cozy at last. "You have not lost it Connell, hang tight." A strange peacefulness descended as I dropped into a deep sleep in the cold night. I awoke freezing and had no idea how long I had slept. I got out of the car to stretch my legs and felt the blood circulate through my body; the sensation was exciting. I thought if I told this to someone, they would think that I was on a trip. Boy was I really on a trip!

I walked for a while in the rain and wind and mused that I was stealing time. Some years ago, I had journeyed close to the Artic Circle, in Norway, living and walking in the wilderness in the freezing rain and snow to become one with the elements. Now, I felt that the rain, wind, and darkness were aware of my journey, each taking turn to feed me life as I wandered in a void where the normality of life seemed gone forever. I got back in the car, dried my face and hair, and felt a gentle peace spread over me.

"I will be okay," I thought as I began saying the Lord's Prayer. By the time I pulled onto the parkway the rain had stopped.

What a whirlwind; while driving my mind raced back over the last few weeks. What would Rachelle decide to do? How would it all finish or would it just fade away? I was feeling rested, replenished, and felt I could now complete the drive. I checked the time; twenty minutes to four in the morning and still a ways to go.

During this ordeal, my body had become extremely tired and my mind could not shut down anymore, yet I was amazed that I could continue functioning. I had developed the instinct of a watchdog, never really relaxing, always on guard. The unknown had taken its toll. The decision that I had made not to bring anyone into the danger zone, I now realized, had not been a smart one. Now it was too late and the imminent danger was heavy in the air. I knew I would be very upset if someone close to me was in danger and had not taken me into their confidence to share the crisis they were going through. The closest I came to share mine with was with Greta, who reached out with great intensity to protect me from danger in the courts. I should have discussed the whole story with her and then explained why I did not want her to get involved or be visible in my life. Rachelle already was aware through the phone messages she downloaded who my friends and contacts were. Her threats to destroy me or those close to me drove me into making the decision to protect them, particularly Greta, who would be the most vulnerable since she would be an easy target on stage. It was one thing to worry about my own safety but to draw Greta into danger and have her get hurt would be more destructive than all that was happening to me. I wondered how things would have turned out if I had made a different decision.

FORTY-FOUR
Fighting Illusions

How lonely my life had become. Even though I managed to hold together some sense of social order, the intimacy of my life had gone, except for Anderson, Natalia, Pamela, Greta, Antonia and Joyce. Without them I possibly would not have made it this far. Why did I protect them from the whole story? But how could I share in depth the ugliness and complexity of the entrapment in which I was now entangled?

The faint greying of the night sky gave comfort as I experienced the slow revelation of the countryside: a soft background to a dark night's journey.

"Connell, this is Rachelle, you had better listen to me. Death will not take you away. I will live in your soul for eternity. You will hear my voice when you think, feel or speak of another's love. I will always possess you; so forget it, Connell."

In the softness of the moment, her voice pierced through me, making me jump: had I dozed off? Thank God the car was still steady on the road. I found myself in a place threatened by despair and was again afraid of falling asleep. I had not only lost my sleep cycle memory but my whole life cycle was seriously disrupted. The anticipation of getting to the safety and the comfort of the cabin was guiding my thwarted reality, which had established its own control. I needed to get "home" at all cost. I continued to push myself even though I knew I was putting my life in danger. My hands began to shake on the steering wheel; my foot trembled on the accelerator, as my whole body began to tighten up.

The battle intensified as I approached the Reservoir in Carmel. In the past, driving across it always gave me the sensation of floating. I usually crossed this expanse in early morning or evening; tonight it was a challenge, a foreboding reality. Could I make it? I felt a lot of apprehension as if I were driving into an abyss, challenging me, threatening me. Crossing the Reservoir made me anxious, as I knew it was a narrow two-way road. What if I dropped asleep and caused an accident? *What if*, had become a constant mantra. All levels of cognitive thinking were seeping away. I could see the dense fog ahead from the parkway; and knew I was close to the last leg of this odyssey. All seemed tranquil as I entered the causeway. The fog was extremely dense, making visibility all but impossible. I had to be extremely cautious, as I desperately needed to make it "home." Nobody knew where I was or about the cabin in the woods. Nobody would connect a car submerged in the icy cold waters of the reservoir, with me. Nobody really knew how lost I had become.

"Don't ignore me, I am right next to you. Look at me you bastard, look at me, you know what will happen if you don't pay attention to me. We have been together for centuries. You exist, only because of me. If you kill yourself, I will also die. I will not allow that. If you don't obey me I will drag you through eternity."

How could I block these intrusions? It was as if she was actually present. I prayed to God to banish her voice forever, and to help me cross through the final barrier.

I wondered where she really was. Had she left the city ahead of me, selected a spot, waited until I passed and then followed far enough behind not to be noticed, or had she discovered my destination and lay in wait?

I recalled that at the end of the causeway, to the right of the curve where the road took a tight left turn was a thicket of sapling trees, briars and thick brush, a perfect place for a sniper. If she were there, I would be in her direct line of fire with no room to turn around. How stupid not to have realized this. I continued to proceed with utmost caution.

Under normal circumstance, this part of the journey was hauntingly beautiful. The heavy fog hung like a tapestry in its opaque and transparent seductive dance in the soft morning light. The water began to shimmer as the light of dawn slashed silver and titanium across its surface, creating light between the surface and the tattered drapes of fog.

I felt as if I was floating into a dream and out of a nightmare. The untouched beauty was so alive in this watery traverse that as the fog lifted slightly and churned around me, it felt as if it was breathing. Forms appeared and disappeared around me as they shifted and changed. Suddenly there were thousands of faces rushing towards me as if they were about to consume the car. They rushed up against the windows, retreating as fast as they appeared, then gathered, swooped faster than before, entering the car through the open side window. Then just as suddenly they were gone:

"It's only fog and imagination, Connell, steady up old boy," I said to myself half jokingly. Everything became quiet for a while.

"Whew! What a vision." The fog got thicker as I approached the middle of the lake. There was an eerie predatory stillness; the shifting forms began to reappear, this time morphing quickly. I could hear them breathing, laughing, jeering, and snarling like a pack of scavengers. Thousands of faces rushed towards me again smashing against the car. I felt helpless; I was terrified. I knew this time I was wide-awake; this was not a dream.

"I must fight these illusions," I screamed. "If I don't fight now, I will die," I screamed again.

My heart was beating so powerfully that I thought it would explode. The pain in my ribs was agonizing. Panic struck, I wanted to get away, swerve off the road; but could not because if I did I would go into the water.

"It is just the beginning of the terror that is in store for you; you are mine now. You did not believe that there was an army of spirits that were working for me. It's too late darling, goodbye; in a few moments, you will be consumed. As your lungs begin to burst and your heart explodes, you will know that I have won. I have become your last earthly thought, not too pretty is it?"

She was in my head, thoughts, voice, and reasoning; I was speaking to myself as if she had taken over. Desperately needing a reality check, I turned on the radio; Jimmy Hendricks was playing. I raised the volume to blast level; the sound of the guitar exploded. Nothing was real anymore.

"I will not empower her to drive me mad, I am not going mad," I screamed and screamed until I was as high as the decibel of the guitar. The fog was empty of any forms as it hung in the heavy dampness of a bad dream. I reached for the radio to turn it off; to my shock, it was not turned on.

There was something primal, ancient and ritualistic about this journey. It was as if I had company all the way, protecting and guiding me through evil and danger, nudging me in a specific direction for an unknown purpose. Such possibilities were easy for me to understand. Why had I not been alert when she first spoke of killing me if I backed out of the poetry project? Her actions alone on Christmas Day were a warning. I should have responded from the very beginning in anger and rage towards her for the destruction of my life and privacy. Why had I not been capable of shattering her instead of succumbing to her blackmail and her threats? Are all voices, images and fears caused by festering doubts? This dialogue was constantly try-ing to find traction, but answers never surfaced. Would anyone really believe my story?

The fog impaired my vision as I continued to drive. Approaching the end of the traverse, I hoped the fog would lift enough to give me a clear view, enabling me to speed through the left curve just in case she was in the thicket waiting for me. My heart pounded at that possibility. I decided to pull over to the side of the road before reaching the curve sensing this was not what she would expect. I turned off the ignition and cautiously emerged from the car in the hope of baiting her. My eyes, sharp as an eagle's, scanned for any movement. My hearing was as keen as a fox in the throws of a hunt. I could hear the lowest decibel of sound. I could hear the air flowing past my face. I listened for any sound from the covered brushes to the right side of the curve. I waited; there was absolute silence. The hunter and the prey, was it possibly this would be the last moment? I believed if she were there, I would be able to hear her. Suddenly there was a rustle of cold crisp leaves; my heart all but stopped. Then I saw a small bird disappear into the fog. I stood still for about ten minutes in the cold; I could hear the steady beat of my heart.

My eyes were glued to the brushes, my ears alert for the slightest sound as I sniffed the air for her smell. The experience was scary and fascinating. I slowly walked towards the edge of the curve, my adrenaline pumping, my body coiled ready to react in a split second, but saw nothing and nobody. However, knowing her cunning, my instincts were still on alert.

The release of tension was such a high that I walked back to the car and with a great sense of relief drove towards the curve. Suddenly, without warning, I felt my body abruptly close down. The release of tension I had just experienced an instant before disappeared; I could barely turn the wheel or apply any pres-sure on the pedals. I was collapsing.

"I must stop immediately."

I backed up into the brushes as far as I could until the car was out of sight. I straightened out the bushes and briars in front to camouflage the car. Feeling secure, I pulled the blanket from the rear and curled up in the driver's seat. I desperately needed to get to the cabin but I needed to sleep; I began to cry. I was so close.

I woke to the chirping of birds; it was eight in the morning. The fog had lifted and the chilled water was glistening in the soft morning sun. Now I had to sustain my sanity since I still had another three and a half miles drive through winding country roads to get to the cabin, the last part of this long and treacherous journey. Eight hours had elapsed from the time I left the city, a drive that usually took no more then an hour. What a struggle to stay alive.

The morning was quiet and I was still in control of my life; with the sunlight came peace. I said a prayer of thanks and gratitude for the guidance and protection that must have helped me through this ordeal.

"What is it all really about," I thought. "How will it end? Will it be quiet and fade away or will it be violent?" In praying for my safety, I called upon God's healing touch to bring peace, balance and closure to her tortured mind and soul. Nobody had the right to play chess with death in order that they can claim they are being loved.

The morning light flashed and danced through the dark damp bare trees. It was as if nature were putting on a show for me. The dark trees swept by as if they were rushing to greet me, to welcome me and to congratulate me on having survived. Approaching the left turn on to Washington Road, I was snapped back into reality by a white American car cutting in front of me, turning into the same road.

"Oh shit! It's her; what now?" But as I made the turn there was no sign of the car anywhere. It was another hundred yards to the road that led to the cabin; I saw fresh tracks in the mud. "Good God, I thought I was safe; she's found me. What do I do now?" I drove past the entrance believing if I did not appear she would eventually come around looking for me, quite possibly making a right turn back to Route 6. I continued further up the road turning the car in such a way that I would be able to see her if she came out, yet was shielded from her sight. My mind was racing, my heart pumping; now what? Was it possible she could have outsmarted me? I was so close to getting "home" now I was caught in a trap. All the beauty of the surroundings seemed to disappear. I sat in the car tucked into the side of the road, not sure if I was the predator or the prey but aware that whichever one of us made the first move, could lose. I could not wait; I had to know. I backed up a few yards pulling closer to the hedge and got out of the car. I walked through the woods, climbed the small hill to survey the cabin and the surroundings from the rear. All seemed clear but I needed to get closer as the cabin blocked the view of the parking area; I approached it cautiously. If she were there, she either would be in the car or would have hidden it on the empty property to the left of the cabin. I felt I was in the sight of her rifle. The hunt was on; I was on full alert. I came around from the rear of the cabin and shed to the parking spot, no car. I examined the parking area for fresh tire tracks: no signs. Good! Walking further, there were fresh tire tracks. A car had driven up, stopped, and turned around. I knew what I was looking for. If it were an old American car, it possibly would have single ply tires that have a distinctive flat surface and no threads on the sidewalls. My car had radial tires that had a specific thread design. I continued to walk further down to where the car would slow down to make a left onto the road. There they were; clear single ply tire tracks, just what I had been looking for. Further down, no more tracks; I was puzzled. She may have been here before and discovered to the left of the driveway a garage and the large empty house being renovated. I went into the woods surrounding the house: still no sign of her. Walking back to the car I had an acute sense of being watched. If she were here, she played a good game of hide-and-seek. I drove onto Route Six, traveled south about a mile and parked: still no sign of her, no white car anywhere. I had enough and headed back. Slowing down to make the left turn onto Washington Road, I was startled by a blast of a horn and a flash of high beams. I was so on edge that I freaked out; it was only a pick-up truck. I made a turn and headed straight towards the cabin. I backed into the parking spot facing the right direction in case a quick exit was needed. I glanced around, chipmunks were busy harvesting seeds; nothing seemed to have unsettled them.

Walking towards the front steps I froze at the sudden sound of leaves being disturbed. It seemed to come from the right rear of the cabin where a loose panel covered the crawl space. The sound stopped when I stopped, then picked up again as I continued to move in its direction. I picked up a shovel from the back of the shed and cautiously approached the panel. Pressing my back against the wall I used the head of the shovel to pull the panel sideways. If she were there waiting, she would assume I would investigate the sound by pulling the panel towards me which would fully expose me to the barrel of a rifle. The sudden action of yanking the panel must have surprised whatever or whoever was there as a scurrying sound could be heard moving towards the other side of the crawl space. She would now be at the front of the cabin, blocking me from getting inside.

I walked back towards the woods and climbed the small rise directly facing the front porch. Leaning against a boulder, I had a clear view of the cabin and could observe any movement. I sat for close to an hour; nothing moved. This game of hide-and-seek was stupid and dangerous. Finally, stiff from the cold, I decided to take a chance and headed for the porch. As I approached the glass sliding doors, I anxiously rummaged through my satchel for the keys.

The next thing I remembered was lying face down on the porch, the back of my head hurting. "What happened?" Feeling dizzy, I tried to get up and reach for my satchel lying nearby, and suddenly felt a rush of adrenaline when I noticed a log of firewood close to my feet. Where had she come from? How could I have missed her? I unlocked the door and quickly went inside. Sliding the door shut I realized that the glass would not be much of a deterrent. One heavy log from the wood stack would be enough to smash the glass.

It was Brooklyn again, me on the inside, she on the outside; but this time there were no fire escapes and no back door.

Joyce's cabin had a false panel behind the refrigerator, which slid open and revealed a stepladder that led to a loft bed. Moving the refrigerator to the left and sliding open the panel, I stepped in and, pushing the refrigerator back, slid the panel close again and with trembling legs climbed the ladder to safety. There it was, a small mattress; it was like finding the Golden Fleece. I collapsed on the bed completely wiped out. Here I was trapped by fear of the unknown; fear of being so depleted that making a fatal mistake would bring me face to face with death. I was on automatic; when I closed my eyes, my sense of hearing intensified. Even the smallest natural sound was magnified and played havoc with my imagination. Was she climbing up onto the roof? I hoped she had not discovered the loose panel in the back of the cabin leading down to the garage. If she were hiding under the cabin where the wood was dry, she could easily start a fire forcing me to run out into her line of fire. If I dropped into a deep sleep, would it be the smoke or flames that got me first? I could not afford to fall asleep.

As I lay there, I became aware of the skylight above and the small oblong window to the left of the mattress. This would be my avenue of escape. I looked around the loft but found nothing that could be used to smash open the window. I went back down to get the poker from the wood burning stove even though having to pass by the glass doors would expose me. With the poker in my hand I now felt empowered; I had a weapon and a means of escape. I returned to the loft and lay in bed clutching the poker. Deep sadness and emptiness overcame me as I slipped into sleep.

I dreamt of two charioteers arguing as they orbited the earth. One said, "Let's get him, it's time." The other one said, "No, wait, it's not time," then in unison, "let's get them." They snapped the reigns but the stallions refused to move.

"Oh, my God, they are coming for me, for her, for us. No I will not go. I am alive."

I screamed, as I awoke in panic, my heart pounding.

It was now already close to noon. I had forgotten that I was scheduled to open the showroom at 9:00 a.m. We did not have a sale staff on Sundays and as the telemarketing manager, I would be there alone. The air was cold and crisp, close to twenty degrees. I moved cautiously throughout the house in case she had broken in. Passing the sliding door and seeing the log of wood on the porch, I realized she could still be outside. Clutching the poker I went into the shower. The cold water was like shards of ice piercing my body. It felt exhilarating to be alive.

I left the house through the trap door to the garage and once outside, scaled the stone wall, and cautiously approached the car. I noticed a scuff of white paint on the right side of the slate blue rear bumper. Had it been there before or happened while I was sleeping? I checked the tires making sure they were not slashed. I looked for tire marks. There they were, single ply: were they new or had they been there before? I opened the door to get in and discovered broken window glass on my seat.

"It's a trap," I thought, "If I bend over to brush the glass off, my back will be vulnerable. No way, grab the blanket and throw it over the seat and get the hell out of here." I sped away from the cabin and my fears. Approaching the city, I felt tension begin to build once more. Rachelle had saturated every part of my life.

FORTY-FIVE

Escape

I turned onto Eleventh Avenue from 56th Street constantly inhaling and exhaling, trying to stay centered. Within minutes of arriving in my office the phone rang. The silver worms began to move within my solar plexus as I reached for the phone.

"Good morning, how can I help you?"

"You are beyond help. You have crossed over into an evil that is so dark, from which there is no return. You have become me. As I die, and it will be soon, you will die with me. We have played a great game together. Now we are on the same orbit but moving in opposite directions; the collision is imminent. Did you enjoy my game last night and this morning? You think that you have outsmarted me?"

I was stunned by her words.

"The courts could not do what I needed to do. You are legally connected to me. No matter what happens to me, you are the prime suspect. I am free to pass judgment and decide on your punishment, which will be within hours. So, Connell, I ask you for the last time to come to me now in humility, beg for my forgiveness, and love me, that is all I have ever asked. You, in your terror of love and its intimacy, have called forth all that is evil and dark. Just ask for forgiveness and I will forgive and we can touch each other's souls for eternity. I am ready."

"Never!" I blasted back finding my voice.

"Don't drop your guard, you bastard. You have one hour to decide. I have no more time. If you want to live, you better keep your guard up. If you don't come to me within the hour, you will be assassinated."

"Goodbye!" I heard her scream as I put down the phone. How could she even think that I would consider coming to her in humility and beg for forgiveness? Her intentions from the beginning were, in her own words, "If you change your mind and don't allow me to publish your poems, I will kill you."

Now, I was invited to come to her place of madness, beg for her forgiveness, and if I did not comply, my life would be threatened. All this, said in one breath, without missing a beat. What did she mean by "Did you enjoy my game last night and this morning?"

Was she prolonging the game of hide-and-seek or was it something more sinister? Had she left ahead of me and set a trap? I had to make a decision before the end of the day as to where the safest place would be for me to spend the night. Returning to Brooklyn was not an option. I considered calling Antonia, and finally decided the cabin would be the safest. She would not expect me to make a return trip there. I counted on her not having access to the car two days in a row.

Phone business was brisk. Several hours went by without intrusion. Suddenly, there she was on the phone again.

"Good afternoon, Connell, I have decided to prolong the game."

"This is a serious situation, not a game of a sound mind."

"Oh yes it is a game, a deadly game. It's my game and I will have the final say. You have no more hiding places; I have discovered them all. You are finally trapped and you don't even know it, you poor fool. Many forces are already in motion that will intensify my attack from all sides, day and night. The world will realize how brilliant a director I am after the last curtain call; mark my words."

"It is all an illusion. To kill me will not stop the living hell you are in. I do not fear your threats anymore. You are a fraud even unto yourself. Take the first step, and get out of my life now."

"You and those closest to you are in grave danger. There will be death before sunrise and you will not be able to prevent it. You were protecting your loved ones: what a horrible joke. They are all set to be my targets."

"You write your lines reasonably well, your script is full of repetitive threats that expose doubt and minimize their effectiveness. In the beginning, I misread you completely. I was a fool to listen to your offer to publish my poetry."

"I was sent to bring you back onto the path of God. The future records of time will state that I succeeded."

"You are not a messenger of God, not the messenger of anything."

"I am not alone anymore. I have made a pact with witches to deliver you to them and cannot fail. Their circle of power is wrapped around you and tightening and will eventually crush you. In order for me to be free you are to be sacrificed for all the horrors that are destroying me. Just hearing your voice earlier made me realize how much I have missed you, and reinforced my commitment to kill you. *You* must go before me; you know what I mean. The time has come for everything to stop."

"Stop all this waste of time. Life is not as horrible as you perceive it to be."

"I no longer need water or solid food. I no longer need to nourish my body; its work is done. We both will be together very soon."

"You are beyond crazy, come to your senses before you go over the brink. Nobody is worth what you are doing to yourself."

The afternoon dragged on. Every time the phone rang, I became more tense and jittery. Outwardly I seemed at ease but in reality I was a nervous wreck. There was nothing but an abyss in front of me. Did I have the where-with-all to cross and survive? I had isolated myself so well that I could not find a way out in order to cry out. The ringing of the phone, making me jump, seemed to explode through my thoughts.

"What time does the showroom close?" a woman asked. I was about to say six o'clock, thinking it did not sound like her, yet the silver worm in my solar plexus had receptors of its own that sensed danger."

"The show room will close at eight o'clock tonight," I answered casually.

"I thought it was 6:00 p.m., sir. Maybe you could answer some questions over the phone."

"Okay, what do you need to know, and to whom am I speaking?"

"What is your name?"

"Chambers."

"Do you have a first name?"

"Connell."

"That's an unusual name. Can I address you as Connell?"

"Whatever, it makes no difference."

"You are an insulting frightened bastard. Don't you know, who the fuck this is? You don't even recognize my voice after all these years?"

"If you stopped the theatrics and all of this vomit, one could possibly get to know who you really are. So what do you want?"

"I was thinking since there is nothing left for me to do, that I should walk away from you and your world and find peace. There is nothing left for me here."

"You sound like a tape that is in repetitive mode; you are stuck."

"Could we meet and have supper together? I promise to behave, respect your presence and put closure to our relationship. I give in; you have won. I may not like that but I have to live with it."

"Why now; why supper?"

"I always knew I was alive during the life of Jesus Christ and that I was present at the last supper. We must have been close during the passion and death of Christ. We had closure then. I want to experience the same intimacy tonight. Grant me this last wish to relive our last supper."

"Enjoy your last supper with your illusionary apostles, and enjoy the bread and wine. I have been assaulted in ways I never thought possible. I don't ever want to face you again, talk to you again, think, or feel anything related to your existence."

"Connell, don't you realize that because of all you have done to me with joy and pleasure, you will burn in hell? You are the one who has no reality. I will still have my last supper as I watch you bleed to death. I will drink it as a victory salute. It was to hell that I was to bring you, not to heaven. What an idiot you've been."

"Be gone from me and take your evil with you."

"I can see you from where I call. Look across the street, can't you see me in the diner? I have perfected my aim; be ready. I am-----------------."

The phone went dead. There was nothing but silence. I looked across at the diner; there was a woman sitting by the window that did not look like her. Immediately the phone rang.

"What time do you close?" Reflex made me answer 6:00 p.m. I was now off guard.

"How can I help you?" No response, just the sound of deep breathing, then, a click.

Now what? As I put the phone down, the other phone rang; I answered.

"Birthing death is just as exciting as birthing life, but you denied me that joy. I have been pregnant with death in my womb for so long that I live off its poisons, yet if you look at me, I look beautiful. As you trapped me, now I trap you, there is no escape this time. Now it will be live fire. Goodbye, you pathetic fool."

I really would be a fool, if I did not intensify my vigilance. I tried not to panic. Was Rachelle really in the diner? Was she still there?

I now had only one thought in mind, to get out of the building without being seen. From her vantage point in the diner, she had full view of the front lot, the doors to the showroom, and the fire escape door on 49th Street, along with both overhead security gates to the service department. There were six new cars parked on the front apron of the building, next to my car, that had to be brought into the service department through the 49th Street entrance, before I closed up.

I decided not to hide and brazenly go about sticking to my routine. If she were to shoot, she would have to come out of the diner to fire. I gambled she would not do so as there would be too many witnesses. I proceeded to bring each car inside, making sure that I always came out again through the showroom door for the next car.

I went out one last time to move my own car close to the showroom door. To my shock, all four tires were slashed; my heart sank. Now what would I do? Without a car I would be obliged to walk; I stayed cool. I glanced towards the diner; she was still sitting by the window and with a gleeful smile waved at me. Putting my hands to my head, as if confused and trapped, I purposely stamped my feet in anger and feigned kicking the car, while my mind raced to formulating a new plan of escape. I got in, started the car then immediately turned it off, as if it would not start. I got back out and opened the hood as if there was a problem. I returned to the car, turned on the engine and with the tires slashed, slowly drove it into the service department.

I came back out to the showroom making myself visible. The telephone rang. I glanced at the diner window before picking up the phone; she was not there. That made sense since the phone in the diner was located in the rear next to the counter. I immediately ran to the front door and locked it from the inside, as I knew if she witnessed it, it would be the trigger for her to make her move. She knew I would have to exit by the front door and now, having no car, would have to walk, leaving me at her mercy.

"Good afternoon," I said as I once again, answered the phone.

"Are you still open and if so, until what time?"

The woman at the other end of the line spoke with a strong Spanish accent.

"We close at 6:00 p.m. Is there anything I can help you with on the phone?"

"No thanks, I will stop by."

By now, it was about four thirty. I glanced at the diner; she was not at the window. Did she manage to leave while I was moving my car?

I counted to ten, feeling that if she were the one making the call, she would now be back at the window. Right on the button, she sat back down and waived. I moved around as if not disturbed. The phone rang again; I picked it up from another desk further back in the showroom.

"Hi Connell," in an upbeat voice; "this is your beloved. I love watching you work. Are you aware you have a very nice walk; it's very focused? I wonder if the first shot should be to your right or your left knee. What do you think?"

"You think you're that good with a rifle?" I asked, controlling my voice, trying to sound calm.

"Yes, I have maimed kangaroos, dogs and other animals. It's more fun with a moving target to watch them react in full stride. They straighten up when hit, then their leg crumbles pulling them down. That's the best time to release a second shot into the other knee; that's when they panic. First, they are frozen, then, terrified. The head is right in sight. You don't shoot immediately, not until they relax from the initial blow. There will be no rush for the last bullet. Connell, you never let me kiss you so as a gift I have kissed the last six bullets so that when they enter you the kisses will explode into your blood like your sperm into my soul that bleeds and bleeds. It is now my time to sodomize you. Just think, as you collapse, I will blow out your elbows and as you fall over, I will fuck your ass up close with a bullet that I have kissed. I will listen to you scream in pain; only then will you know the screaming pain in my womb."

"I have no response to your grotesque fantasy. Your threats no longer have substance. You are a frightened being with no identity. You are still the frightened child who stole the bread to give to the monsters so they would not kill you, and now *you* have become a monster. I hope you don't get too impatient sitting there waiting for me. Now, I've got to go."

"Connell, please don't go. I can't walk, please help me. I am not evil, I am afraid."

"One has to walk to get from the window to the phone in the Munson Diner. Goodbye."

She was desperate. I was at wits end and in extreme danger; I felt it in my being. I was convinced that there would be no tomorrow and I had to get out of there now.

I decided to leave all the lights on and go about attending to business as usual. I panicked, realizing it was already five forty-five, and she now knew, I would leave at six o'clock. I quickly went into the service department, removed the plate from my car and put it on a used Honda, driving it up to the 50h Street exit. It was the only exit completely out of her line of vision. I had to locate the switch that controlled the overhead gate since I was not familiar with the service department controls. I eventually found the main switch in the service manager's office. Success, it will open.

I ran back to the showroom, and stayed visible. The phone rang; I hesitated for a moment, and then decided to answer so that everything seemed to be on an even keel.

"Connell, before I approach you when you leave the showroom, I want to ask you for forgiveness for what I am about to do. I have to kill you as soon as you exit; I must, otherwise I will have failed. You must understand that you have to die before I do. I am sorry, but it is the only way. You have to be destroyed before I am," she said pleading. "Please," she added in desperation.

I froze at her words, and had to disavow what I had just heard. If I wanted to survive, I would have to play her game.

"Okay, whatever you want; I guess it is your last wish. It saddens me that I will not be able to see the dawn, as you have said. The showroom will close at six. You must be focused and quick to achieve your dream. Give me a moment to turn off the lights and set the alarm. You know everything must be in order. Do you realize you have created so much destruction for so little a prize? I am so tired I can't go on anymore. So why don't you leave the diner now so we can meet at the glass door? It is so sad that I will not be able to tell you how your kissing bullets felt."

"Do you really mean that?"

"Yes."

"You bastard, you won't even give me the pleasure of killing you; you have turned it into your ritual. How dare you. I am leaving now."

"Goodbye."

I hung up the phone; it was 5:57 p.m. I put out the lights, and calmly walked to the back of the office. Once out of her sight, I ran to the service department and jumped into the Honda and drove it out through the 50th Street exit. I got out of the car, ran back down into the service manager's office, and pressed the down switch, then raced back to the overhead gate as it was closing, barely making it out. Once in the car, I got the hell out of there, and headed east towards safety; I could only imagine how livid she would be realizing that the door was locked. She possibly would believe I was going to stay in the building all night. I still felt the panic within me and knew I had to get away from the city as quickly as possible, but where to? I thought again of going to Antonia's apartment, or maybe once more to the cabin, finally deciding to first head to Brooklyn. My heart was racing. I was excited that I had outmaneuvered her but still scared that I may have miscalculated. Going home was taking a gamble. By now, she may have realized that somehow I had managed to escape; I could not afford to rest.

I arrived at my house, collected the mail accumulated on the steps that led to my apartment, quickly gathered what remained of fresh clothes, plucked the tape out of the answering machine, and ran back down the stairs out the door. I scanned the street for the white Dodge, jumped into the car and without a moment's hesitation, automatically headed to the cabin. It was 6:58 p.m.

Once I was on the parkway, my body began to relax. I could not believe that I had outwitted her, yet I was still in grave and serious danger. For awhile I mulled over the thought of driving north to Canada to my brother Daniel's home in Toronto, but decided instead to go straight to the cabin. I kept glancing in my rear view mirror for a sign of the white Dodge. I wondered where my life would take me and how it would all end. Would her twisted, obsessive passion for me explode in my face?

FORTY-SIX
The Witches Chant

The drive out was smooth and the weather calm. Until now, I had forgotten about the tape I had taken from the answering machine. I slid the tape into the slot; messages from Anderson and Natalia, Joyce and other personal calls; then silence. Good, no Rachelle. The tape continued for a few more minutes with only the soft hum, then suddenly,

"Connell, where are you, something is going wrong in me. I am so weak I can't stay standing. Are you trying to drain my energy; what should I do? Connell, where are you? I can't make any psychic connection anymore. Maybe you are killing me in some cultish way. I have become frightened of you. I am crumbled on the ground talking to you. I need you to get here as fast as possible. I am frightened." The message stopped. I was unmoved by the words.

My thoughts were abruptly interrupted by a blood-curling scream coming over the tape, followed by three more screams full of rage and anger, sounding like a trapped animal.

"I will destroy you before the sun sets today. I have become one with the forces of death. There is no escape from me. If you live for a while after me, I will be present, except for my body, which is rotting away inside from your poisonous soul sperm. Maybe I am pregnant with a demon from you. The witches are physically here with me; listen."

All of a sudden I heard what sounded like the bubbling of water, then of animals and people screaming, of babies crying and what sounded like a cleaver dismembering limbs, all evoking some sort of ritual. Then there followed the sound of wood crackling and of something heavy being dropped. A chant followed in full rhythm with the words, *boil and burn, entrails,* accompanied by the sound of stirring.

"Connell, the fire is red hot; the iron cauldron is full of boiling water and oil. We are coming for you to submerge you and to direct your spirit to the eternal world of everlasting torture and endless pain. You will forever experience being alive in the boil, and forever being alive as the demons of the darkness feed off your flesh. The head witch will now appear to you, in order that you experience it all through her."

She was consumed with Macbeth, once again using Shakespeare's words as her own.

"Connell, the final act, Act IV is upon us. The cauldron is boiling in the middle of this cold and dark cave. The messengers have turned away leaving me in the absolute of my desires; stop the fight and come to me now, allow yourself; there is no return from here. We have taken all of your resistance away; you are being drawn to my soul right now and there is nothing you can do. The spirits that came in with me to bring you to my path are here, as are the power witches. They have prepared the cauldron of boiling oil into which you will be submerged to boil away all that is evil about you. I want you to experience the roaring thunder and the fierceness of the forks of lightening as it spreads its spears of death through the cave. Soon you will be here. There will be three signs as your death approaches. First will be when; *'Thrice the brinded cat hath mew'd.'*

Then the witches together will chant, *'tis time, tis time.'* As the ritual begins the Priestess will give the order."

She continued to recite the text right up to the lines,
> *'Double, double toil and trouble,*
> *Fire burn and cauldron bubble.'*

"You will experience shortness of breath, tightness of chest. Connell, your life force is being sucked out of you by powerful witchery. You will experience a fever that you have never felt before as if you are boiling. The weaker you become, the stronger your presence materializes where we are. Listen to the witches chant, fire burns, and cauldron bubbles,
> *'Fillet of a fenny snake,*
> *In the cauldron boil and bake,*
> *Eye of newt, and toe of frog,*
> *Wool of bat, and tongue of dog, . . .'*

You look so innocent and peaceful as your life forces are being transferred to this side. It could have been so simple: just a kiss, a wish to be held, a walk in the park, to dream in your arms, to spend the rest of our lives together. But no, you denied me everything. You will become the walking dead when your spirit is extracted from you before your death. Your body will boil forever and your soul will be trapped in the oil, which is full of witches' power; you will forever be tormented. You often spoke of hell, well, you bastard, welcome.

You claim never to kill life or eat the flesh of any creature," she said as she laughed, "Look at where you have finished up; in the horrors of everything you have avoided. I will now place my hands on your skull and push you below the surface of the oil. Now you will be among,
> *'Gall of goat, and slips of yew*
> *Sliver'd in the moon's eclipse, . . .*
> *Double, double toil and bubble.*
> *Fire burn and cauldron bubble.*
> *Cool it with a baboon's blood*
> *Then the charm is firm and good.'* "

She begins to chant, then scream, ending in blood-curling laughter.

"I now own your body and your soul; you are becoming me, soon there will only be one. A man who was a poet now drowns in the scaling moat. You may have outsmarted me on the plain we played. If I die I will be living inside of you; you will never be released from my grip. We have been one since the beginning of time. Don't ever think that I will disappear. It will never be over."

The tape finished; there was an eerie quietness. Was she so consumed by her drama that she possibly believed that I would be terrified by the fact that she was deeply immersed in witch-craft? She seemed unaware of the fact that I would recognize that her words were verbatim from the mouth of the witches of Macbeth. I was somewhat amused by her approach, yet glad that her conversation was on a Panasonic ninety-minute tape rather than a conversation over the phone. All of her craziness had fes-tered and spewed from her mouth; it really was beyond anger and frustration, designed intentionally to terrify. Was I frightened by it? I don't think so, yet it tugged at every part of my being. There possibly were powers within the unknown that could make good on her threats. This worried me quite a bit. As I passed over the reservoir, I began praying and asking for protection.

Finally arriving at the cabin, I decided not to park in the driveway, but by the house being renovated. Though weary, I needed to walk and try to clear my head before going in. It was hard to believe I had managed to escape, and was still alive. Nothing seemed real. The moonlight cast a soft glow as I walked warily along the reservoir. I walked for about thirty minutes; nothing made sense anymore; I was exhausted. I had become a sleepless warrior; robbed of all that comforted me. I entered the cabin, opened the window facing the water, and wrapping myself in Joyce's thick goose eiderdown, snuggled in the corner of the couch.

Once I returned to the city, I knew I would experience the raging turmoil of her attack. I decided to meditate, but there were so many elements, it took me a while to quiet down. When I surfaced, my face and nose were cold yet my body was relaxed and warm; it was one o'clock in the morning. I walked to the sliding doors still wrapped in the eiderdown and stepped out into the chilly night. The sky was black marble punctuated by twinkling stars. The moon was bright as it softly penetrated the naked trees. Wrapping the eiderdown tighter around me, I walked up the small hill and sat down upon the rock I loved. The soft hoot of the owl was comforting. The sound of life in the woods and across the lake was like an orchestra playing at low volume. I forgot all and felt at one with everything around me. I returned to the cabin in a deep meditative state.

I was in this situation because of poetry. Poetry lived in my mind, body, and soul. It was who I was. I loved the word "poetry" even in its written form. Never in my wildest dreams could I have ever perceived the danger that emerged from what seemed an innocent encounter by someone interested in publishing some of my poems. Through those dark days where fear existed in every breath, I never stopped writing.

In absolute despair, I managed to keep the books in my car that were inspirational and comforting to me throughout my life. "Hymn of the Universe" by Pierre Teilhard De Chardin, "Return to the Center," Bede Griffiths, and "Sparks of the Truth" by Meher Baba. Along with these were books of poetry by Alfred Lord Tennyson, Pablo Neruda, Galway Kinnell and Thomas Kinsella. These poets and writers spoke profoundly to me through their works. Now they became traveling companions and my solace.

I climbed up the ladder to the loft-bed and was consumed by the rapture of safety and slumber. I woke early and well rested. I felt a tranquility that had been lost to me over the past months.

Though events had taken such a drastic turn, I trusted myself to the unknown of tomorrow, and the knowledge I would make it to the other side of this ordeal. It reminded me of the time when I was about three years old, and Victor my eldest brother, guided me out into the middle of a river, let me go, and told me to swim to the riverbank. I succeeded because I did not know about drowning or that I could not swim, and I made it. I was a strong believer that "thought manifests itself in reality." Now years later I knew I had to swim and must make it to the banks of the river of sanity.

I was surprised that I had left the cabin, had got in the car, and had driven away without caution. I wondered how long it would last once I returned to the city.

FORTY-SEVEN

The Verdict

I was not privy to what Sophia had prepared for the court date, but I had to put my trust in her and tried to release the tension that permeated my life. Sophia informed me that she had confirmed Rachelle's new address and planned to proceed with the EBT (Examination Before Trial), which was a formal interrogation of parties and witnesses before trial. It was also her intention to file a motion for dismissal based on the result of the EBT.

The morning of the 7th was chilly as I headed into the Court House. The regular bustle of the people was comforting. I took my seat and observed as the benches filled; again no sign of either Sophia or Rachelle. However, when the case was called, on cue, they both appeared. Rachelle, dressed in her faded down overcoat moved towards the bench; Sophia followed. I was filled with apprehension. Rachelle, seemingly somewhat subdued, did not look at me and never gave recognition of Sophia's presence. The judge requested both of them to approach the bench but I was not within earshot of what was being said. After a brief exchange, the session was concluded. Rachelle left without even a glance towards me. As Sophia past me she quietly said, "You can leave now. I will call you."

I sat for a moment totally disconnected from it all. I felt deserted in a room full of people while trust and doubt played havoc with my thoughts. I walked cautiously to my car, constantly on the lookout for Rachelle. I left the parking lot and arrived at my office without incidence.

On arrival I was quickly sucked into the whirlwind of a busy day. I tried to put the experience and the frustration of the morning aside for the moment and not to let my thoughts jump ahead anticipating Rachelle's next move.

I was extremely busy returning calls and doing phone business that time flew by very quickly. As I automatically picked up another call, a female voice using my first name with familiarity asked to speak with me, putting me on alert.

"This is Sophia Algoni." I apologized for not recognizing her voice immediately.

"Rachelle changed her claim to state that what caused her emotional and mental stress was the fact that you had stolen her passport and that she could not work without it since she was here on a Journalist's Visa."

"Passport? She admitted she had dropped her passport outside my apartment the day she assaulted me, which was in turn immediately returned to the police precinct. Sophia, that was over nine months ago."

"We know, what you just said was already confirmed."

"So where does the case go from here?"

"Nowhere. The case has been dismissed. It's over. Just be careful."

I thanked and told her I appreciated all of the work she had done behind the scenes, and slowly hung up the phone. I sat numb for a moment feeling exhilarated yet at the same time experiencing a mounting fear.

Now that the court had dismissed her case, Rachelle would be in a rage, furious, and in a state of desperation as she tried to churn the brew that no longer worked. Since she was directing her play on the theatre of life and the climax was imminent, I understood the time was up for her, for me, or for both of us. I was now running on the fumes of survival.

FORTY-EIGHT
Naked Rage

A s I approached my office on Monday morning, I won-dered why the hell I was going there. I was in an altered state of reality. How could I even begin to perceive the idea that I could function in business when Rachelle could mate-rialize at any second? All fibers of my being were threadbare capable of snapping at any second, yet I had to trust, and focus on my work.

At 10:00 the phone rang,

"Chambers, here."

"Chambers, here too." I recognized my sister's voice.

"We just received a very strange call from the Brooklyn police. I am not sure what it is really about, but I thought I should call you. There was a person by the name of Randall Richmond found dead in a car in Flushing with a bullet wound in the head. Do you know anyone by that name?"

"No, why would they have called you?"

"When I answered the phone, they asked for Tom."

"Is he sure of the name?"

"Yes, he seems to be," she said, "but Tom's an Irish man and in his part of the world, the local folk get all discombobulated when a constable comes to their door. Tom wants to have noth-ing to do with the police, even if it's only on the phone."

"So anyhow, Teresa, what makes it so important that you had to call me?"

"Connell, why would the police call and inform us that this man found dead in Flushing had our name, address and phone number on his person?"

"Maybe someone gave him Tom's name as a business referral. It could be just as simple as all that."

"Yes, that's possible, but I have a gut feeling that there is some connection between you and Randall Richmond."

"Like what? I don't know anyone by that name."

"What was the name again of that weirdo woman you brought over that Christmas?"

"What's that got to do with the person found dead?"

"I don't really know, but I think there's a connection."

"Her name was Rachelle Ri . . . chards."

Both of us went absolutely silent. I broke the silence,

"It's close but Randall Richmond is a man's name and Rachelle Richards is a woman."

"It's her. I know it's her. As I told you, since it was a police officer on the phone, Tom only half heard the name."

"Well what happened with this person, was it a woman or a man?"

"I really don't know, but according to my husband, the person is dead and had our number."

"Did Tom get the name or the number of who called; I need to check it out?"

"I think he at least did that. Let me ask him, hold on."

As I held on, my mind began to race. I wondered about the true identity of the person found. Was this possible? I knew Rachelle's mind and her ability to manipulate facts. Teresa returned to the phone and gave me the name of a detective Napoli at the Fresh Meadows Police Station, and the phone number.

"Let me follow through and call you back."

I called Detective Napoli and after identifying myself, asked if the person found dead in the park was Rachelle Richards. He asked me if I was a relative. I answered no, but needed to know the cause of her death. He suggested I call Queens General Hospital and the Medical Examiner's office.

I had no confirmation that the person found dead was Rachelle Richards. Knowing her, it was possible that she was not the person found in the car. Could it be possible that Rachelle shot another woman and made it look as if she was the victim by placing her own identification on the corpse? How could the body be properly identified with a blast in the face? Anything was possible where it concerned Rachelle. If it was a set-up, it had moved to a more dangerous level. The moment was guarded and terrifying. If this really were true, it was all over. What was the truth? I needed closure. I had to know if the body found was really that of Rachelle. I contacted Detective Dragonetti to inform him of what had happened.

I needed to clear my head and refocus. I headed to the diner for a cup of coffee. I walked to the crosswalk and before crossing, waited for the light to turn Green; drivers always jumped the lights on 11th Avenue. I had almost reached the other side when I slowed my stride to look down at a license plate of a car that caught my eye: the word, *LOVE*, spelled out in bold colored aubergine letters. A cab jumping the light on the inside lane, like a yellow blur, shot right in front of me. Taking those few seconds to look down at the word *LOVE* possibly saved my life. For the first time in two years I had dropped my guard and was nearly run over by a cab. I never caught a glimpse of the driver.

On Tuesday evening, December 12, at 9:50 p.m., I called Detective Napoli back.

"I have been informed that you are the detective involved in the case of the death of Rachelle Richards in Flushing. I need to know how she died and how she was identified."

"What do you have to do with this case," he barked.

"I had an order of protection issued against her; she in turn issued a Civil Court summons against me, which she just lost in the court. There are records as recent as six days ago in the Criminal Court System and the Civil Court that this person has threatened my life."

"Then what do you want?"

"How do you know if the body you found is really Rachelle Richards, and not someone on whom she planted her ID? Detective Dragonetti, of the 78th Precinct, stated I would be needed to identify her."

"Since you're not a relative it's none of your business; only family members. Her brother in Australia is on his way here. Don't go anywhere. Everybody we talked to stated you had driven her to her death. You are the prime suspect."

What had he just said, "Prime suspect?" Was he crazy?

He advised me I would be needed if any information surfaced, and hung up. His attitude was very hostile.

How had all this come about, from reviewing poetry to threats on my life and now being a suspect in her death? I needed to call someone who had witnessed this story. Everything was so dark, so empty, so final, and yet clear about why she would take her own life.

On Thursday I called Dragonetti and shared the abrasive and confrontational dialogue I had with Napoli. Knowing the complete story, he assured me he would bring Napoli up-to-date and after speaking with him, would get back to me.

After a short while, Dragonetti called.

"It is true; the woman found dead has been identified as Rachelle Richards. Connell, it *is* true that Rachelle Richards is dead. It seems she had a new boyfriend in Queens. They had an argument over something sexual and she ran out naked."

"A new boyfriend! That's news to me. Have you any idea how it happened?"

"Well, I'm not sure I have it right, but this is the story I got. The guy who had called the police told them that he had interviewed her for a job and agreed to employ her on an editorial level for a monthly magazine called *Light Beam*. She told him that she had just won a Civil lawsuit awarding her a large sum of money, and she had lost her lease at Garfield Place where she lived, and that her new lease would not become active for another twenty-four hours; therefore, she had no place to sleep that night.

He said he told her that if she had no problem sleeping on the couch, he and his wife would have no problem accommodating her. When they arrived at his home, the wife was not present, and Rachelle immediately made sexual advances that, he said, he vehemently rejected. He left the room for a moment and when he returned, he found her standing there completely naked. He asked her what the hell she was doing and she answered, 'I want you to fuck me.' He rejected her again, at which point she became enraged and attacked him physically, demanding him to respond. He became so angry that he picked up her clothes and threw them at her, telling her that she was a crazy maniac and to get out of his house. The last thing he remembered was that she ran out of the apartment stark naked into the street. He immediately called the police precinct to inform them of what had just occurred and that she had run out naked and was acting irrationally.

After a couple of hours, a police officer phoned him asking if he knew Rachelle Richards. He answered yes, he knew her, and that she was the woman he called the police department about two hours ago. The officer told him that they found her dead from a rifle shot, in a car parked at 138th Street and Hoover Avenue in Flushing. When he told the officer he could not believe she was dead, the officer informed him that it looked like a suicide, and that the rifle had been purchased in Long Island."

When Dragonetti finished relating the story, I was without response. After more then two years of living hell, it was over, or was it? Rachelle had so well perfected the theatrics of her life, and played them out, as in the Shakespearian tragedies she studied and loved. She was the tragédienne drawn to the darker characters of these plays, and was capable, like them, to conjure up evil, even after death. That is, if she were really dead.

My mind flashed back to the incident with the cab, realizing that it was possible after all that she was not dead. I never really got a glimpse of the driver of that cab.

Or was it also possible that in her absolute despair and clinging to the tattered, frayed, and weakened threads of her reality, feeling that she had nothing else to offer, but her physical nakedness, and if that were rejected, all was lost?

"Connell, are you still there?"

"Yeah, I'm still here. What do you think really happened?"

"She was psychotic. We were aware she had purchased a short-barreled rifle. This is a scary story, Connell. It looks as if it's really over. Her brother is flying over from Australia to claim her body."

"What do I do right now? I know her, and I know what has gone on and I can help the police department."

"You can do absolutely nothing. Why do you think you can help?"

"Everything recorded in the Criminal Court system and the Civil Court system will identify who I am in relationship to her life. Why can't I help?"

He repeated, "You can do absolutely nothing. You are the prime suspect in her death."

"What do you mean the 'prime suspect' in her death?"

"When the police contacted people who knew her, they all pointed the finger to you, describing how you abused her and had driven her to her death. Napoli concluded that you had caused her death. That's why he was so abrupt."

"Abused her? What do they mean *I* abused *her*? I spent close to two years of my life trying to help this person. *I* was the one who was abused," I said in frustrated anger. "I am the one who couldn't live in my home, couldn't sleep, stalked, day and night. Mike, how could that be perceived as abuse, and as someone guilty of her death? Over this time period, I tried to understand the confusion and complexity of her life. All this is crazy. Do you realize what is being said here? I am a suspect of a death?"

"Prime!" I was stunned and felt so isolated.

"I need you to share with Napoli your role and experience in this case. You've got to talk to him for me. Will you do that?"

"Yes, Connell, I guess I do know more than I realize. I'll let you know. Don't weaken now. You've stayed strong through all of this."

"Thanks." With that, I said goodbye. Was she *really* dead? Now, in the moment of emptiness, strangely, I also felt relief. It was over and I was still breathing, but I desperately needed to be sure she was really dead.

For the next few days, time stood still. My mind was racing trying to be one step ahead of her, to sense danger, to be alert to all possibilities, to all of the end games. Where would she spring her traps? I had begun to think like her, and my instincts had become so finely tuned to her predatory movements.

I believed Dragonetti would not let me down. Time was passing and each moment without the response I was waiting for, turned my anxiety into fear and insecurity. Had Rachelle set a trap? Knowing how strongly I had battled for my safety, if I was to be informed that she was dead and believed it, I would have become her ultimate prey and she would have won. I felt she was still out there and her final plan for my demise could come at any moment. For the first time in twenty-four months, I really knew raw fear. Was I in her rifle sight? As I moved through the following days, the tension got worse. I prayed for Dragonetti to call me.

It was not until Tuesday morning, December 19, that I received the long awaited call,

"Sorry I couldn't get to you any sooner. It was impossible for me and Napoli to get together until yesterday."

"Thanks Mike, I must have lost about ten pounds waiting for you to call me back. So what happened?"

"Well I shared with Napoli your desperate need to identify her and why, and my own personal account as a detective, with a woman of the same name claimed to be found dead. I told him, the whole story that I am going to share with you now."

Dragonetti began telling me that when he phone Rachelle advising her that he was coming over to serve her a summons, filed by me issued by the Criminal Court, she didn't sound at all bothered. When he arrived, she invited him in; he found her to be charming and polite. He noticed a table set for two, with lit candles and an opened bottle of wine. Since it was apparent she was expecting a guest for dinner, he apologized for intruding, but his job was to serve her the summons and leave. At which, she answered him, teasingly, 'You are the guest; I have never dined with a detective.' He didn't know whether or not this was her sense of humor, but skipped over it, and went on to explain her responsibility in response to the summons. She then asked him to sit down.

"Connell, all I can say is that I was a lucky man to be married, with a good wife, a home and a reliable job." He told me he found her attractive, and seductive, and questioned my description of her behavior. He began to believe he was issuing the summons to the wrong person.

"I told her your side of the story. Nothing I said about it seemed to bother her. She shared with me the work she was doing in the theatre, in meditative groups, and with homeless children. She said that if she were really like the obsessive personality that you claimed her to be, why would she be attending Saint Xavier's Church, and intend to become a Catholic. I told Napoli, that right in mid-sentence, while she was talking about Catholicism, something very strange happened to her. It was as if now, somebody else was sitting right in front of me. She was speaking in a low growling angry voice, claiming that you raped her everyday. However, in the next moment she was talking about how from time to time she enjoyed having dinner with you. When I asked her if you made any sexual advances she answered, 'absolutely never.' I questioned her about her claim that you raped her every day, and asked how that could happen without you making any sexual advances. She said that it happened a long time ago in other lives; 'We were having holistic sex.' Connell, I'm not a believer of life outside this one so this is very confusing to me. Honestly, when I got home I had to look up the word holistic. She went on about her love for you, saying you were very kind, caring and respectful, and spoke about the stress she was under over your ignoring of her. When I inquired once again how it was possible for you to rape her, if, she only saw you over casual dinners, she answered in a deep dark tone, 'It's in my mind; it's psychic rape every day. I am exhausted from it. He never stops. Somebody has got to stop him.' My head was spinning with this shitty freak stuff. I had to get back in control and focus on why I was there. I told her what her rights were regarding the Order of Protection and that we had the authority to arrest her if she refused to obey. She said she didn't care, that she had nothing to live for except your love, and that love, conquered all. I've never studied this psychological stuff. I was shocked with what I was hearing. I needed to get out of there. I told her, she would be put into jail with prostitutes, dope pushers, and addicts, and asked her why would she want to subject herself to this depravity? 'I have no problems going to jail if it will bring him to me.' I remarked she was a beautiful, educated, and well-bred woman with a job, apartment, and so on, and questioned why would she want to lose all of that for a man who did not love her? 'Love will always endure,' she answered, 'I don't relate to earthly discomforts. You don't understand what this is all about.' As I looked at her, I felt as if piano wire was tightening around my testicles. I told her I had to go; an officer was waiting in the car down stairs. As I was about to reach the door, I heard her say, 'No, you cannot leave. Here, let me serve you some wine.' Before I had a chance to respond, I heard a swish in the air, as a full bottle of wine went flying past me and exploded against the door. I couldn't believe it; she had just assaulted a police officer. I don't know what prevented me from reaching automatically for my gun. I couldn't get out of there fast enough. As I rushed down the four flights of creaking stairs, I prayed that they wouldn't collapse before I reached the street."

Dragonetti said that none of this made sense. Those who knew her, though they never had met me, claimed I was hurting her, but there was no proof of any of these claims. However, he said, they still had to place me under surveillance and report as to where I stayed, the church I attended, and every part of my social life. They could find no pattern in my life that substantiated Rachelle's story and that not one of her claims proved to be factual. They concluded that everything I had told him, was true.

"You always checked out as consistent, and honest. I had no choice but to believe you. So, I decided to check out who her psychoanalyst was. I called up Doctor Rambert and informed her as to what was happening. She found it hard to believe. She blamed you for her death. She kept on repeating that you refused to compromise. It appeared to me Rambert was afraid that if what I was telling her were true, it would expose her of not being professionally aware of the complexity of her patient's serious psychotic problems."

Mike explained to Napoli that Rachelle was dangerous and crazy. That I had never done anything to harm her, and that is why I couldn't understand why he was so abrupt and nasty when I offered to help identify the body.

"You know, the car doors were locked. The rifle and the keys were inside the car. There was no sign of foul play. They can confirm who shot the rifle. There was a powder burn detected on her hand.

I really don't know how you worked and endured your life. It must have been a terrifying nightmare. There was nothing in your presence that would reveal to anybody what you were going through, you always seemed in excellent spirit. I liked you from the beginning and was always glad to see you. Not many people could have lived through what you experienced. I honestly don't know how you survived; you're a lucky man. You are one hell of a person to have never changed; you never blew your cool. I have great respect for what you did alone."

"Mike, I prayed a lot and kept very close to God."

"I don't know about God, but I live by my morals and conscience. I learned a lot through this episode."

I told Mike she had a way of speaking that made one feel she was innocent and a victim. You'd be moving along with her feelings and emotions and yet somehow feel contradictions within yourself as to what was going on. Then all of a sudden she would flip to different personalities. She would be a child of four or five, then, a sixteen or seventeen year old and begin to speak of sexual situations, then suddenly, a sophisticated adult, the celebrity, then flip into this soul-mate psychic stuff, always catching me on the wrong foot.

"Weird, Connell, fucking weird. I asked her how she was able to talk to you daily if she did not know where you were. She said, spirits always told her. They would find her walking on God's path and would speak to her everyday. She was told to use her machine to talk to your phone. As long as the connection was made with some material object, the commitment was in place. This would suffice for lovemaking. But since you did not respond, she would feel as if your machine was using her, and this usage to her was psychic rape. This did not matter because she loved you. She believed you being in her life, confirmed to her, that you were soul mates. That was all; nothing else mattered. You know, Connell, it's sad, really sad; at moments she seemed so tender and beautiful. It's sad, such a waste of life. When you called me and told me Rachelle was dead; I was shocked. It was a real fatal attraction.

Connell, life is so weird. New York City has a lot of crazy people. I don't know what is happening, but I want to get out. I want to move to the country. Do you know how many cases of aggravated harassment, robberies, and assaults take place each day? Innocent people like you get hurt."

He told me that after he spoke with the police department, he was told to let me know, I would not be brought in for questioning.

Nicole Ruth Richards' brother arrived from Australia, made a positive identification, and arranged to take the body back home to Australia.

In my absolute quietness, I remembered the last words Rachelle said to me,

"If I die, I will be no further away than your shadow. I will never give up."

Epilogue

I lived with the possibility that it was not really Rachelle who was found dead on that December 10th date; there was no way of confirming the report. I lived with the fear that one day she would surface. It was not until fifteen years later, after exhausting many avenues, that I made a connection with the New York City Medical Examiner's office, and that I received the conformation I was seeking.

Receiving this information overwhelmed me with a sadness I did not expect. What was her true story? Were the events of her childhood real? So many questions left unanswered.

When encouraged to write this frightening episode that occurred in my life, I collated my myriad of notes, transcripts, court papers and letters that were stacked away unread for twelve years. The process of reliving the events and the retelling of the story triggered much stress often causing me to stop writing for long periods of time before resuming once more.

I also had to accept the fact that she contacted friends whose names she took off my answering machine, as she did that of my brother, and made true her threats to isolate me from society with her vicious accusations. This, I now realize, resulted in the abrupt silence of a few.

What a tragic end for a lost and disturbed soul. She inflicted so much havoc in my life. I suspect there may have been others before me. I was fortunate to have survived.

Author's Note

There was no way to anticipate that a casual meeting involving a work project would lead to such a terrifying nightmare and the possible destruction of a life. By writing the story I hope to draw the reader into the complexity and initial confusion, the psycho-drama taking place, and the seemingly innocent way predators weave their web to draw in their unwittingly naïve prey.

Stalking has become a national phenomenon of our times. It is a major issue that touches and affects millions of lives. Many victims are helpless with limited resources available to them for their defense. They are often left with psychological damage, nervous breakdowns and panic attacks, and need legal protection from their stalkers. An order of protection does little to protect them. More has got be done to heighten public awareness and bring stalking to the forefront as a topic of national concern.

The prism of stalking and the risk it involves continues to frighten and fascinate.

About the Author

Connell J. J. Chambers: The Hill of Slane, Ireland

Connell J. J. Chambers was born in Dublin, Ireland into a family where literature and poetry were an important part of daily life and where he honed his passion for the written word. Attending Ballinafad College in the province of Connacht, he studied the writings of the mystics of the Middle Ages and developed a kinship with Irish Bards. In this rarefied atmosphere, his poetic voice and gift of the spoken word took root.

After travelling extensively throughout Europe for several years, studying the arts, and spending time in the renowned cities of the Middle Ages, he settled in London before migrating to the United States. Connell now lives in New York City where he continues to write.

In The Dark Night

Mist rises at dawn from the lake,
Rises from the ancient depths of memory,
Soft at first
A bird flies through, silent wings.
Was there love in the dark night?
Or, is it a flight of escape
Heavy eyelids fear openness, lest dream's
Picture fails.
There is fear as the dawn sun warms the air.
Mist rises; nakedness stands chilled.
Turning back to the warmth of blankets,
The landscape is barren, we scream.
To awake to a nightmare from a dream,
Frightens more, than to awake from a dream.
How frightening the breeze has become.
Naked, terror rips our faces open.
A child runs towards us from the mist.
We are speechless as the morning lark
Pierces the dawn.

Connell J. J. Chambers

©

www.ingramcontent.com/pod-product-compliance
Lightning Source LLC
Chambersburg PA
CBHW020602270326
41927CB00005B/142